Mac
for Beginners

Imagine Publishing Ltd
Richmond House
33 Richmond Hill
Bournemouth
Dorset BH2 6EZ
☎ +44 (0) 1202 586200
Website: www.imagine-publishing.co.uk

Editor in Chief
Dave Harfield

Production Editor
Jon White

Design
Dani Dixon, Charles Goddard, Annabelle Sing

Photo Studio
Studio equipment courtesy of Lastolite (www.lastolite.co.uk)

Printed by
William Gibbons, 26 Planetary Road, Willenhall, West Midlands, WV13 3XT

Distributed in the UK & Eire by
Imagine Publishing Ltd, www.imagineshop.co.uk. Tel 01202 586200

Distributed in Australia by
Gordon & Gotch, Equinox Centre, 18 Rodborough Road, Frenchs Forest,
NSW 2086. Tel + 61 2 9972 8800

Distributed in the Rest of the World by
Marketforce, Blue Fin Building, 110 Southwark Street, London, SE1 0SU.

Mac for Beginners Vol 3 © 2011 Imagine Publishing Ltd

ISBN 978 1908 222 022

IMAGINE
PUBLISHING

Contents

Feature

8 Ultimate guide
Introducing you to everything you will need to know about your Mac

Getting Started

Using iLife

Welcome to...
Mac
for Beginners

Welcome to **Mac for Beginners**. If you are new to the wonderful world of Mac, then this is the place for you. We'll take you through everything your shiny new machine has to offer, from turning it on and sending emails to an introduction to iLife and creating spreadsheets in iWork. There are also guides to iTunes and the brand-new Mac App Store, along with over 20 pages of reviews of the very best apps currently on offer. Covering everything you need to get up and running, you'll be a master of your Mac in no time at all… so let's get started!

"Your Mac offers you a wealth of opportunities, and they're all covered in this complete guide"

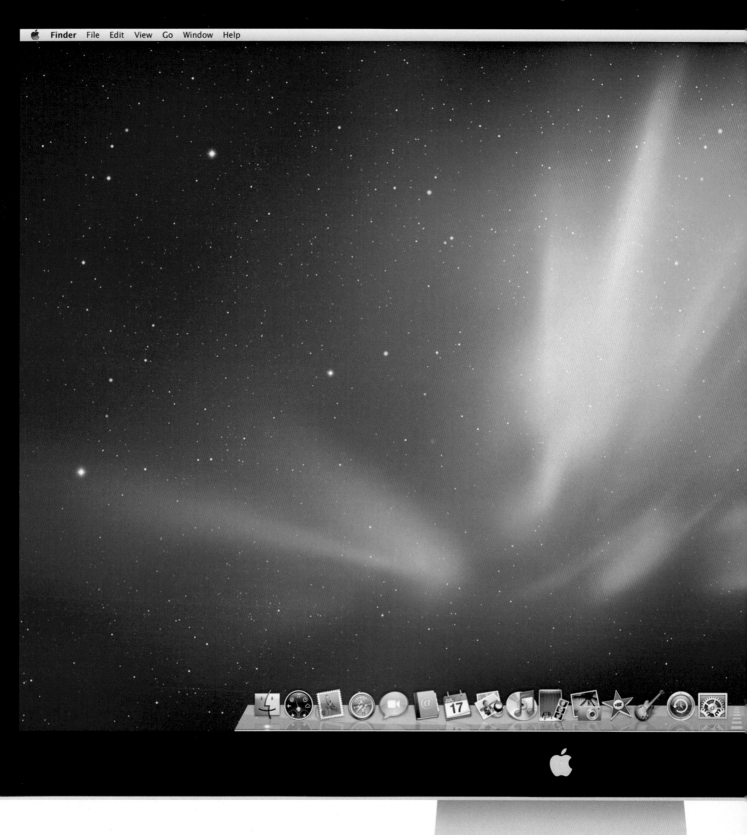

🍎 **Finder** File Edit View Go Window Help

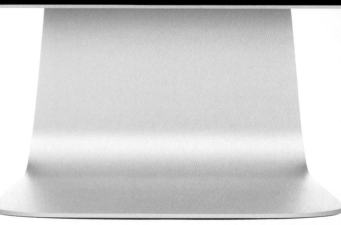

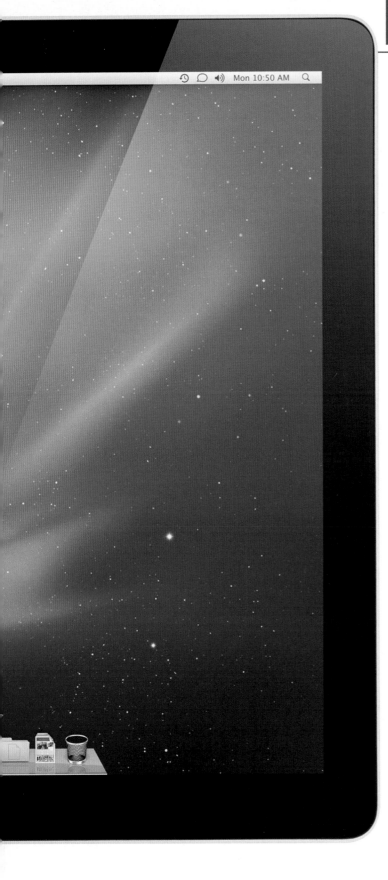

The ultimate guide to your Mac

Taking you through everything you need to know to get started on your Mac

Welcome to the Mac, and welcome to the Mac community. If this is the first time you've owned a Mac, trust us: you're in for a treat. The Mac is a multi-talented computing phenomenon: part entertainment device, part office workhorse, part creative tool, part media hub. But among all its talents, there's one constant: you'll enjoy using it. If you're used to fighting to get a PC to do the simplest thing, you'll find your new Mac a breath of fresh air. It doesn't get in the way. But many of the joys of discovering the Mac's benefits lie ahead.

However easy the Mac is to use – its reputation in this regard is well earned – it's also true that starting out on a new computer or on a new platform can seem daunting at first. Parts of it will inevitably seem unfamiliar at first. And that's where this book comes in. Over these pages we'll take you through everything you need to get going and start enjoying your iMac and MacBook. Soon you'll be taking off with the Mac. It won't be long before you find yourself offering tips you've discovered to other Mac users – and gently extolling the benefits of the Mac to others.

Ultimate guide

iSight camera
This built-in camera lets you video-chat with friends using apps like iChat

SuperDrive
Read and write double-layered DVDs and CDs by popping them into this slot

SD card slot
Pop the memory card from your digital camera in here and import your photos!

Magic Mouse
Intuitively interact with your iMac by swiping this Bluetooth-enabled mouse's touch-sensitive surface

iMac

The iMac is the perfect combination of form and function. Its slim anodised aluminium frame is an all-in-one mix of computer and display. Although it has a small footprint on your desk, the iMac provides a generous amount of screen space for you to work or play in (especially if you're the proud owner of the 27-inch display!). As it chats wirelessly to the Magic Mouse and keyboard that ship with it, there are no cables to clutter up your desktop.

The iMac is not just a pretty face – it's easy to get on with too. There's no faffing around installing additional drivers and software before you can watch a DVD, import photos or surf the web, for example. Movies and photos look stunning on the LED-backlit display, which has a 16:9 aspect ratio that's perfect for enjoying a widescreen Hollywood blockbuster. Your iMac isn't an island either, thanks to four USB ports that are used to connect other devices like digital cameras or external hard drives.

Under the bonnet a powerful Intel Core processor ensures that Apple's Snow Leopard operating system runs quickly and smoothly, enabling you to enjoy the ultimate desktop experience as you interact with various applications in the iLife suite. By default the iMac comes with four gigabytes of RAM to help run applications even more efficiently, but this can be upgraded to a whopping 16GB on models like the 27-inch version! And with up to 2TB of storage space to play with, you can install professional video editing software like Final Cut Pro to extend your iMac's functionality.

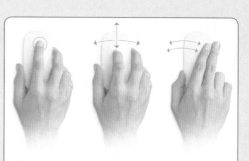

Mouse moves
The Magic Mouse allows you to click anywhere, single-finger swipe to scroll and double-finger swipe to advance through pages in Safari or images in iPhoto.

USB ports
Connect a host of devices to your MacBook. The MacBook Pro has an additional USB port

MagSafe power port
The power cable attaches magnetically, so there's no danger of you accidentally pulling your MacBook off the table!

SuperDrive
Read and write double-layered DVDs and CDs by popping them into this slot

MacBook

The laptops in the MacBook range run the same Snow Leopard operating system that you enjoy on the iMac and give you full access to the iLife software suite. Thanks to the MacBook range's portability, you can break free of your office to work and play on the move. Indeed, the entry-level MacBook (pictured) is just 1.8 inches thin and weighs in at a lightweight 4.7 pounds, so you can enjoy watching content on its 13.3-inch LED-backlit screen in a coffee shop or on a train! Things get even lighter if you have a MacBook Air, which is the first ever Mac to replace the usual spinning disc-based hard drive with a lightweight flash storage drive.

Despite the entry-level MacBook's relatively compact size, it packs a generous 500GB hard drive, so you can store lots of documents, apps and photos on it. The Nvidia graphics processor enables you to push polygons around with ease, so you can enjoy 3D shoot-'em-ups at a suitably fast frame rate – and the battery should give you seven hours of action! At the top end of the range is the 17-inch MacBook Pro, on which you can squeeze 750GB of storage and 8GB of memory. The MacBook Pro models use an Intel HD Graphics 3000 processor, so you can enjoy a true HD movie-going experience, edit in HD and even view HD-quality video when making video calls using FaceTime. The MacBook Pro models also boast a Thunderbolt port, so you can export and import video much more quickly than you can using USB or FireWire connections.

"Thanks to the MacBook range's portability, you can break free of your office to work and play on the move"

iSight camera
Make video calls and chat to family and friends. Higher-spec MacBook Pros use a FaceTime HD camera

Ultimate guide

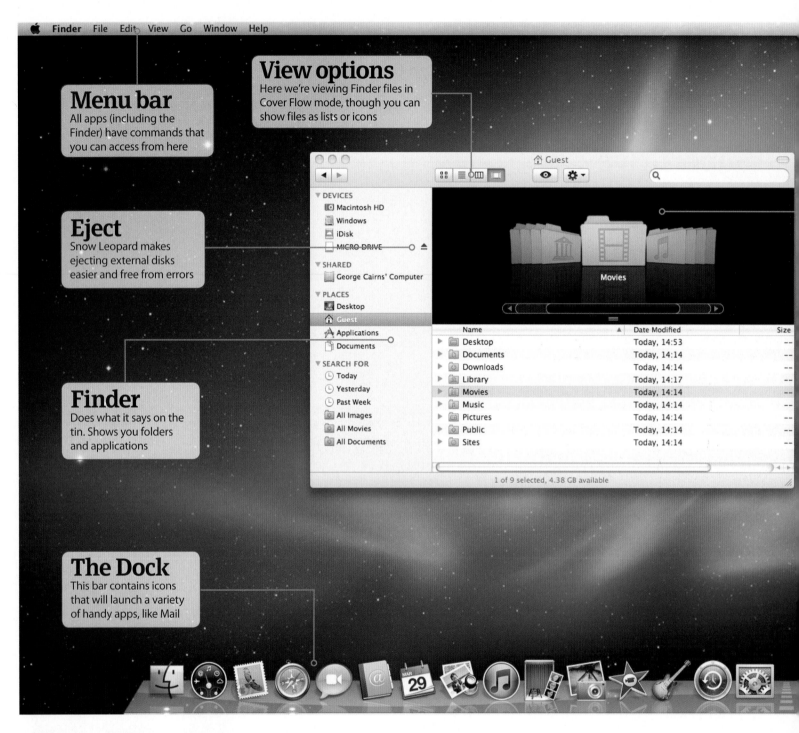

Menu bar
All apps (including the Finder) have commands that you can access from here

View options
Here we're viewing Finder files in Cover Flow mode, though you can show files as lists or icons

Eject
Snow Leopard makes ejecting external disks easier and free from errors

Finder
Does what it says on the tin. Shows you folders and applications

The Dock
This bar contains icons that will launch a variety of handy apps, like Mail

Finder   File   Edit   View   Go   Window   Help

Guest

▼ DEVICES
🖥 Macintosh HD
🖥 Windows
🖥 iDisk
MICRO DRIVE ⏏

▼ SHARED
🖥 George Cairns' Computer

▼ PLACES
🖼 Desktop
🏠 Guest
🅰 Applications
📄 Documents

▼ SEARCH FOR
🕐 Today
🕐 Yesterday
🕐 Past Week
All Images
All Movies
All Documents

Movies

Name	Date Modified	Size
▶ Desktop	Today, 14:53	--
▶ Documents	Today, 14:14	--
▶ Downloads	Today, 14:14	--
▶ Library	Today, 14:17	--
▶ Movies	Today, 14:14	--
▶ Music	Today, 14:14	--
▶ Pictures	Today, 14:14	--
▶ Public	Today, 14:14	--
▶ Sites	Today, 14:14	--

1 of 9 selected, 4.38 GB available

OS X

The advantages of the sophisticated Mac operating system

OS X is the operating system that all Macs use to run their software. Each incarnation of the OS is named after a member of the cat family (that's big powerful cats like Cheetah, Puma, Tiger and so on – we're unlikely to see OS Kitten any time soon). The latest OS (version 10.6) is called Snow Leopard, though Lion is waiting to pounce later on in 2011.

OS X Snow Leopard is designed to make it quicker and easier for you to interact with your Mac. For example, if you open multiple documents using different applications, you could take a while to find a specific file, as all the open windows will overlap each other. OS X's Exposé feature enables

you to tap a single key (F9) and view all of the open documents as tiled thumbnails, so you can find what you're after in an instant.

Snow Leopard takes up a smaller amount of disk space than older Mac operating systems. This smaller footprint enables you to fill your hard drive with more apps, videos and photos. Like its predecessors Snow Leopard is a very stable OS, so crashes are the exception rather than the rule.

Searching for a particular file can be a challenge on a

Date & Time
You can view the time as an analogue or digital clock by clicking and holding the mouse button here

Cover Flow
You can view folders and their contents as scrollable thumbnails in Cover Flow mode

Background
The desktop wallpaper is set to Aurora by default, though you can change this in the System Preferences' Desktop & Screen Saver menu

PC, but with the powerful Spotlight OS X search engine you can find files (or the contents in a note or email, for example) with ease. Spotlight works so quickly because it automatically indexes the files on your Mac.

Entertainment

The Mac has made a name for itself as a creative device, but if you're just looking to relax, it will happily fill that role too. In the mood to watch a movie? iTunes has expanded from its original role as a music player and organiser, and now it can handle your video collection just as easily as it does your audio library. At the same time, the iTunes Store also holds a growing video collection that you can either rent or buy and watch on your Mac. Both current and classic films are available, and there's a good choice of TV episodes too, particularly when it comes to comedy. Don't forget podcasts either. Some of the video podcasts in the iTunes Store – all free, remember – offer excellent quality.

But what's the best way to watch this downloaded content? You can play video full-

Browsing

If we were to make the bold claim that the Mac offers the best way to browse the web, you would probably ask for evidence.

So here's exhibit one: Safari, the Mac's built-in web browser. It's not only one of the fastest and best-looking browsers around, but it also complies with modern web standards, which means that the latest cutting-edge websites should appear exactly as they were intended. Safari also comes with clever features such as private browsing, which hides your browsing history from prying eyes, and a neat 'Top Sites' view that presents small previews of your most-visited sites on one page and lets you visit them with a single click. Very convenient. In Top Sites view, Safari even lets you know when new content has been added to these sites.

"On a Mac, the web really isn't something you worry about. It's something to enjoy"

screen from within iTunes, although some users – particularly those who own big-screen Macs and an Apple Remote remote control device – enjoy sitting right back and watching their movies through Front Row. This is the Mac's built-in media software that allows you to easily navigate your iTunes music and video content or iPhoto pictures.

And, of course, AirPlay – Apple's wireless streaming technology – lets you stream video as well as audio from your Mac over a Wi-Fi network to your Apple TV. So even if you download your videos to a MacBook, you can still enjoy them on a really big screen.

Don't forget that you can also watch live or archived TV footage on your Mac through a web browser. The BBC's iPlayer (**www.bbc.co.uk/iplayer**) has earned a fine reputation, but several other channels also offer either a live view or an on-demand service archive of previous shows.

If your entertainment interests are more cerebral, what about reading a book? Your Mac might not be the first choice for reading, but if your iPad or Kindle device is out of reach, you can still browse books on your Mac. Amazon's free Kindle application for Mac lets you read books you've downloaded from the Kindle store – it will also synchronise bookmarks and annotations with other Kindle devices.

Another great feature, for those of us who hate the ads that clutter webpages, is Safari's Reader mode. With a single click, webpages are transformed to show the important text in a simple scrolling, image-free window.

Exhibit two: choice. It might surprise many, but Macs come with a far bigger range of web browsers than PCs do. You may not find Microsoft Explorer here, but you won't find anyone missing it either. As well as other big browsing names (Chrome, Firefox and Opera), there are delightful niche alternatives such as Omnigroup's OmniWeb (**www.omnigroup.com**) and Camino (**caminobrowser.org**) for you to try.

Exhibit three: security. You'll be more comfortable browsing the web on a Mac because you're far less susceptible to viruses or other malware than you would be on a PC. That's not necessarily because the Mac is immune, but because malicious software tends to target Windows PCs, you don't have to worry nearly as much about the risk of malware infecting your Mac. And if it's the kids you're worried about, you can rest assured that Mac OS X comes with parental controls – found in System Preferences – that can be configured to block websites unsuitable for younger eyes before they are displayed. On a Mac, the web isn't something you worry about. It's something to enjoy.

Music

As the creator of the iPod, the most successful music player in history, Apple has long had a special relationship with music. "Why music?" asked Apple CEO Steve Jobs rhetorically in 2001, the year iTunes was launched. "We love music. It's part of everyone's life." Nowhere is this view more apparent than with iTunes, the hub of all music operations on your new Mac. It's a fantastically versatile program. Some will use it as a simple music player, either with music you have imported (stick a CD into your Mac and it will convert its tracks and add them to your iTunes library automatically), by importing digital music from another source (iTunes can automatically convert music held in Windows Media format), or by buying it from the iTunes Store, which you can reach through iTunes. Here you can browse and preview short samples of tracks, buy them with a single click, and be listening to them on your Mac seconds later.

But others will use their Mac as an audio hub. iTunes can sync your music library to iPods, iPhones and iPads, so you can take your tracks wherever you are. iTunes also comes with a cool feature called AirPlay. If you have a compatible device, such as AirPlay-enabled speakers, an AirPort Express wireless device or an Apple TV, you can stream your music straight from your Mac to them. Another feature, Home Sharing, allows you to share your music with other iTunes users (Mac or PC) over your home network.

The Mac isn't just great for listening to music. You can create it too, thanks to GarageBand. GarageBand is part of the Mac's bundled iLife suite and allows you to create your own music, either using the program's built-in software instruments, or by recording a real instrument by plugging it into your Mac.

Even if you're an absolute beginner, GarageBand can be fun. You can drag pre-built 'loops' of audio onto tracks to build up a song, and even begin to learn how to play an instrument by downloading free basic music lessons from within the program.

Top 10 tips

Tip 1

USING SPOTLIGHT

Spotlight enables you to find text, image or movie files anywhere on your Mac (even if they're buried deep in an old email). Click on the Spotlight Icon at the top right of the screen and type a phrase into the search field. Click Show All to see search results from a variety of sources.

Tip 2

CHANGING BRIGHTNESS/ VOLUME

We all like to work in different ways, especially in relation to sound volume and image brightness. You can control sound volume using sliders within an app like iTunes, or drag the master volume slider up or down from the top right of the main menu bar. To change Brightness, use the slider in the System Preferences>Displays option.

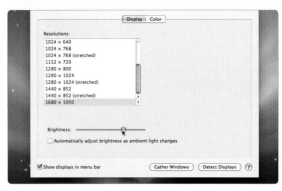

Tip 3

SETTING UP PASSWORDS

If you pop out of the office and leave your Mac unattended, you can get it to lock when the screensaver activates. Go to Apple>System Preferences and click on the View drop-down menu. Choose Security. In General, tick 'Require password after sleep or screensaver begins'. Choose a time for this password protection to kick in.

Tip 4

MINIMISING/MAXIMISING WINDOWS

The desktop can soon get cluttered with multiple open Finder or app windows. You can use Exposé (F9) to tile them, then click on the one you want to view full size. Alternatively, click on the yellow Minimize icon at the top left of any window and it'll shrink to the Dock. The green Maximize icon will make the window expand to full size.

Mac OS X is a joy to use compared to Windows, with many user-friendly and powerful features to make your life easier. Here are some top tips to get started with OS X, from changing the desktop appearance to creating multiple user accounts and securing your system

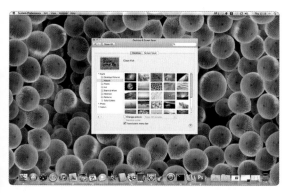

Tip 5

CHANGE THE BACKGROUND

To make yourself feel more at home you can change the default desktop background. Go to Apple>System Preferences>Desktop & Screensaver. Browse through a variety of themed folders for an eye-catching image (or rummage through your iPhoto Library for something more personal). Click to select a new background.

Tip 6

SET UP MULTIPLE USER ACCOUNTS

To stop others tinkering with your files or settings, give them their own user account. Go to Apple>System Preferences>Accounts. Click the padlock and enter your Admin password. Click '+' to add a new account. This user can choose their own password. Any changes they make to things like the desktop background will be unique to their account.

Tip 7

CREATE AND RENAME FOLDERS

To create a new folder, click the Gear icon at the top of an existing folder and choose New Folder from the drop-down menu. Alternatively, on the menu bar, go to File>New Folder. By default, each folder is labelled as 'untitled'. Click on the label and type something more informative.

Tip 8

ADD APPLICATIONS TO YOUR DOCK

Docking a favourite application makes it easier to access. Browse to the Applications folder to see a specific application's icon and then drag it to the Dock. You can then launch it by clicking on its docked icon. Remove unwanted docked applications by dragging them from the Dock. They'll vanish in an animated puff of smoke!

Tip 9

SAVE EDITED FILES UNDER ANOTHER NAME

Let's say you've adjusted the colour of an image using Preview. Go to File>Save As and give the file a name. Click on your house-shaped Home directory and browse to the Pictures folder. Click Save. The edited version of the shot can be found and reopened by going to the Pictures folder.

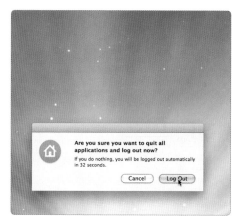

Tip 10

LOG OFF AND SHUT DOWN

To log off after a hard day's work (or a fun gaming session) go to Apple>Log Out. Click the Log Out button. This will take you to the Mac OS X screen, where you can click Shut Down (or let someone else log in to use their own account). Alternatively, press your Mac's power button and choose the Shut Down option.

The Dock

The Dock at the bottom of the screen enables you to access commonly used applications with ease…

Finder

Think of this as a doorway to other folders and applications. The Finder helps you find and access any file

Safari

Fire up Apple's native web browser by clicking here, then enjoy a safe and pop-up-free surf

Address

Add your friends' contact details to cards in your Address Book. You can use the iSight camera to snap your own contact mugshot

Preview

Preview enables you to view images with ease. You can also edit their colour and mail them from within the app

Photo Booth

This fun app uses your iSight to generate a variety of shots. Use them as your iChat Account Picture or mail them to a mate

Dashboard

Click here to access a variety of handy floating widgets including a clock, calculator, calendar and even a weather forecast

Mail

Launch the Mail app by clicking here and follow the step-by-step instructions to set up an account

iChat

Have video or text chats with your online chums. Use Video Effects to creatively enhance your streaming footage

iCal

Keep track of important dates and events using this powerful but easy-to-master calendar app

iTunes

Import music from disc or the web and play it on your Mac. Check out the video tutorials to help you get started

Photos

If the extent of your photo organisation in the past has been to loosely organise them in folders on your PC, or even just to shove prints in a shoebox, you'll be stunned by the organisational prowess of your Mac's iPhoto application.

iPhoto gives you a whole new way to easily sort and group your photos. For example, its Faces feature automatically recognises faces in images and lets you add names to them. iPhoto learns from your choices and can suggest other photos that might include that person after a while, this automatic recognition gets very good. You can then browse your photos in a special Faces view which gathers all photos of one person together.

In the same way, iPhoto's Places view uses location information often embedded in a digital image to display their location on a map, while an Events view groups photos by the date they were taken. And if that's not enough flexibility, how about iPhoto's Smart Folders, whose contents automatically update to hold images depending criteria you set.

If there's a downside to digital photography, it's the tendency for shots to be kept on your computer rather than shared. But iPhoto encourages you to post images to Facebook, Apple's MobileMe gallery or online photo sharing site Flickr. And if you're after permanent keepsakes, it can design letterpress cards, books and calendars which can be ordered from within the program.

Storing photos in iPhoto also makes them available in other iLife and iWork programs, making it easy to put your slideshows to DVD using iDVD, or home movies using iMovie. iPhoto isn't an all-singing, all-dancing photo editor, but it will happily hand off such chores to other applications, such as the excellent Mac-only Aperture or Photoshop Express. Even so, it does the basics very well. You can crop, straighten and correct odd colours in a photograph easily and its tool to correct red-eye is almost foolproof. You can also add smart-looking effects to an image without worrying about damaging the photo, as iPhoto always keeps a copy of the original that you can revert to.

iMovie
Organise your ever-growing collection of video clips and edit them into polished productions

Time Machine
If you plug an external hard drive into your Mac, you can use this app to back up the entire contents of your computer

Open in Finder

About Downloads.pdf

Stacks
Click on a docked folder to view its contents as a Stack. You can then click on a Stack item to open or launch it

iPhoto
This powerful app enables you to store, edit and share your photos on popular sites like Facebook

GarageBand
If you have even a hint of musical talent, this app will help it grow. Contains synthesized instruments and musical loops to play with

System Preferences
You can do a host of things here, from changing the desktop wallpaper to modifying the size, shape and location of the Dock

Applications
On this side of the dividing line you can store favourite folders like Applications. Minimised windows hang out here too

Trash
Click on this icon to have a quick check of its contents, then Control+click to empty it!

Video

What do *True Grit* and *The Social Network* have in common? Apart from being two recent box-office blockbusters, both movies were edited on a Mac using Mac-only software. It's a growing trend, and one that's becoming accessible to more people – not just professional film-makers. Ten years ago you would need to have sold your house to be able to afford that sort of editing functionality, but now you can do it using equipment costing a few hundred pounds.

If you've got a video camera and a Mac, you already have all the hardware you need. If your camera is a relatively recent model, it's a decent bet that you'll be able to start working with it without even having to install drivers or tweak settings.

While many top-of-the-range movies are edited using the high-end Final Cut Pro and the Mac, iLife's own bundled iMovie is the gold standard of home video editing. Editing in iMovie is as simple as importing your footage and then dragging it into a project area. Simply drag and drop to add transitions between scenes or titles – and there's a full array of sound effects that you can use to enhance audio. Even if your original footage isn't top quality, iMovie can improve it. It has a stabilisation tool to correct shaky video, and individual clips can be colour-corrected. The professional look is

enhanced through iMovie 11's templates that help you to quickly create short and memorable trailers for your work.

The real beauty of iLife applications is the way they work together. With the iLife media browser, you can add a soundtrack from iTunes or images from iPhoto or export your video to iDVD to create permanent keepsakes on disc. That's not the only export option either: you can share directly to popular video-sharing sites such as YouTube, Vimeo or Apple's own MobileMe.

And naturally, there's an easy transition to even more powerful tools. Final Cut Express isn't an expensive purchase, yet is only a slightly cut-down version of the high-end studio application. It imports existing iMovie projects while allowing you to work with multiple audio and video tracks.

Gaming

It used to be said that the Mac lagged behind Windows when it came to games, but that's far less true now. There are plenty of reasons for this change. The attention of games developers has been grabbed by the Mac's ever-increasing market share. And the Mac's transition to run on Intel processors a few years ago resulted in both performance improvements and easier porting of games from the PC platform.

The arrival of the Mac App Store has also proved critical. It has given exposure to Mac games developers who would otherwise struggle for the limelight. That has benefited the developers of games like *Call Of Duty* and *Rome Total War*, which have been some of the App Store's biggest sellers since it launched in January 2011.

The arrival of the Mac App Store has also encouraged existing iPhone and iPod games developers, already familiar with the App Store format and Apple's development tools, to try their hand with Mac games.

The conversion process is comparatively simple and as a result, titles that originally grabbed attention on the iPod, such as *Angry Birds*, *Flight Control* and *Rugby Nations*, have been ported successfully to the Mac. Crucially, in many cases, this transfer has come ahead of their arrival on PC or console systems.

And Mac users don't just have a better choice of games now. The Mac App Store means no more hunting around the recessed corners of computer shops to find a compatible game. Like the iTunes Store, gratification is instant: purchase, download and run games within seconds of buying them.

There's another reason for the Mac's growth: the arrival on the Mac platform of Steam, a digital distribution platform that boasted 25 million user accounts before it arrived on the Mac. But now Mac gamers have feature parity: Steam games release simultaneously on Windows, Mac and the Xbox 360. And if you're a Windows Steam user, there's great news: if you already own the PC version a game on Steam, you get Mac versions at no extra charge.

Shortcut tips

The brilliant thing about OS X Snow Leopard is the way it lets you control the way your Mac behaves with a few taps on the keyboard. These keyboard shortcuts can speed up the way you interact with your Mac, so you can clear away clutter, find files fast or jump between open applications in a click. By knowing the keyboard shortcut for a command, you no longer have to drag the mouse up to the main menu and rummage around in submenus! We'll cover shortcuts that work with OS X, plus show you some generic key combinations that will work in most applications (like copying and pasting). Many shortcuts use the key with the Apple logo on it – we'll refer to this as the Command key in our tips (since some wireless keyboards don't feature the Apple logo on the Command key). The key with Alt on it is the Option key.

COMMAND+Z
This is the Undo function in most applications.

OPTION+SHIFT+COMMAND+ESCAPE
If you hold these keys down for three seconds, you'll Force Quit the currently open app. Only do this if an app freezes up.

COMMAND+C
Copies selected text, documents or even images.

COMMAND+SHIFT+3
Takes a screenshot of your display and saves it as an image file to the desktop.

COMMAND+V
Pastes anything you copied with the Cmd+C shortcut.

COMMAND+S
This shortcut saves the current document, using the same name.

COMMAND+N
This will give you a new document in any application you're using.

COMMAND+TAB
This activates a handy mini-Dock. Keep pressing tab to switch between currently open applications.

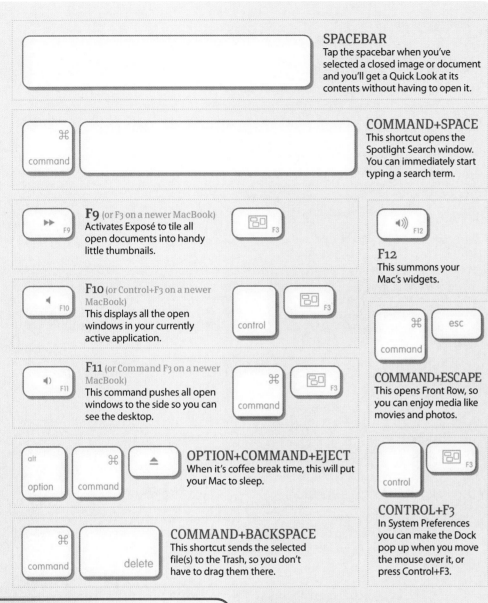

SPACEBAR
Tap the spacebar when you've selected a closed image or document and you'll get a Quick Look at its contents without having to open it.

COMMAND+SPACE
This shortcut opens the Spotlight Search window. You can immediately start typing a search term.

F9 (or F3 on a newer MacBook)
Activates Exposé to tile all open documents into handy little thumbnails.

F12
This summons your Mac's widgets.

F10 (or Control+F3 on a newer MacBook)
This displays all the open windows in your currently active application.

F11 (or Command F3 on a newer MacBook)
This command pushes all open windows to the side so you can see the desktop.

COMMAND+ESCAPE
This opens Front Row, so you can enjoy media like movies and photos.

OPTION+COMMAND+EJECT
When it's coffee break time, this will put your Mac to sleep.

CONTROL+F3
In System Preferences you can make the Dock pop up when you move the mouse over it, or press Control+F3.

COMMAND+BACKSPACE
This shortcut sends the selected file(s) to the Trash, so you don't have to drag them there.

"These shortcuts can speed up the way you work"

MacBook Air

MAGIC MOUSE

RIGHT CLICK
If you do this while selecting a word in Safari, you can choose 'Look Up in Dictionary' from the context-sensitive pop-up menu.

SCROLL BUTTON
By default this activates Spaces, though you can use System Preferences to change its behaviour.

CONTROL+SCROLL
This combo enables you to zoom in to get a magnified view of what's on the screen.

Office

If you didn't think of the Mac as an office workhorse, think again. As a work computer, the Mac has a lot more going for it than many beige PC boxes. Easy to use, supremely resistant to viruses and coming with a reputation for reliability, Apple desktops and laptops tick plenty of hard-nosed business boxes.

But what about the software? The good news is that the dominant office software is available on the Mac – and it's just as good as the one on Windows. Microsoft Office 11 for Mac has virtually the same functionality as its PC sibling, but looks better. You can swap Word and Excel files with PC users and even share Outlook calendars on a connected server. And recent Macs come with built-in support for Microsoft Exchange Server 2007, so if you use Exchange at work, chances are you can access all your emails and calendars at home too.

But Apple has been making its own steps in the office space. Its Mac-only iWork suite, which comes in a fair bit less expensive than Microsoft's offering, also features word processing, spreadsheet and presentation capabilities. If its word processing and spreadsheet tools lack the complete range of functions of Microsoft's equivalent tools, they are at least arguably easier to use. iWork's Keynote presentation software is generally accepted to be better than PowerPoint, with more polished templates and more impressive transitions.

iWork files are also Office compatible: files saved in Office on the PC can be opened in Pages, Numbers and Keynote, while you can export them from iWork in PC format too. The only thing missing in both Microsoft Office and iWork suites is a decent database. But even here you're spoiled for quality Mac choice: pick between the excellent Filemaker (**www.filemaker.com**) or its budget equivalent, Bento (**www.bento.com**).

Office work isn't all about spreadsheets, letters and slideshows, though. What about managing your accounts? There's plenty of choice here. AccountEdge (**www.mamut.com/uk/mac/accountedge**) and Business Accountz (**www.accountz.com**) are both capable desktop applications – but the Mac is also open to the growing number of excellent web-based alternatives, such as Xero (**www.xero.com**) and FreeAgent (**www.freeagentcentral.com**).

Ultimate guide

Productivity

Keeping yourself organised has never been more demanding. But your Mac, and its built-in iCal calendaring application, can help you to keep on top of things. iCal supports multiple calendars – so you can track work and family commitments separately – and you can view calendars in several ways: by day, week or month. You can invite others to events you create, and set an alarm to remind you before it starts.

iCal also lets you sync appointments with iPhone, iPod touch or iPad calendar apps using iTunes as a handy go-between (if you subscribe to Apple's MobileMe service, you will also have the ability to sync your calendar without an actual physical connection, and you will also be able to share calendars between multiple Macs).

Beyond iCal, the Mac has been built to take control of the chores while you do what you want to do. For example, every computer user knows they ought to back up regularly, but the organising of backup discs and choosing what to copy invariably gets in the way. Not on a Mac. Here, backing up is as simple as attaching an external drive. Apple's Time Machine backup utility takes care of the rest.

To be truly productive, you need to get as much done while avoiding those repetitive tasks that can use up a lot of your time and become quite frustrating. Automator is a drag-and-drop tool for automating common chores. You build a workflow by piecing together actions and the saved result automates the task in the future. With some applications you can just record your mouse and keyboard movements and save the result to an Automator workflow, where they can be stored and replayed. It's like programming without the hard work.

Another often overlooked productivity treat for many Mac users is Services, small pieces of functionality that can be shared between different applications. Accessed from the application menu (if you are in iTunes, for example, Services can be found under the iTunes menu), services suitable for the current application automatically appear – so if you're working in a word processor, you might see a service to send the currently selected text in an email. And if you don't find a service you would like to see, you can easily build one of your own, using Automator of course.

iTunes top tips

Organise your entire music collection with iTunes, rediscover favourite tracks from yesteryear and sync songs with mobile devices

The way that we manage music has changed dramatically since iTunes and mobile devices like the iPod and iPhone came along. Once you've copied your CDs into your iTunes app, you'll rediscover music you haven't listened to for years. Think of iTunes as your personal digital jukebox! You can use it to store and organise your music collection, as well as discover and buy new music (or movies) via the iTunes Store. Your digital tracks can be turned into Playlists (like cassette mixtapes of old!) and transferred to your iPod or iPhone to be enjoyed on the move. Here's how to transfer (or sync) music from your iTunes library to your mobile device, such as an iPod, iPhone or iPad.

MacBook

Tip 1

NEW SOFTWARE

Like other apps, iTunes is always evolving to include improved performance and extra features. You may be informed that newer versions of iTunes are available when you open the app, but you can also check out any updates by going to the Apple menu and choosing Software Update. You can then download and install the latest version of iTunes.

Tip 2
MINI PLAYER
To reduce the size of the iTunes interface, simply click the small green circle at the top-left of the interface. This turns iTunes into a small floating mini player that enables you to perform useful commands like playing, pausing or jumping forward to the next song. You can adjust volume too.

Tip 3
CREATE A PLAYLIST
It can be daunting deciding what songs to listen to in a huge music library. Thankfully, you can create Playlists of your favourite songs. Click the '+' icon at the bottom left of the iTunes window. Label your Playlist. Click on Music in the Library section. Drag tracks from the Library into the Playlist. When you click on the Playlist, only these selected songs will play.

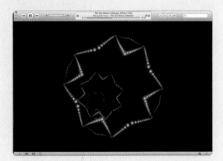

"Once you've copied your CDs into your iTunes app, you'll rediscover music you haven't listened to for years"

Quick iTunes tutorial

01 Plug in your gadget
When you plug your iPad (or iPhone) into your Mac via a USB cable, click on the relevant icon under Devices. Click Summary. Tick 'Open iTunes when this iPad (or iPhone) is connected'. Tick 'Sync only checked songs and videos'.

02 Choose content to sync
Click on the Music tab in the main window. Tick Sync Music to see songs on your Mac. Tick Selected playlists, artists, albums and genres. Tick the playlists or albums that you want to sync onto your iPad/iPhone.

03 Sync!
You can also tick boxes to sync apps, movies, TV shows and photos. Use the Info tab to sync Contacts and even Safari bookmarks. Click Apply to start syncing. This will transfer content from your iTunes Library onto your mobile device.

Tip 4
VISUALIZER
By pressing Command+T you can activate the Visualizer and enjoy real-time animated graphics that react to the track you're currently playing. To see different types of graphics, go to View>Visualizer and choose an option like Jelly. By pressing Command+F you can expand the Visualizer to full screen and create a psychedelic light show to accompany your music.

Tip 5
GET ALBUM ARTWORK
An Album gets some of its character from the accompanying cover artwork. To enjoy this important aspect of any album in your collection, go to Advanced>Get Album Artwork. iTunes will then trawl an online database for appropriate covers. You can display and browse through downloaded album covers using Cover Flow.

Ultimate guide

Mac App Store

Browse thousands of Mac applications, all located in one convenient App Store

Launched back in July 2008, Apple's original App Store was initially accessible via an app on the iPhone – and subsequently the iPod touch and iPad – enabling users of those devices to peruse thousands of downloadable apps designed for iOS devices. Apps span a wide range of categories (from Photography to Education) and let you extend your iPhone's functionality in many exciting ways. The iPhone-centric App Store has proven incredibly successful, so there was little surprise when a Mac OS X App Store appeared earlier in 2011. On its first day, the new Mac App store sold a million apps.

The Mac App Store enables you to find useful software for your iMac or MacBook in one convenient place, without having to trawl the internet. To browse it, you'll need the Mac App Store app, which is available when you use your Apple>Software Update menu command to install the latest version of Snow Leopard. Once you've updated Mac OS X, the Mac App Store will appear in your Dock. Double-click on the app's icon to fire it up.

As there are thousands of Mac apps to explore, it can be a daunting task finding what you need, so it's worth starting with a rummage through one of the 21 categories. As on the iOS App Store, these Mac app categories cover a wide range topics, including Games and Social Networking. Once you've found a category that you're interested in, you can refine your hunt by looking at the Top Paid or Top Free Apps to see what is popular. Alternatively, you can search the App Store with a relevant keyword. Once you've clicked on an app that catches your eye, you can find out more about it by viewing screenshots of its interface. More importantly, you can read the reviews of people who've already downloaded the app to see whether it's worth your time (and money!).

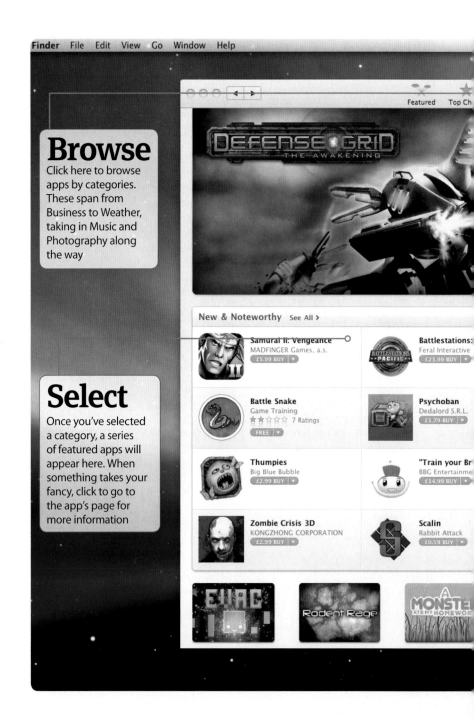

Browse
Click here to browse apps by categories. These span from Business to Weather, taking in Music and Photography along the way

Select
Once you've selected a category, a series of featured apps will appear here. When something takes your fancy, click to go to the app's page for more information

Quick tutorial

Locate an app
Use the Categories list to home in on the type of app you fancy, then check out other users' ratings and reviews to see if it's worth downloading.

Download it
Click on the app's price (or the Free icon) and sign in using your Apple ID. The icon will change to 'Installing' and you'll see the app downloading in your Dock.

Launch it!
Once the app's download progress bar disappears, it's ready for action. Click on the app's icon in the Dock to launch and explore it!

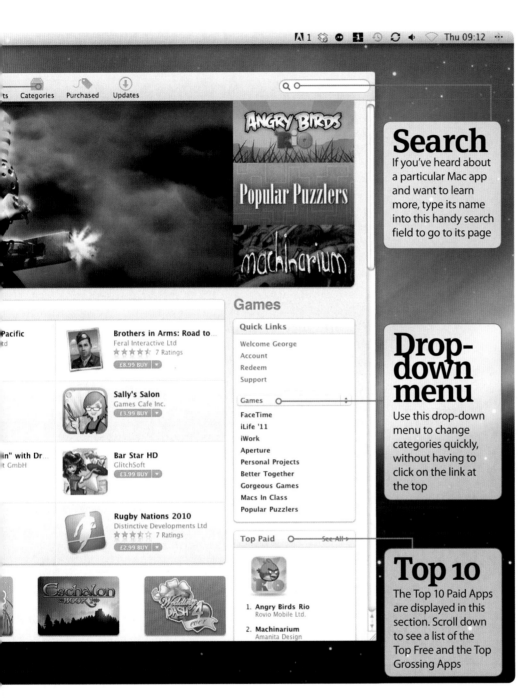

Search

If you've heard about a particular Mac app and want to learn more, type its name into this handy search field to go to its page

Drop-down menu

Use this drop-down menu to change categories quickly, without having to click on the link at the top

Top 10

The Top 10 Paid Apps are displayed in this section. Scroll down to see a list of the Top Free and the Top Grossing Apps

Creativity

The Mac, at its heart, is a creative tool. It seems to have always been that way. The desktop publishing industry began on the Mac back in the Eighties and 30 years later, today's web design industry still favours the platform. How can that be? Perhaps the Mac's ease of use has something to do with it, or the fact that creative peripherals, such as drawing tablets, are designed to work seamlessly on it.

It's as likely, though, that the quality of Apple's hardware strikes a note with creatives. And that applies from a practical, as much as an aesthetic, point of view. Those Mac screens – particularly the larger iMac displays – not only look great, but offer great colour reproduction. And the Mac's built-in Colorsync technology ensures that what's great-looking on screen will look just as good (and colour-accurate) when it prints out.

Above all, it's the software that appeals. A quick scan of the Mac App Store will reveal dozens of cool budget drawing and illustration tools – not forgetting Pages' superb layout tools – while the industry-standard design applications all work well on the Mac, from QuarkXPress to Adobe's Creative Suite, which comprises popular applications such as image editor Photoshop, drawing tool Illustrator and page layout application InDesign.

The web is the catalyst for much creative work nowadays. For those who want to put a creative site together without having to get their hands dirty with code, iWeb, which comes as part of the iLife suite, is a great start. You can base your website on pre-built templates and customise it by dragging other iLife components – video from iMovie, images from iPhoto or audio from iTunes – into it. Instead of having to hand-code functionality to add features such as embedded YouTube video, you can just drag a widget to your page. Publishing to the web is a single click away.

If iWeb whets your appetite to get more serious about web development, there are plenty of more powerful tools available to help. Another Mac-only tool, Coda (**www.panic.com**), offers a single window coding environment that's popular with Mac web coders and developers.

"There are dozens of cool budget drawing and illustration tools in the Mac App Store"

Apps to download right now!

Comic Life 2

This app provides comic-book-style graphics and fonts that enable you to turn your photos into panels from a graphic novel. See page 238 for a full review.

PRICE: **£11.99**

Twitter

Keep tabs on the latest tweets on this popular social network, or send out tweets of your own to inform your Followers. See page 248 for a full review.

PRICE: **FREE**

Pixelmator

Edit and enhance your images with this pixel-pushing app (and it's much cheaper than the popular Photoshop Elements!). See page 236 for a full review.

PRICE: **£34.99**

Ultimate guide

FAQs

Common OS X questions answered for you…

How does Spaces work?

A *Spaces lets you set up four different windows to work in. Click the Scroll button to activate Spaces, then drag various open documents into their own space. Click on a space to work in it. Use Control + the arrow keys to jump between spaces.*

How can I reposition the Dock?

A *Go to the Apple menu and choose Dock. You can then tick an option to position the Dock left or right. If you click on Dock Preferences, you can change the size of the Dock so that it can display more icons, and turn on Magnification.*

How can I change the Dock's contents?

A *Simply drag an application's icon to the Dock to add it. You can then launch that application from the Dock. Drag unwanted applications from the Dock and they'll vanish (though they'll still be accessible in the Applications folder).*

How can I make certain apps open automatically upon startup?

A *If you always check your mail after starting up your Mac then go to Apple>System Preferences>Accounts. Click Login Items and tick the + icon, then browse to choose Mail from the Applications folder.*

How can I stop pop-ups when browsing the web?

A *Open Safari. Go to the Safari menu at the top left and choose Block Pop-Up Windows (or press Shift+Command+K). This will keep those pesky adverts out of your hair!*

How can I save battery power on a MacBook?

A *Go to Apple>System Preferences and click Energy Saver. Click on Battery. Tick the boxes that make the hard disk sleep whenever possible and set the display to dim a little when being powered by the Mac's battery.*

Accessories

Expand your Mac with a variety of add-ons

Microphones Your Mac comes with a built-in mic so you can enjoy a video chinwag with your mates. However, if you're into video editing and need to record high-quality voice-overs then you'll need something like the Microsoft LifeChat LX 3000 headset, which reduces ambient background noise and enables you to produce more professional-sounding recordings.

Remotes If you're enjoying music via iTunes, or have your MacBook plugged into your HD TV to watch a video clip then a remote control device will let you control the content while keeping your feet up. The Apple Remote interacts with Front Row, so you can enjoy all your Mac's media (or download rentals from iTunes).

Protection plans You may be very dependent on your Mac, especially if it helps you earn a wage. You get complimentary technical support up to 90 days after purchasing your Mac and a one-year limited warranty. The Apple Care Protection Plan enables you to extend this support to three years. See the Apple Store for more details.

AppleCare
Protection Plan

Communication

The Mac is all about communication, whether by email, text message or video. Apple Mail, the email program that sits in the Dock of every Mac, is a superb way to keep in touch with friends, family and colleagues. It can handle multiple email accounts and, thanks to the Mac's

External speakers Your MacBook or iMac provides many ways for you to enjoy music, like playing MP3s in iTunes or streaming songs via Spotify. For a richer range of sounds, get hold of a speaker system like the Harman Kardon Soundsticks. This gives you a wider stereo field and a deeper bass thanks to its subwoofer.

Printers It's all very well sharing photos via Facebook or Flickr, but nothing beats a hard copy print that you can frame. You may also need to print a boarding pass before you can fly. The all-in-one, Mac-compatible Epson Stylus SX525WD consumer inkjet printer is one of the best available on the market.

External drives No matter how large your Mac's hard drive is, you're going to fill it! An external drive (like the Seagate GoFlex for Mac) will give your Mac's OS space to breathe. You can set up new iPhoto libraries on an external drive too, and tell Time Machine to back up the contents of your Mac onto an external drive.

Memory sticks If you have a MacBook and a desktop computer like an iMac, you may want to transfer files between your machines. One way to do this is to plug a memory stick into a Mac's USB port, then copy files onto it. Once you eject the stick, you can pop it into your other machine and transfer files to its hard drive.

Bags and cases When you're out and about, you'll need to carry your MacBook in a bag or case to keep it safe. A shoulder bag like the Small Alley will enable you to carry and protect a 13" MacBook plus other bits and bobs like cables, mouse and iPhone.

Spotlight search engine, all its messages can be searched in an instant. Want to add files or photos to your email? Just drag them over your message window or use Mail's photo browser to grab snaps from your iPhoto collection. In Mail, email doesn't need to be drab: you can style it using beautifully designed templates.

Mail is clever too, analysing the contents of incoming messages, not just to check whether they contain spam – in which case they will be neatly removed from view – but also to interpret the contents. So if you get an email asking you to meet someone tomorrow at one, you can click on this

invitation to add it to your iCal calendar. And Mail works neatly with the Mac's own application for storing contacts – Address Book - which syncs with your iPhone or iPod, so your contacts are with you all the time.

Facebook is becoming an ever more popular way to communicate and while most people are happy using the Facebook website, there are plenty of Mac applications that integrate with it. Even iPhoto offers a way to upload your images directly to your Facebook account – and comments about the photo made by Facebook friends can be seen within iPhoto.

You can also use the web to keep up with your Twitter contacts – although it's easier to use one of the Mac's own applications: the Twitter application itself is a free download from the Mac App Store.

FaceTime is a feature of Mac OS X 10.6.7 that allows you to have a video chat with other FaceTime users, whether on the Mac, iPhone, iPad or iPod touch. Another application, iChat, offers similar features, but also supports text messaging. And if you want to keep up with friends using other text messaging services, such as Microsoft Messenger, look no further than the excellent Adium (**www.adium.im**).

Getting Started

All the basics are covered right here to get you in control of your Mac

Tip 1
Master Finder

Tip 5
Set your Trackpad

"Your Mac, just like anything else that you own, needs to be properly cared for"

Tip 2
Screensaver
slides

Tip 3
Preferences
& Exposé

Tip 4
Audio MIDI

About Finder
Preferences...   ⌘,
Empty Trash...   ⇧⌘⌫
Secure Empty Trash...
Services   ▶
Hide Finder   ⌘H
Hide Others   ⌥⌘H
Show All

Where is everything kept on your Mac?

A common problem is keeping track of your files and folders. Let's put an end to that…

I t's nothing to be ashamed of and it happens to even the most experienced of us – you absent-mindedly put something somewhere and the next thing you know you're searching around wondering where you had it last. It happens to your car keys and it happens to the files and folders on your Mac. Luckily your Mac makes it easy to save your stuff in the right place, quickly and often without having to think about it. The key to this is how your Mac handles Home folders, which are a special set of folders that are automatically created for each person that has a user account on your Mac. Know your way around here and you may never get lost on your Mac again!

Get to the right folder quickly

Finder window sidebar
On every Finder window you'll see a column of helpful shortcuts to the common folders in your Home folder. Click one to head there quickly.

Head home
Set new Finder windows to open your Home folder (see the steps below) and you'll have all your common folders quickly to hand.

Keyboard & menu shortcuts
There are a host of helpful keyboard and menu shortcuts to get you to your favourite or recently used folders – check them out in the Finder's Go menu.

Step-by-step: OS X

Tweak your Mac to get around quicker

01 A home in every window
To set any new Finder windows you open to automatically show your Home folder choose Preferences from the Finder menu.

02 Home sweet home
Make sure the first tab, General, is selected and then choose Home from the New Finder window's open menu to set your preference.

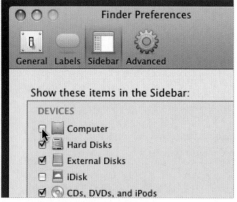

03 Trim Finder window sidebars
Click the Sidebar tab and you can choose to turn off any Finder window sidebar shortcuts that you don't think you'll need.

04 Getting ticked off
Just click the checkboxes next to the options to remove them from every sidebar. You can always change your mind later if you wish.

05 Set your own shortcuts
To get your own folder to appear in every Finder sidebar so you can get to it quickly, start by finding the folder on your Mac.

06 Drag it on, drag it off
Click on the folder and drag it into the sidebar and your Mac will pop in a shortcut. To get rid of it just click on it and drag it back out again.

Folder by folder: What's where on your Mac…

Take a moment to snoop around your system and you may quickly become overwhelmed at the array of folders hidden away. Luckily, you only really need to know about just a few of the important ones…

Macintosh HD
This is the first folder that contains everything else. Think of it as a filing cabinet. It represents the physical storage device inside your Mac, called the Hard Drive. You can personalise the name if it's on your desktop.

Applications
Here's where you'll find all of the software that came with your Mac, and it's a good idea to install any new applications in here as well.

Users
This folder contains the Home folders for every person that shares your Mac. This helps to give everyone the ability to have their own personal settings, music, bookmarks, photos, emails and documents. It doesn't have to all be separate though, there's a shared folder in here – and with applications like iPhoto and iTunes you can easily share photos and music between different people.

Utilities
Inside the Applications folder on every Mac is a folder called Utilities. In here you'll find all the little programs you'll need (or more often not need) for making tweaks and changes, setting things up, turning things on or trying to find out why something isn't working!

The Library and System folders
As you snoop and pry around you can do so secure in the knowledge that if, by mistake, you move or delete something, you won't break your Mac. That rule does not apply here. With the innards that make your Mac tick exposed, it's best to steer clear of these two folders!

Your Home folder
This is where you'll find everything that makes your Mac yours! Your files, folders, photos and settings – even your Desktop. They're all in here and only viewable by you! Luckily Mac OS X makes it pretty easy to find, and so this is the starting point for finding or saving your documents. Learn the shortcuts (Shift+Cmd+H) to get here fast!

Shared
Any files or folders stored in here will be accessible to all the users of the Mac – great for sharing whole photo albums or documents that more than one user might need.

The Home folders for all the other people that use the Mac
Even if it's your Mac, you won't be able to see what's inside the Home folders of the other users. All you'll find inside are Keep Out symbols and a couple of shared folders.

Desktop
Anything you dump on your desktop (the background behind your other windows) is really kept in this folder.
Used by: You, when you want to dump a file somewhere quickly!

Documents
This is your general storage area for all your everyday, miscellaneous files and folders.
Used by: Most well-behaved applications that don't use one of the other folders.

Downloads
When you download a file from the internet, or save it from iChat, the chances are it'll be saved to this folder. It's a good idea to give it a good clear-out now and then!
Used by: iChat and Safari.

Library
This version of the Mac's Library is used to save your personal preferences, settings and fonts – helping you to personalise your Mac.
Used by: Most applications.

Movies
This is where iMovie will save projects, and so it's also where the other iLife apps will look for your videos if you want to add them to other projects.
Used by: The iLife apps, especially iMovie.

Navigate the folders in your Home folder

Your Home folder is your 'safe place' on your Mac – it's where you'll save your files, folders, photos, movies, music and more. Learn your way around it and you'll go a long way to mastering Mac OS X and your Mac!

Music
The first time you boot up iTunes it will create a folder in here for its library; adding any tracks you rip as well as music, movies or TV shows you buy from the iTunes Store.
Used by: iTunes.

Pictures
This is the default folder for your pictures, so is naturally used by iPhoto for its library. iChat and Photo Booth also use it for saving their snaps.
Used by: iPhoto, iChat and Photo Booth.

Public
These last two folders are the only ones that other users can look inside. As the Shared folder inside the Users folder does a better job then you'll probably never use them!
Used by: Not many people.

Sites
If you're up for some tricky setting up, you can publish a website from your Mac. Most people won't bother though.
Used by: Possibly even fewer people than the Public folder!

Make the most of Finder

The Finder is an effective way to work with the software, documents and folders stored on your Mac

There is a wealth of fantastic software running on a Mac, but perhaps none more iconic than the Finder. It is the first program a user interacts with after first booting up a Mac, and it is responsible for the general look and feel of your machine. Many aspects of your work are based on, and take advantage of, one of its features, so it's definitely worth getting to know what's going on back there!

Its windowed view of the content of your system not only allows you to open and launch the applications and documents that are present on your system, but can also be tailored to suit your specific needs. Furthermore, the Finder leverages the services provided by built-in Mac OS X software and eases the access to shared resources and networks. But for all its promise, the Finder can sometimes be overlooked or under-utilised, due to not being thoroughly understood. In this tutorial we aim to familiarise you with the various aspects of this essential tool, allowing you to get the most out of your Mac and guiding you through all the little details it has to offer that you may never really notice. In no time at all you'll know exactly what that smiley little face on your Dock is up to, and you'll be grateful for all its hard work…

> "Many aspects of your work are based on, and take advantage of, one of its features"

Finder interface

Familiarise yourself with Finder and all its functions

The Finder menus
The Finder menus allow access to a number of menu items and actions, such as Finder Preferences

The View buttons
Four buttons allow you to choose how to view the content of files and folders, so choose the one that suits your needs

The search field
Enter any word in the search field to look for, and then find all of the matches in any chosen location

Hide/Show button
This little button hidden away in the top corner is very handy to show or hide the toolbar and sidebar when necessary

The Close, Minimise and Maximise buttons
These buttons provide a recognisable colour scheme: red for Close, green for Maximise and yellow for Minimise

The Back and Forward arrows
These arrows let you navigate through the chronology of previously visited locations within the current window

The Quick Look button
This toolbar button lets you see the content and information for the selected file or folder

The Finder content pane
This Finder pane displays the content of the current location using any view style chosen

The sidebar
The sidebar stores shortcuts to folders and shows connected or networked items

The Action button
An easy way to access the most common actions to perform on files and folders

Knowledge base

Finder views

The choice of view styles available covers all your needs for exploring any folder or device. The Icon view displays an icon for each item. The List view lets you sort items alphabetically, by size or type. The Column view makes exploring the folder hierarchy simple. Finally, the Cover Flow gives a visually elegant flow of previews for the contents of folders.

Knowledge base

Finder sidebar sections

The four sections of the sidebar represent four categories of items that encompass your digital world. The first two, Devices and Shared, expose your surrounding network and storage hardware: hard disk, DVDs etc. The third section, Places, is made up of files and folder shortcuts. The last section, Search For, contains smart folders showing matches for custom searches.

Step-by-step: OS X Discover Mac OS X Finder

01 The Finder environment

The Finder comprises a menu bar at the top, the Dock at the bottom and the desktop in the background. It can also display floating windows.

02 The menu bar

The menu bar displays various menus; first the Apple menu, then the menus for the currently active software and finally a number of items.

03 The Dock

The Dock shows icon shortcuts for some of the software installed on your Mac, as well as file or folder shortcuts and the Trash further to the right.

04 The Dock's Finder icon

The Finder will always be the first icon on the Dock; one single click on it is the simplest way to activate the Finder.

05 The Finder window

The Finder's window is a toolbar with various buttons (at the top), a sidebar with up to four sections (to the left) and a central content pane.

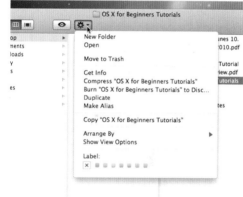

06 The Finder window toolbar

The toolbar includes buttons allowing different actions to be performed on the window itself and on the selected file, folder and application.

07 The Finder window sidebar

The sidebar presents shortcuts for resources, files and folders, applications, networked or connected devices and search results.

08 The Finder content pane

There are four view configurations for the content pane; Icon, List, Column and Cover Flow. They are useful for browsing networks, folders and files.

09 The Finder menus

The Finder's menus regroup actions that can be performed on files. The Finder's Finder menu gives you access to the Finder's Preferences.

Working with applications

Without applications your Mac would just be a beautiful table decoration – pretty to look at, but nothing but a blank screen. Time to fire up some incredible creative tools…

It's easy to think of your Mac as a wonderfully creative toolbox, packed to the brim with inspirational tools to finely hone your projects. Those tools are the software saved on your hard drive, the applications. Software, for the most part, is kept in the Applications folder – a shared folder that any user of the Mac can see and open applications from. The beauty of Mac OS X is that each user's version of an application can behave differently and use different files, the same way that each user can have an individual iTunes library. Of course, before you start learning how to use specific applications, it's worth taking a moment to look at how you open, close and switch between them, which is just what we're going to do here…

Five ways you can start an application

You need to open an application before you can start playing with it. Luckily your Mac makes this really easy to do, and gives you a few options as to how you go about it…

1: Launch it from the Dock
Apple conveniently places the most used application icons in the Dock, where they simply require a single click to launch. You can also add your own favourite programs by dragging the application's icon down among the others.

2: In the applications folder
If there's a program you want to launch that's not in the Dock, click the Applications shortcut in a Finder window sidebar, and scroll through the software listed until you find it. Simply double-click its icon to launch it.

3: Double-click a file
Mac OS X is smart enough to launch the right application when you double-click a file that belongs to it. This is often the quickest method if you're working on a specific project – you'll be ready to go with just two clicks of the mouse.

4: Launch it using Spotlight
Here's one for the speed freaks! Press the Cmd key and the Spacebar to open the Spotlight search window, then start typing the name of the application you want to launch. When it appears, and it's highlighted, just hit Return.

5: Plug something in
There are some applications that are smart enough to launch automatically when you need them – iPhoto can launch when you plug in a digital camera, as can iTunes when you attach an iPod or iPhone.

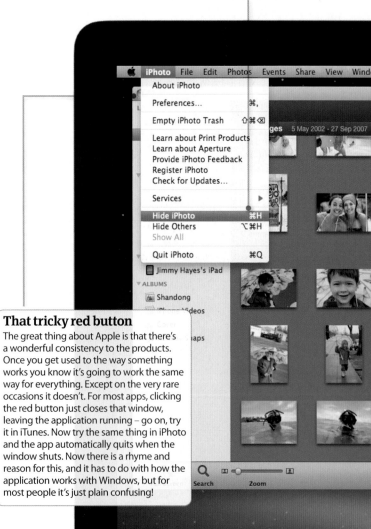

The Application menu
Clicking an application's name in the menu bar gives you a few options for how you see (or don't see) it…

Hide The application's still running, but it will be hidden from view. Click its Dock icon to bring it back.

Hide others Want to focus on just one app? This option clears your screen of all other software.

Show All Brings back all the applications you've hidden.

Quit Closes down the application you're working in, giving you the option to save any unsaved work.

That tricky red button
The great thing about Apple is that there's a wonderful consistency to the products. Once you get used to the way something works you know it's going to work the same way for everything. Except on the very rare occasions it doesn't. For most apps, clicking the red button just closes that window, leaving the application running – go on, try it in iTunes. Now try the same thing in iPhoto and the app automatically quits when the window shuts. Now there is a rhyme and reason for this, and it has to do with how the application works with Windows, but for most people it's just plain confusing!

The little blue light
Wondering how many applications you have open? Each one has a little blue indicator dot underneath it. If you have lots and lots of lights you need to check out the five ways to quit applications at the top of the opposite page!

Five ways you can close an application

Finished playing? Close it down…

1: Application menu
Click on the application's name in the menu bar and choose Quit from the options.

2: Learn the shortcut
Even quicker, press the Cmd key and Q together to gracefully exit the software.

3: Click the Dock icon
Click the Dock icon, keep the mouse button held down, and a menu containing Quit appears.

4: Click the red button
Some apps, like iPhoto, quit when you close the window by clicking the Red button.

5: Application switcher
Press Cmd+Tab, release Tab, then press it repeatedly to get the app's icon. Then press Q.

Application windows
You can have more than one application open at once and most applications can have more than one window open, which can make for a lot of screen clutter if you're not careful! Luckily you can hide windows, minimise them down to the Dock (click the amber window widget) or use advanced features like Spaces or Exposé to manage your windows

Click an icon, watch it bounce
When you click an icon in the Dock to launch an application it can take a few seconds before any new windows appear. No need to panic – so that you know something is happening in the guts of your Mac, the Dock icon will bounce happily while everything boots up

Applications that just won't quit
Sometimes applications run into trouble, and when that happens they'll often just show you a spinning rainbow cursor and refuse to quit. Should that happen to you, just press Alt+Cmd+Esc to bring up the Force Quit window. Click the name of the problem application and then click the Force Quit button to shut it down

Getting Started

Customise your Mac's desktop and Dock

Much like its real-life equivalent, personalising your Mac's desktop and keeping it neat and tidy can make a huge difference to your working day or creative play. Here are the tips and techniques you need to know…

Straight out of the box, there's a wonderful cleanliness to the Mac OS X desktop. Everything is fresh and everything is new; a blank canvas for your creative endeavours. Give it a while though and you'll no doubt start wanting to make it a little more 'you'. Just like the urge to start redecorating once you moved into a new house, there's a definite urge to stamp your personality on your creative workspace. Thankfully, Apple makes this simple. It's incredibly easy to change your desktop picture, keep the icons on it neat and tidy, or shift the Dock around to suit the way you work. If you've got an album of your favourite photos in iPhoto it's even easy to set them as a constantly revolving slideshow on your desktop. Here's all you need to know…

Options for icons on your desktop

If you're ready to start making your own additions to your desktop, there are a number of ways you can go about filling that vast purple space…

1: Set which discs and drives appear on your desktop
To set whether CDs, DVDs, hard drives, iPods or external hard drives appear on your desktop, choose Preferences from the Finder menu.

2: Tick the boxes
Click on the General tab if it isn't already selected and right up the top you'll see checkboxes to set which drive icons will appear on your desktop. Should you choose to rid yourself of any you'll still be able to access them from Finder windows.

3: Set how icons are arranged
To keep your desktop nice and tidy you can control the arrangement of any folder or document icons you keep there. Click on your desktop picture to double check it's active and then choose Show View Options from the View menu.

4: Set the settings
In the pane that appears you can then set the size of your icons to your desired dimensions, decide what information is displayed alongside them and how they are arranged on the screen.

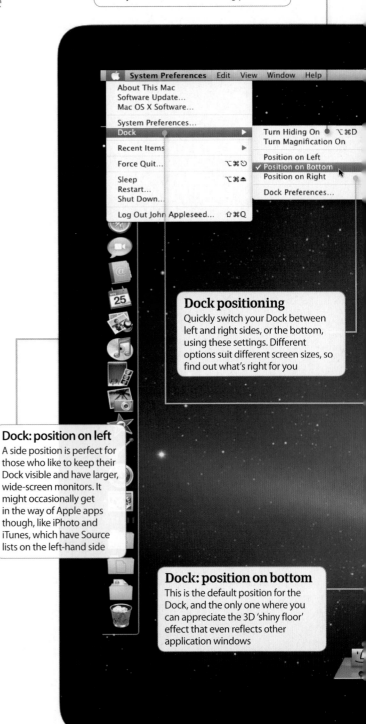

Get a shy Dock
Looking for a perfectly minimal desktop? Turn 'Hiding' on and your Dock will politely disappear when you're not using it, only to slide helpfully back into place when you move your mouse near its hiding place

Dock positioning
Quickly switch your Dock between left and right sides, or the bottom, using these settings. Different options suit different screen sizes, so find out what's right for you

Dock: position on left
A side position is perfect for those who like to keep their Dock visible and have larger, wide-screen monitors. It might occasionally get in the way of Apple apps though, like iPhoto and iTunes, which have Source lists on the left-hand side

Dock: position on bottom
This is the default position for the Dock, and the only one where you can appreciate the 3D 'shiny floor' effect that even reflects other application windows

Changing your desktop background

Don't be stuck with the standard Mac OS X background picture when you can easily change it for one of your own. Here's how…

1 Open up System Preferences

The control system of how your Mac operates, System Preferences, collates many of the most useful settings and options together. You'll find it under the Apple menu in the top-left corner of your screen. Once it's open, click the Desktop & Screen Saver icon (it's the second one in the top row).

2 Choose your picture

On the left side of the window is a panel containing sets of folders. The top set, under Apple, is the collection that comes free with your Mac. Underneath these are your iPhoto pictures, any of which you can select as a background. Finally you have the option of adding any additional folders of photos you hay have by clicking the '+' underneath the panel.

Add picture folders
This is the button to click if you want to add your own folder of pictures to the Desktop preference pane – allowing you to create custom collections of photos

3 An ever-changing slideshow

While you can just click on a photo in the main window to select it as your background, you can also set your Mac to softly change the desktop picture at set intervals to another from the folder you've selected on the left, perfect for a permanent background slideshow.

Searching your Mac's hard drive

One of the most frustrating things for any computer user is to lose a file or folder on your hard drive. Luckily the searching features built-in to Mac OS X make it easy to find those wayward documents

If you've been using the internet for any time it probably feels quite natural to head over to the top-right corner of your browser window to search on Google (or another search engine). Mac or PC, there's a search field up there on almost every browser and it's how most people find what they're looking for. The good news is that it's exactly the same if you want to search the hard drive inside your Mac. There's a search field in the same place on every Finder window and there's even one, called Spotlight, in the top-right corner of your desktop, just at the end of the menu bar. Learn how to use these to search the contents of your Mac's hard drive and you need never be stuck looking for a file, folder or application again.

Searching a specific folder

If you've misplaced a document or are suffering from a bad case of amnesia, Apple has made it easy to search for and track down those missing files…

1: Open up the folder
Open up the folder so you can see all the contents listed. Your search will include all these items – including the contents of any folders.

2: Type in the search field
Click by the magnifying glass in the top-right of your window and start typing your search. The results will automatically start appearing in the menu below.

3: Narrow it down
These results will be from everywhere on your hard drive. To narrow it down, click the name of the folder you started in (it's located at the top in quote marks).

4: Filter and find
Now the results will be filtered to only include the ones that are inside this folder. Find the one that you're looking for and double-click it.

Narrow down the search
If you're searching from the search field in the top-right corner of a Finder window, you can easily narrow down where you want to search by clicking these headers. The 'This Mac' tab will search your entire computer, while the tab named with your account name (in this case John) will search only your files and folders. You'll also get the option to search only the folder you started from – useful for when you know you're in the right place but just can't find that file (see the step-by-step bottom left)

Two easy ways to find the file you're searching for

The searching features of Mac OS X make any file or application only a couple of clicks away…

Spotlight preferences
Spotlight has its own pane in System Preferences (you can get to it from the Apple menu, or from the option at the bottom of the Spotlight menu during a search). From here you can specify how your search results will appear, what Spotlight will search for and exactly where it's allowed to search should you want to exclude private files and folders, for example

Saved searches
Every Finder window comes with a preset list of Searches in the sidebar. Click one to search for files created recently, or of a specific type

Search by more than just name

Can't remember what a file was called? No matter, you could still find it…

1: Start a search
Press the Cmd+F keyboard shortcut to open a new Finder window with a blank search.

2: Chose your criteria
Before typing your search, use the pop-up menus to choose what you want to search by, including date created.

1 Type into a Finder window's search box
If you already have a Finder window open, the quickest way to find a file anywhere on your hard drive is simply to click and type into the search field in the top-right corner of every window. The search results will appear below.

2 Type into the Spotlight search box
It can be just as quick to click on the magnifying glass icon in the top-right corner of your desktop and type in your search. The main benefit of this approach is that the results are clearly organised by types, such as Applications, PDFs, Music, Contacts, Photos, etc.

Spotlight search results
As you type your search the results will start to pop up in the menu below. If you see what you're looking for then click it, otherwise click Show All at the top

Shortcuts to Spotlight
Want an even quicker way to search your Mac? Using a keyboard shortcut to bring up Spotlight makes searching for your files incredibly quick and works from any application

Saving a search
Do you find yourself doing the same search again and again? Click the Save button to save it as a Smart Search in the Search For section of the sidebar in your Finder windows

Getting Started

Use the Put Back function in Finder

Everyone puts files in the Trash by mistake, but by using the Put Back feature you can instantly restore those files to their old position

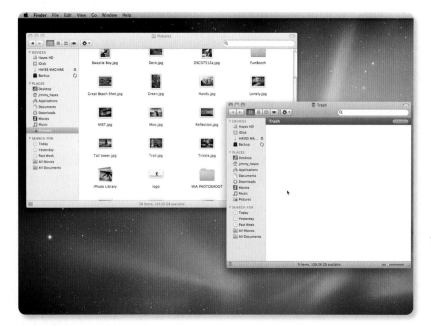

It really does seem as though hard drive space is always at a premium, and as a result it's no surprise when we put things in the Trash by mistake. The trouble with this predicament is that, should we have the foresight to remember before emptying the trash, we have to remember where the file belonged and restore it to the right place. This can be more than tedious and can get pretty frustrating if it happens quite a lot.

Luckily, Snow Leopard has the answer. Yet again the guys over in Cupertino have anticipated our frustrations and built in a very handy feature to solve the problem. The Put Back function will instantly restore the files you have trashed to their original positions. Please do remember though that this will only work for items you can see in the trash folder – anything you have deleted by emptying the trash will require a trip into Time Machine or recovery software.

"Put Back will restore the files you have trashed to their original positions"

Mac OS X Restore accidentally deleted files with Put Back

01 Drag and drop

The drag and drop function is so easy that sometimes we can send the wrong file to the Trash by mistake. When this happens just open the Trash by clicking the bin.

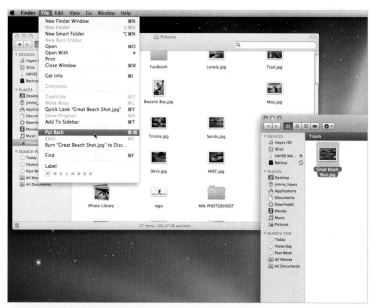

02 File menu

Once the Trash is open select the file that you wish restore to its original position. Now go to the File menu and select Put Back. There you will also see the keyboard shortcut.

Save items from the Trash

Undo your mistakes and save files you accidentally dumped

Empty space

You'll be surprised how often you get that 'I'm sure there should be more files in here' feeling. That's when you need this cool trick

Knowledge base

Time machine

Always make sure you back up your files as the Put Back solution only works for those files in the Trash folder. Once you've emptied that folder you'll have to delve into Time Machine. But the cool thing is that you can use a similar process to get back what you lost from there too. Apple really does think of absolutely everything…

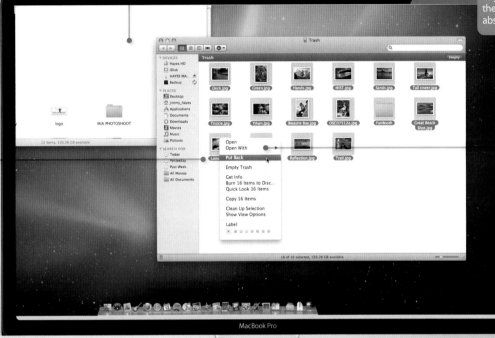

Multiples

You can restore as many files as you like by selecting them all and using the Put Back function

Plenty of choice

The option to use the contextual menu, file menu or keyboard shortcut means you can complete the manoeuvre in whichever way suits you best

Packed bin

You will also be surprised how often you get the 'did I really want to delete all these files' feeling!

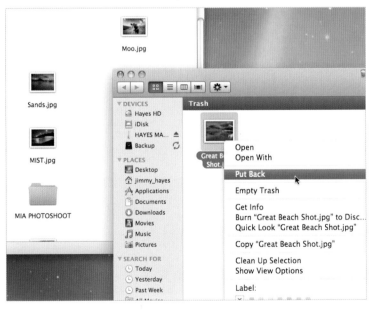

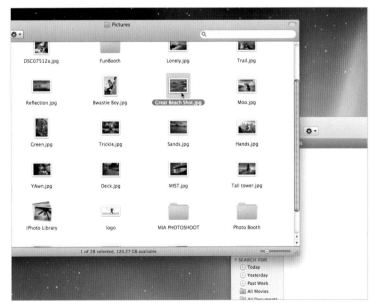

03 Contextual too

For those of you who are right clickers you can also bring up a contextual menu on the selected file and select the Put Back option. To set up the right click on your mouse go to System Preferences>Keyboard & Mouse.

04 It's like magic

Once done the file you trashed is instantly restored to its original home, saving you the need to drag and drop it somewhere and possibly misplace it again.

Remove purchased apps from your Mac

While installing new software from the App Store is straightforward, deleting it securely is a little trickier

After setting up your profile in the App Store, installing a few freebies and moving on to install some commercial software too, you find yourself with a cluttered Dock and the need to recover some disk space and have a thorough tidy up at the same time. Indeed, with such a great tool as the Mac App Store, it is extremely easy to overburden your system with unnecessary software, free games and applications that you've played around with for ten minutes but the novelty has now worn off. The problem is that, unlike the average document that has been downloaded from the internet, these software packages can often be rather large and will not only fill your Applications folder, but could also litter your Dock and desktop with all manner of shortcuts and preference files.

Recovering free disk space on your system and de-cluttering your environment is an essential part of maintaining a healthy system and a productive work space. This tutorial will help you keep your cool when considering the somewhat daunting and risky task of removing unwanted software from your system.

"Litter your Dock and desktop with all manner of shortcuts and preference files"

Delete unwanted apps

Clear up your desktop and save some space for new purchases

The App Store Purchases list
The App Store Purchases list can be viewed by clicking on the Purchases button. This list shows a catalogue of all the applications bought through the App Store software buying and installing facility

An installed application
Applications bought and installed from the App Store appear as new rows in the Purchases list. On the right-side of each row, a button labelled 'Installed' indicates the activated status of the software

The Trash menu
It is not necessary to open the Trash Finder window to empty the Trash. Click on its Dock icon and hold your click until the contextual menu appears. Then choose Empty Trash to start the emptying procedure

An uninstalled application
Once software bought on the App Store is uninstalled, the button on the right-hand side of the Purchases List will change from Installed to Install, indicating the changed status

Knowledge base
Why am I asked to enter an admin password?
Installing an application through the App Store facility is the equivalent of having the system install the application for you. Conversely, when performing a regular installation, the user installing the software is also the one who owns it. Therefore, if the same user wants to remove an application, no special access rights are required.

Knowledge base
Thoroughly clean your system
Software packages are self-contained and seldom install files outside of the Applications folder. Nevertheless, to maintain application settings and user preferences, Mac OS X requires the creation of a few files, mostly in your system's Library folder. For safe and secure removal of these files, it is best to use a software tool such as AppZapper.

App Store   Remove unwanted App Store purchases safely

01 Locate the application

Every software application bought on the App Store is installed in your Applications folder. Open a Finder window and navigate to the software.

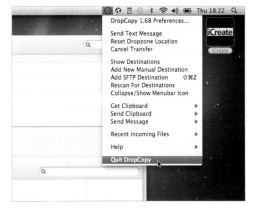

02 Is the software running?

For menu bar utilities, use the respective Quit menu item to close. For regular running software, switch to an active window and hit Command+Q.

03 Locate the Dock shortcut

With most applications, a Dock shortcut is created. Browse through the Dock and look for a pictogram of the software.

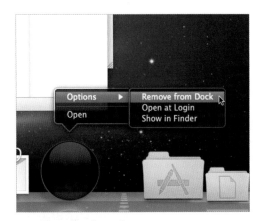

04 Trash the shortcut

If the shortcut is present, click and hold until the contextual menu appears. Choose Options and then Remove from Dock to remove the shortcut.

05 Trash the application

Return to your Applications folder, click and hold on the software to be deleted and move it on to the Trash icon in the Dock. Click delete.

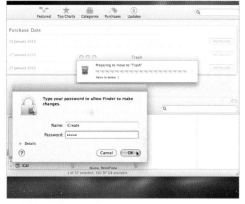

06 Are you authorised to do it?

When an App Store purchase is dropped onto the Trash, a dialog box opens, asking you to enter an administrator password. Enter one and click OK.

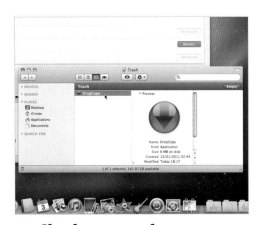

07 Check your work

Click once on the Trash icon in the Dock and the Trash Finder window appears. Check that the application is listed in the contents of the Trash.

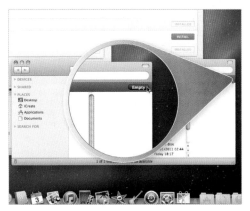

08 Empty the trash

With the Trash window open, start the emptying procedure. Click the Empty button on the right-side of the Trash banner.

09 A word of warning

In the second step of the removal process, a warning dialog box opens. Click Empty Trash to delete the software.

Delete files securely from your Mac

Safeguard your privacy, enhance the performance
of your Mac and recover valuable disk space

I n this day and age, ID theft is more than just an idle threat. Overloading
your Mac with irrelevant or no longer needed documents means that there
is always a possibility that, if your machine was stolen, the information could
be put to illegal use. Therefore, removing data from your system and keeping as
much available disk space as possible should be part of your daily routine. Privacy
is not only a personal matter, it is also a highly relevant topic when considering
client information, whether this belongs to former or currently employed staff
and/or confidential company data. Furthermore, having a system cluttered
with irrelevant files, either downloaded from the internet or copied onto your
system, can vastly hinder your Mac's performance and limit your ability to use
very valuable disk space. Follow these steps and we will show you how to delete
unwanted files safely and securely, so you know you are always protected.

"Removing
data
should
be part of
your daily
routine"

Gone for good

Permanently delete files from
your Mac to keep them safe

Finder menu items
You can empty the Trash from the
Finder menu by selecting the
Empty Trash or the Secure Empty
Trash menu item; do so while
holding the Option key for a
prompt-free procedure

Finder Preferences
Activate the Finder by clicking on its
Dock icon. From the Finder menu, select
the Preferences menu item and click on
the Advanced tab; the third and fourth
options are the Trash preferences

The Trash window
The Trash window aspect does not vary
greatly from a standard Finder window.
It differentiates itself with a Trash
banner below the toolbar and a button
to the right-hand side of the banner

**The Empty Trash
Securely button**
Once the Empty Trash Securely
option is selected in the Finder
Preferences Advanced tab, the
Trash window's Empty button
changes to Empty Securely and
this option becomes the default
file-erasing method

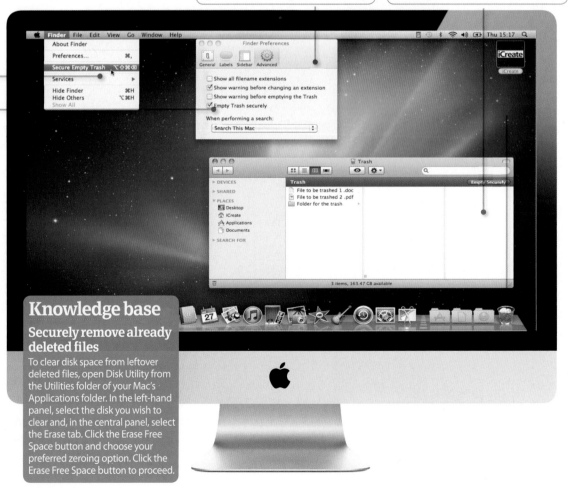

Knowledge base

**What is so special
about securely emptying
the Trash?**
When using the 'regular' method
for deleting items, your system
makes them invisible and the disk
space occupied by their content is,
if needed, marked as rewritable. In
addition, the Securely Empty Trash
writes a random series of ones and
zeros (up to 35 times) on that same
disk space, making the content of
the file impossible to retrieve.

Knowledge base

**Securely remove already
deleted files**
To clear disk space from leftover
deleted files, open Disk Utility from
the Utilities folder of your Mac's
Applications folder. In the left-hand
panel, select the disk you wish to
clear and, in the central panel, select
the Erase tab. Click the Erase Free
Space button and choose your
preferred zeroing option. Click the
Erase Free Space button to proceed.

Mac OS X Permanently remove files/folders from your Mac

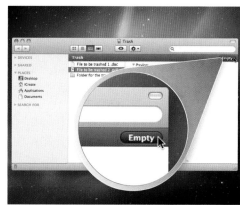

01 Select an item to delete
To delete a file/folder, click on it and, without releasing your click, move it on top of the Trash icon. Release the click to put it in the Trash.

02 Check what you delete
Check that the intended item is in the Trash. Click on the Dock's Trash icon and, in the window, your file/folder should be in the contents of your Trash.

03 Empty the trash
At the top-right of the Trash banner in the Finder window, click on the Empty button to empty the Trash and effectively delete the trashed items.

04 Are you sure?
Upon clicking on the Empty button, a dialog box will ask you to confirm the operation. Click Empty Trash to delete, or Cancel to abort the operation.

05 Empty the Trash securely
To make a trashed item irretrievable, select the Secure Empty Trash menu item in the Finder menu. Click Empty Trash to delete the file.

06 Bypass the warning message
To erase without verification, press the Option key when using the Empty button or the Empty Trash/Secure Empty Trash Finder's menu items.

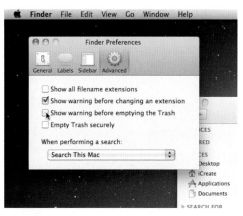

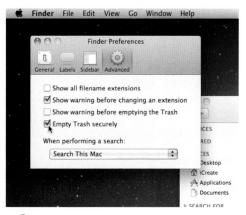

07 Warning messages
From the Finder menu, select Preferences and Advanced. To disable the confirmation dialog, untick 'Show warning before emptying the Trash'.

08 Security as standard
From the menu, select Preferences and click the Advanced tab. Tick the Empty Trash Securely option to enable this method of erasing items.

09 Know your shortcuts
Use Cmd+Delete to move an item to the Trash. Add Shift to empty the Trash, or Shift+Option to empty without a confirmation dialog box.

Inside System Preferences part 01...

Learn how to tinker and tune the inner workings of your Mac by following this simple, four-part guide to the System Preferences. First part: the Personal settings...

Many Mac users are happy to leave their Mac set up the same way it was the day they opened the box. That's fair enough – after all, why fix what isn't broken? But, if you're prepared to take a few minutes to delve into the wealth of settings at your fingertips you may just find a few that could change the way you work, make your Mac a safer place, or just spruce the ol' gall up a little. In the first of a four-part guide, we're going to take you, icon by icon, through the top row of the System Preferences window: the Personal settings...

Dock

With these settings, you can easily control how the Dock (the bar of icons along the bottom of your screen) looks and behaves.

Desktop & Screen Saver

Desktop

Set the background picture on your desktop to one of the Apple-supplied images, one of your own photos from iPhoto or one you've downloaded from the internet.

Screen Saver

Set an animation that automatically starts when your Mac hasn't been used for a while. Choose from one of Apple's, or automatically create a slideshow from your iPhoto albums.

Exposé & Spaces

Exposé

Sometimes you can't find the window you need among the many you have open. Exposé provides handy shortcuts to display all of your open windows or application windows, or to clear everything to give you access to just the desktop.

Spaces

Screen feeling a little cramped? Using Spaces, you can set up a collection of 'virtual screens' that you can quickly flip between, saving you digging through windows. You can even lock Applications to Spaces, so you'll know where the windows will be.

Security

General

By setting your Mac to require a password when you wake it from sleep or the screen saver, your Mac will automatically lock itself while you're away. You can also set it to only respond to a certain remote control.

FileVault

By using FileVault you can automatically encrypt every file on your Mac – great for security-conscious laptop users worried about losing their computer, and the sensitive data it contains.

Firewall

It's no myth that Macs are safer on the internet than Windows-based computers, but if you'd rather be safe than sorry you can turn on the Firewall to monitor and block potentially dangerous connections from the net.

Scroll bar controls

With a scrolling mouse, you may never have used the scroll bars on the edge of every window, but there may still be settings here that you'll find extremely useful – such as the Jumping options

Text smoothing options

Without smoothing the words on your screen can appear harsh and jagged, but you might find text too fuzzy to read comfortably at smaller sizes. You can fine-tune the effect here

Search System Preferences

If you know there's an option you'd like to change but can't remember where it is, try entering its name into this search box to see matching icons dynamically highlighted

Appearance

In this pane you'll find the settings that affect how your windows and menus appear. You have the choice between the usual Blue theme, with shiny blue controls and red amber and green window widgets, or – if you find all the colour distracting – you can switch to the Graphite theme where all the controls are grey.

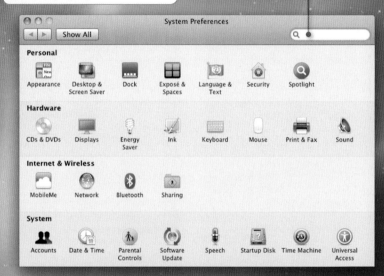

Language & Text

Language

For most users this will come preset, but if you're multilingual (or fancy learning a new language) you can quickly change the language of menus and controls.

Text

Not only can you set your Spell Checking options here, but you can also set your Mac to automatically replace certain typed shortcuts with special symbols, like automatically swapping (c) for ©. This can be extremely useful, but it only works in supported applications.

Formats

Dates, prices or times not displaying the way that you would like? You can easily change how your Mac automatically formats certain numbers using this Control Panel. Presets for most regional variations are already included.

Input Sources

Great for giving you shortcuts to switching to different keyboard languages, but the thing most users will find useful is turning on the Keyboard and Character Viewer, which gives you a map of those hard-to-find symbols on your keyboard, like the é, ü or °.

Spotlight

Search Results

Always searching for phone numbers but never emails? You can trim down exactly which results Spotlight displays using this list.

Privacy

You may have personal data that you don't want to include in Spotlight searches, in case it pops up in the results. Drag those folders into this list.

Inside System Preferences part 02…

Get to grips with the technology inside your Mac by following this simple four-part guide to the System Preferences. Part two: get your hands dirty with the Hardware settings…

T he simplicity of Mac OS X means that you don't have to become an expert on computer hardware to enjoy using your Mac. For most peripherals you can just plug in and play; at the worst you may have to install the occasional driver. But with improvements made with Mac OS X Snow Leopard, even these installs are becoming fewer and farther between. This ease of use doesn't mean there aren't any settings to fiddle with though – System Preferences has a whole row of icons dedicated to fine-tuning the hardware settings of your Mac, and a few well-chosen tweaks could vastly improve the way you work…

Displays

Make sure you're using the optimum viewing settings to get the most from your monitor

Display
Everything seem a little small on screen? The higher up the list you set the resolution, the bigger everything will get (but you'll fit less on, and it won't look as sharp).

Arrangement
If you're sporting more than one monitor (a great idea, especially when you're at home with a laptop), this panel let's you tell your Mac how they are positioned and which one you want the Menu bar to appear on.

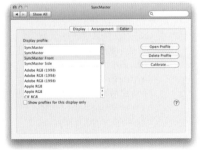

Colour
Ensure you're seeing the correct colours on your screen by either selecting the correct Display profile or, even better, by clicking the Calibrate button to create a bespoke setting.

Schedule
Want your Mac to be on when you wake up or get home from work? Use the Energy Saver schedule to set when your Mac turns on, turns off, goes to sleep or wakes up

CDs & DVDs

It sounds a simple thing, but it makes a great deal of sense to set up how you'd like your Mac to behave when you slide a disc into the drive. Want blank CDs to appear on the desktop? Just set the blank CD action to 'Open Finder'. Don't want the DVD player to open when you pop in a movie disc? Just choose 'Ignore' from the video DVD menu, or set it to open in Front Row if that's how you prefer to watch your films.

Keyboard

Keyboard
Considering how much of the time you spend sitting in front of your Mac, you also spend time tapping away at your keyboard, so it's good to make sure you've got it set up perfectly. If you're a slow typist then increasing the 'Delay Until Repeat' setting is an especially good idea if you often find yourself typing repeating letters.

Energy Saver

Possibly the most useful of this row of preferences, the Energy Saver settings do much more than cut down your electricity bill. The Computer Sleep slider sets how long you'd like your Mac to stay on when you're not using it, while a second slider lets you set the same for just the Display.

Keyboard Shortcuts
Mac OS X comes crammed with many keyboard shortcuts that can speed up how you work, saving your hand a trip to the mouse or trackpad. Not only can you discover what they all are from this pane, you can also tweak and change them to better suit your fingertips – a great way to personalise your Mac for the way you work.

Print & Fax

With every new version of Mac OS X, Apple has significantly improved the printer installation experience. So much so that many users will never need to visit the Print & Fax preference pane – simply plug in your printer and most times it will just work. That said, it's still useful to set your default paper size or check the amount of ink in your printer by clicking the Options & Supplies button.

Sound

Sound Effects

Your Mac makes a number of small noises to give you feedback on certain events. Choose which ones you'd like to hear, and how loud you'd like them to be.

"If you're the arty type and use a graphics tablet, then you might want to have a play with the handwriting recognition built into Mac OS X"

Output

On most Macs there are a number of ways to pipe the audio out – through headphones, the built-in speakers or through a digital optical cable, for example. You can choose which one to use from this pane.

Input

The audio input options are less useful to most users, until you decide to try Skype, record a movie voiceover or experiment with GarageBand. Choosing the right input device will depend on the equipment you use, but it is vital for a great result.

Mouse/Trackpad

The pane that you see here will depend on whether you use a laptop with a trackpad, a Magic Mouse, Mighty Mouse or a third-party mouse. As with the keyboard settings, considering how much time you spend controlling a cursor, it's important to get these settings perfect – especially the tracking and double-click speeds.

Ink

If you're the arty type and use a graphics tablet, then you might want to have a play with the handwriting recognition that's built into Mac OS X. Ink allows you to enter text using your pen and tablet instead of the keyboard, and it can be great for taking notes. You can also set up gestures to control your Mac with the pen.

Inside System Preferences part 03...

Get to grips with the technology inside your Mac by following this simple, four-part guide to the System Preferences. Part three: get generous – share and share alike...

There's one aspect that sets the computers of today far apart from those we were using just ten years ago: networks. Back in 2000 the internet was only just starting to become commonplace, and if you did have it you probably only had it on one computer in the house (which wasn't really a problem, as most houses only had one computer). Now, with the advent of easy Wi-Fi and cheaper computers (plus iPods and iPhones), many houses have a handful of connected devices sharing the airwaves and, with a little setup, sharing their connections, files and data too. The Internet & Wireless row of icons in System Preferences is all about your Networks – local and worldwide – how you interact with them and how you choose to share across them; be it sharing your files, screen, printer or even disc drive.

Network

For most users this should hopefully be one of those 'set it and forget it' preference panes, if you ever need to set it at all. With most modern networks you should find your Mac just connects and configures itself. Bliss.

Bluetooth

Check out the status of the Bluetooth peripherals you have connected to your Mac. To add a new Bluetooth device, like a mouse, keyboard or phone, click the '+' button.

"With most modern networks you should find your Mac just connects and configures itself"

Sharing

DVD or CD Sharing

Share your DVD drive with a Mac that either has a broken drive or doesn't have one at all, like the MacBook Air or new Mac mini server.

Screen Sharing

Allow another computer (or iPhone) on your network to see your screen, and even control your Mac remotely.

File Sharing

Make files in certain folders available to other computers on your network. You can control who sees what.

Printer Sharing

With a tick of a box you can share any printer connected to your Mac with any other local computer.

Scanner Sharing

Save yourself the hassle of unplugging and swapping one scanner between Macs by sharing it over the network.

Web Sharing

Mac OS X has its own pretty serious web server built right in, which can be enabled by ticking this box.

Remote Login

For those users happy typing commands in Terminal, this setting allows remote login to the Mac.

MobileMe

Account

Get an overview of your account status, including how long you have until your account needs renewing.

Sync

Syncing across MobileMe allows multiple Macs and iPhones, even those in different locations, to share the same bookmarks, address books, calendars and more.

iDisk

The MobileMe iDisk is your virtual hard drive on the internet. You can use it to store photos, movies and files, or to host your iWeb pages and iPhoto galleries. This preference pane lets you check your space and control the security settings.

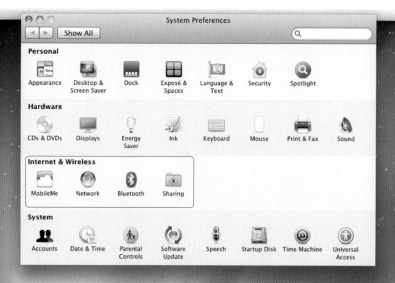

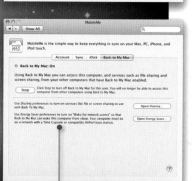

Back to My Mac

With Back to My Mac turned on you can access your files, folders and applications from another Mac over the internet anywhere in the world. You can even use Screen Sharing to control the Mac as if you were sitting right in front of it.

Remote Management

A step-up from Screen Sharing, Remote Management allows system-level control of your Mac from afar.

Remote Apple Events

For the real power users, Remote Apple Events allows your Mac to be automated by other computers.

Wake it up when you go, go
If your Mac is connected to the internet through a recent Apple AirPort Base station or Time Capsule, you can set your Mac sleeping when you leave the house and it will automatically wake up should you want to access it using Back to My Mac

Stay safe
You don't want to let just anyone send your files over Bluetooth, especially if you use a laptop in crowded areas like airports. To be safe, tick both 'Require pairing' boxes and leave the 'When' options as 'Ask What to Do'

Xgrid Sharing

Share extremely intensive tasks, like video rendering, across multiple Macs using Xgrid – for power users only!

Internet Sharing

Share your internet connection with another computer by ticking the box and selecting the correct ports.

Bluetooth Sharing

Share photos, ringtones and more with a mobile phone using Bluetooth Sharing to create a short-range network to pass files across.

Getting Started

Inside System Preferences part 04...

Get to grips with the technology inside your Mac by following this simple, four-part guide to the System Preferences. The last part: delve into the final row – the System settings

The System settings, like the Network row above them, get deep down and dirty into the depths of Mac OS X. Many of the changes affect all users of the Mac, and it's here where you'll discover the tools you need to control which users can do what. It's also where you'll find Universal Access, the first place you should go if you have physical difficulties that make it hard for you to enjoy your Mac.

Startup Disk

For power users, with different versions of Mac OS X installed across multiple hard drives, this pane enables you to pick the drive you'd like to start from.

Date & Time

Always be sure that your Mac's clock is bang on time by setting it to automatically stay synchronised with Apple's time servers over the internet.

Time Zone

Let your Mac know where you are in the world by clicking the map near where you are, then choosing the closest city to you from the pop-up menu at the bottom of the screen.

Clock

Set how your Menu bar displays the date and time. If Menu bar space is at a premium you can choose to see a tiny analog clock, or even get rid of it completely and have your Mac announce the time on the hour, every hour.

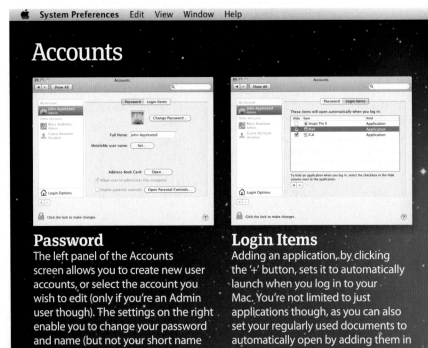

Accounts

Password

The left panel of the Accounts screen allows you to create new user accounts, or select the account you wish to edit (only if you're an Admin user though). The settings on the right enable you to change your password and name (but not your short name that's used elsewhere on the system).

Login Items

Adding an application, by clicking the '+' button, sets it to automatically launch when you log in to your Mac. You're not limited to just applications though, as you can also set your regularly used documents to automatically open by adding them in the same way.

Speech

Speech Recognition

Chances are you may not have realised that it's possible to control your Mac using your voice. Okay, so it's not perfect – in fact, it's likely to turn into one of the most frustrating experiences you've had on a Mac, but it's still cool. And for the rare few that have it working perfectly, invaluable.

Text to speech

Not only can you talk to your Mac, it can talk straight back at you. Text to Speech can give you valuable audio feedback when your Mac requires your attention, speaking alert boxes and more. You can also choose your Mac's voice from a wide range of styles and speeds.

Time Machine

Mac OS X comes with what is arguably the best 'set it and forget it' back-up utility: Time Machine. Turn it on, select a disk and rest assured that your data is safe.

Parental Controls

Kids spending too much time on the Mac? Heading to unsuitable websites or playing too many games? Parental Controls give you the power to manage their Mac use.

Universal Access

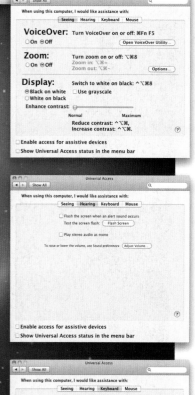

Seeing

For those of us with less than perfect sight, Universal Access aims to improve how you interact with your Mac – you can even have every element on screen read out to you using VoiceOver.

Hearing

If you have trouble with your hearing, Universal Access has two very simple settings to help you out. The first will flash the screen every time an alert sound is played, while the second checkbox plays stereo sound equally between left and right speakers – great if you suffer from deafness in one ear only.

Keyboard

If you have difficulty operating your Mac's keyboard, then this Universal Access pane could make your life a great deal easier. You can use Sticky Keys to help with key combinations and turn on Slow Keys to turn down your keyboard's sensitivity and avoid any unwanted key presses.

Mouse

Turning Mouse Keys on enables you to use your keyboard to move the mouse cursor, which many people with limited mobility will find easier than the arm and hand movements that are required to move the mouse itself. You can also make the on-screen cursor larger if you have difficulty seeing it.

"You can choose how often you would like it to check for updates or run a manual check yourself"

Software Update

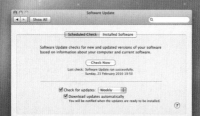
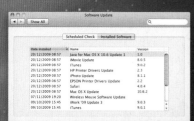

Scheduled Check

Software Update runs automatically to ensure your Mac is always running the most up-to-date version of any Apple software you have installed, including Mac OS X, iLife and the Apple Pro applications. You can choose how often you'd like it to check for updates or run a manual check yourself.

Installed Software

By using this pane you can quickly check the version numbers of any Apple software you have installed and when it was last updated. This can come in handy if you're trying to troubleshoot a problem and think it might be down to a recent update or software install.

Setting up your Magic Trackpad

Get multi-touch on your desktop with Apple's newest peripheral

We love the fact that Apple takes its line of peripherals as seriously as it does its computers, iPhones, iPods and iPads. The company has been innovating in this area ever since the infamous 'hockey puck' mouse. The latest device for input that looks likely to revolutionise drag and drop is the Magic Trackpad. It brings all of the multi-touch gestures available on the MacBook range and offers it to desktop Mac users. It is almost exactly the same hardware that is found in the MacBook, except of course for the Bluetooth chip and batteries to power it. Setting up the device isn't quite as simple as just turning it on and plugging it in like a normal mouse, however. You need to download an update to OS X to allow your iMac, Mac mini or Mac Pro to accept and use the device and you'll also need to pair it with your Mac too, as there are no cables involved. The process is very simple, here's how...

Configure your Trackpad

Take multi-touch to a new level and navigate with ease

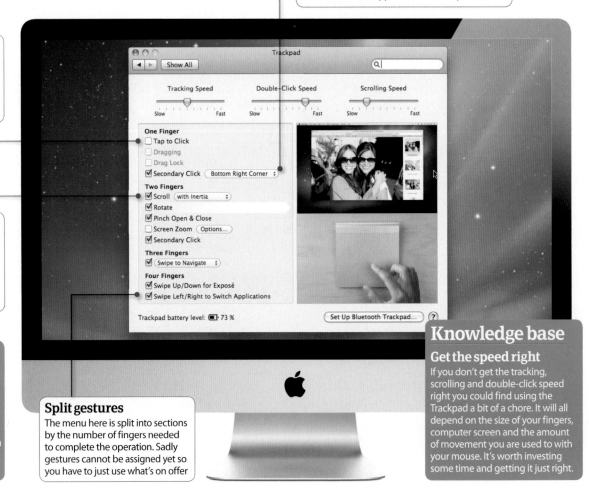

No right click?
People always say that about Macs but even the Trackpad can have a right click. You can even decide where it happens on the Trackpad

Tap to Click
This is one of the most important decisions you'll make on a Trackpad. Without tap to click you'll need to fully depress the button to make a selection

Inertia
Choosing to scroll with inertia will tell the Trackpad to measure momentum of swipes so that webpages will continue to move even after your finger has left the Trackpad

Knowledge base

Hard surface
The clicking mechanism actually works through the feet of the Trackpad so you need to make sure it's always on a hard surface. You'll find that if you try to use the click on your leg, for instance it wont work nearly as well.

Split gestures
The menu here is split into sections by the number of fingers needed to complete the operation. Sadly gestures cannot be assigned yet so you have to just use what's on offer

Knowledge base

Get the speed right
If you don't get the tracking, scrolling and double-click speed right you could find using the Trackpad a bit of a chore. It will all depend on the size of your fingers, computer screen and the amount of movement you are used to with your mouse. It's worth investing some time and getting it just right.

Mac OS X Dock   Getting started with Magic Trackpad

01 Update or find
You should have downloaded the Trackpad update but you can get it from **http://support.apple.com/kb/DL1066**. Just hit download.

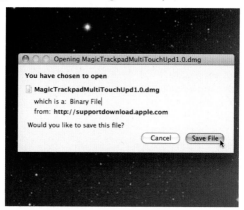

02 Prompts
You will then be prompted to save the file. The download should be quick. When it's done head to your downloads folder.

03 dmg
The dmg file will be in your downloads folder. Like an application, you'll need to double-click on this and OS X will begin installing it.

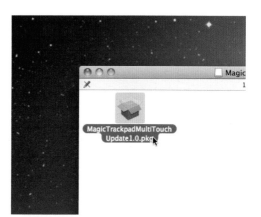

04 pkg
You will now see that OS X has unpacked another file. Double-click on this and a new window will then appear.

05 Good guide
You will now be given easy prompts to finish the install. Then your Mac will need to reboot so it's worth saving any work you have been doing.

06 System Preferences
You can check it has installed by opening System Preferences. You will see a Trackpad section next to Mouse. Now it's time to turn the Trackpad on.

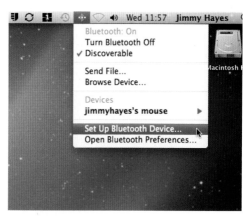

07 Bluetooth
Click on the Bluetooth icon in the menu bar and then click on 'Set Up Bluetooth Device'. Your Mac will now start to scan for available devices.

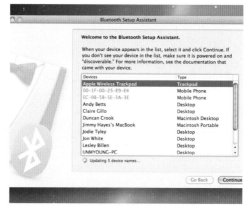

08 Find it, pair it
Your Trackpad should appear in the list of devices. Click on the Trackpad and click Continue. The device will then pair and you can use it.

09 Return to the Prefs
Go to System Preferences and click on Trackpad and you will see the options. The newest is a three fingered selection and dragging control.

Configure a Magic Mouse

Learn how to apply the clicks and swipes that make
your new mouse such a magical tool for your Mac

I f you're lucky enough to have one of the latest iMacs, you'll have
been bestowed with one of the finest control devices Apple has ever
created. For the rest of us, the Magic Mouse is a quick trip to the Apple
Store away and, in our opinion, worth every penny. The touch controls across
the back of the mouse mean that the swipes you're used to on an iPhone, iPod
touch or iPad can be used when browsing the web or flicking through photos.
When you become accustomed to such luxuries on your iPhone and iPod, and
even on the new MacBook trackpads, it's a shame to have to go back to the
old Mighty Mouse that was once seen as such a brilliant tool.

In this tutorial we'll show you how to make the most of your Magic Mouse,
set the buttons up as you wish and make use of the swiping and scrolling
features across its Multi-Touch surface. It's a simple task that requires a couple
of clicks within your Mac's System Preferences and can make all the difference
to the way you work.

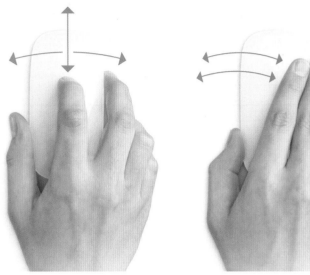

Magic Mouse Preferences

Customise the settings to suit
your requirements

Mouse speed
Using the sliders across the top
of the display, you can adjust the
speed your cursor moves and your
mouse scrolls. You can also reduce
or increase the delay between
double clicks

Swiping
Two fingers sliding across the
back of the Magic Mouse add
even more control options,
such as flipping through
pictures and moving between
pages in your web browser

Scrolling momentum
Momentum means that you can flick a finger and
let the display scroll freely rather than stop when
you lift your finger. It also feels great to do!

Video preview
These little videos show
you what changes you
have made to your
Magic Mouse and how
to make use of them

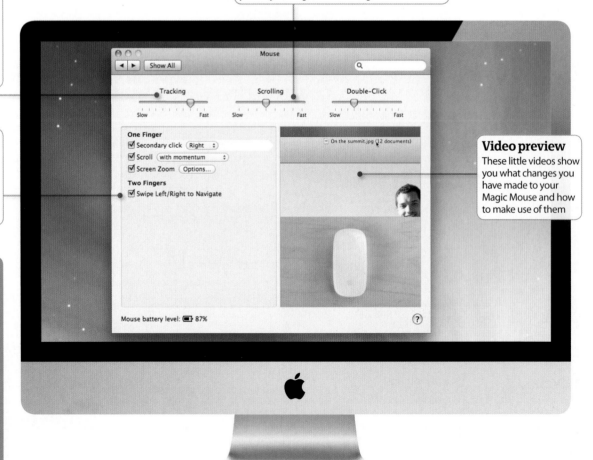

Knowledge base

**Available Magic
Mouse functions**

Click - One finger to select an item
or button

Two-button click - Both fingers
together makes a secondary click

360-degree scroll - Scroll in any
direction using one finger

Screen zoom - One finger plus the
Command key

Two-finger swipe - Two-finger
swipe for web or image viewing
confidence to try more complex
tasks and procedures

Mac OS X Magic Mouse settings

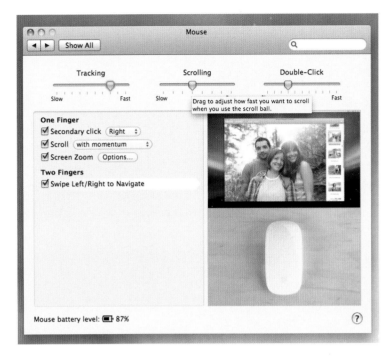

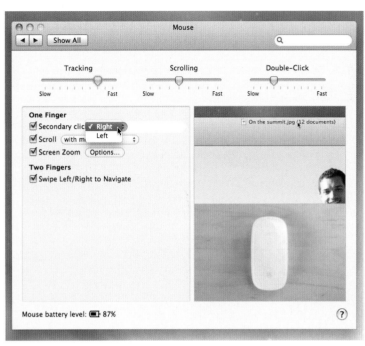

01 Track, scroll and click

Under the Mouse section of System Preferences, the first set of sliders sets speed. Tracking determines the speed the cursor moves, Scrolling sets the scroll speed and Double-Click sets the speed for double clicks.

02 Right (or left) clicks

Using the drop-down menu below One Finger, under Secondary click, you can set which finger you will use to left- or right-click your mouse. The video on the right will show you your choice in action.

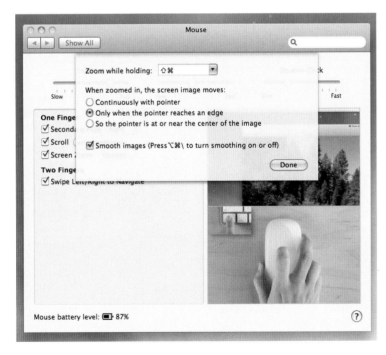

03 Screen zoom

Clicking Options next to Screen Zoom, you can determine which key you can hold down in order to zoom in on your entire screen. Further options allow you to focus your zoom by moving the cursor.

04 Swipe navigation

The Two Fingers section allows you to turn on the ability to swipe back and forth between pages in Safari, files in Cover Flow or across pictures in iPhoto. Many apps make use of this feature, so try it out.

Adjust Date & Time settings

For the truly international Mac user there are a wealth of options hidden in the Date & Time section of System Preferences…

We admit that this probably isn't the most thrilling topic in the world, but there's no doubt that when you travel abroad, having the right time and date on your Mac can be a life saver. So, you need to be able to get in there and make changes very easily. This is the kind of stuff OS X is great at doing. With a couple of clicks you can change your time zone, calendar type, the view that you get on your Mac, as well as a host of other options. And don't worry, none of the changes are permanent – just go back in and change them again whenever you need to.

Once you get used to the system, even if you're as frequent a flier as Steve Jobs, you will always know whether you're in time to get a drink at the bar or if the hotel you're staying in is still serving breakfast. And you certainly don't want to be late for that meeting you've flown out for!

"With a couple of clicks you can change your time zone, calendar type and more"

Of course, this isn't the only use of this essential feature. We trust our Macs to tell us the correct time and date, and not even changing to British Summer Time should confuse your computer. But if you ever find that the time is slightly out, or even the date, it's useful to know how to change these setting manually. It shouldn't happen very often but the option is always there.

Customise Date & Time

The options on your Mac are plentiful and will keep you up to date

Drops and buttons
The combination of drop-down menus and buttons means that making changes isn't an overwhelming mess of screens. It always feels as though you're on the same page

Changeable
Everything in System Preferences can be easily switched back to the way it was, so if you are travelling you can simply switch everything back when you return

Lockable
Prevent other users from changing settings by clicking the lock shut every time you finish making a change

Knowledge base

Safety first
System Preferences are password protected to make sure that only a Mac's administrator is able to make changes. The lock is retained even for single users in order to prevent any kind of malicious or would-be-funny changes being made by a guest in your account.

Easy examples
Snow Leopard gives you examples of the way dates can be displayed, so you can choose the one you like best or take elements from it before you make the changes

Step-by-step: OS X

Time it right, make it a date

01 Preferences
Load System Preferences from either your Dock, Applications folder or from the Apple menu. Now head down to and click on Date & Time.

02 Automatic and easy
If you are connected to the internet, your Mac can quickly and easily set the time and date from a network server. Just tick the box.

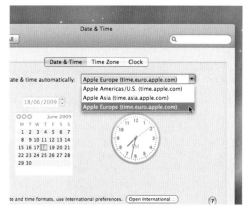

03 Pick a zone
You will, however, have to make sure that your Mac has the right time zone, so use the drop-down menu and pick the one that applies to you.

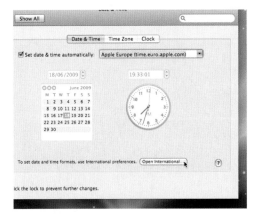

04 Get international
If you want to make further changes to time and date formats then just click the Open International button under the clock.

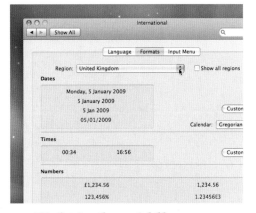

05 Right in the middle
Now that you're on the International page, click the Formats tab. Here you can begin by selecting your region from the drop-down menu.

06 Drag and drop
If you click the first Customize button you'll see this drop-down window. Here you can drag-and-drop different elements into the format bar.

07 Time to get detailed
When done with that one click OK and then hit the second Customize button to do the same thing with the time settings.

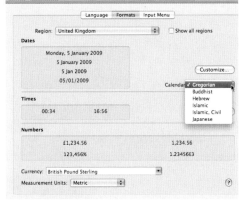

08 Calendar
Again, click OK to save the changes and return to the Formats screen. You can now use the drop-down menu to select the calendar to use.

09 Back to the lock
When you are happy with the changes, use the back button to return to the Date & Time page. Now click the lock to prevent further changes.

Set up security on your Mac

If there's more than one person who uses your Mac, protect yourself against unwanted system changes by setting up some security

When you first buy a Mac it's very easy to get caught up in the bells and whistles of the iLife suite and the great creative projects that you can complete by using it. So this usually means that OS X, and especially security, can accidentally be overlooked.

Your Mac, just like anything else that you own, needs to be properly cared for. And in most cases your Mac will be used by more than one person, so changes to the system can easily be made without you even being aware of it. These changes could affect the way you use your computer and cause you a lot of unwanted grief. It could also use up a lot of your time having to constantly go back and return the settings to the way you want them every time someone has fiddled with things. But protecting your Mac against these accidental – or indeed intentional – changes is extremely easy and will mean that anyone wishing to

make system changes will require a password to do so. Sometimes it's the only way you can stop your kids from putting that Mickey Mouse screen saver on every time they use the computer! It will only take a few minutes of your time, and it will ensure that you remain in control at all times, even when someone else is using your machine.

> "Your Mac, just like anything else that you own, needs to be properly cared for"

Make your Mac secure

Remain in control of your settings and stop others from fiddling!

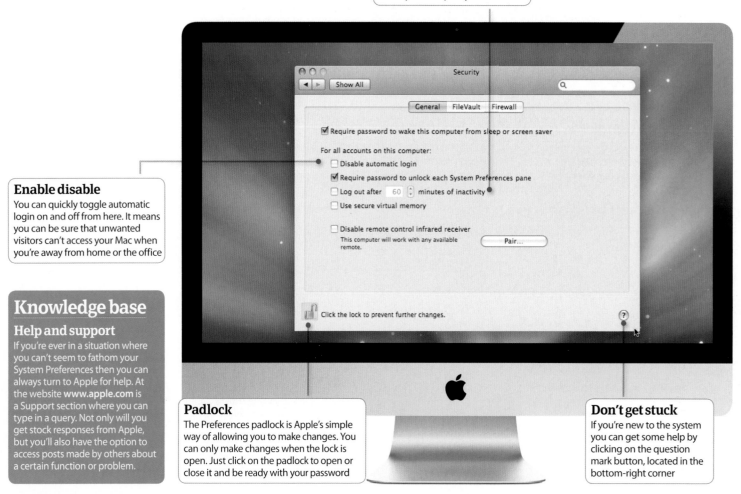

Log out time limit
Use this setting to action a time out for inactivity. The system will require you to log in if the computer is inactive for a certain time period, which you can specify

Enable disable
You can quickly toggle automatic login on and off from here. It means you can be sure that unwanted visitors can't access your Mac when you're away from home or the office

Padlock
The Preferences padlock is Apple's simple way of allowing you to make changes. You can only make changes when the lock is open. Just click on the padlock to open or close it and be ready with your password

Don't get stuck
If you're new to the system you can get some help by clicking on the question mark button, located in the bottom-right corner

Knowledge base

Help and support

If you're ever in a situation where you can't seem to fathom your System Preferences then you can always turn to Apple for help. At the website **www.apple.com** is a Support section where you can type in a query. Not only will you get stock responses from Apple, but you'll also have the option to access posts made by others about a certain function or problem.

Finder   Keeping you safe and secure

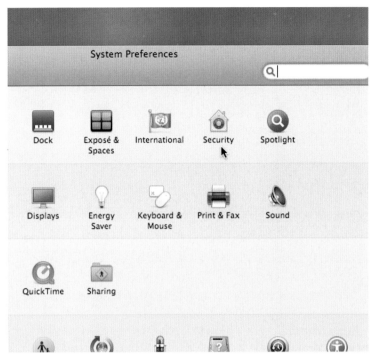

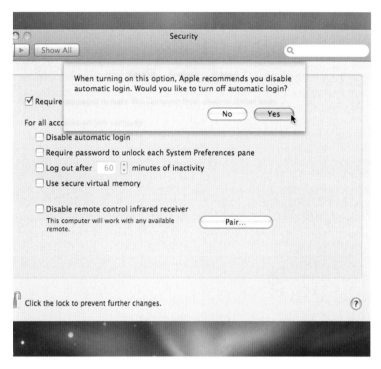

01 It's all about Preferences

Open up System Preferences. Do this either from your Dock or by clicking the Apple in the top-left of your screen and selecting System Preferences from the drop-down menu. Now click the Security icon.

02 Tick the boxes

Tick the top box to set the system up to require a password when waking, either from sleep or from the screen saver. This will then prompt you to decide whether to disable automatic login. Click Yes or No.

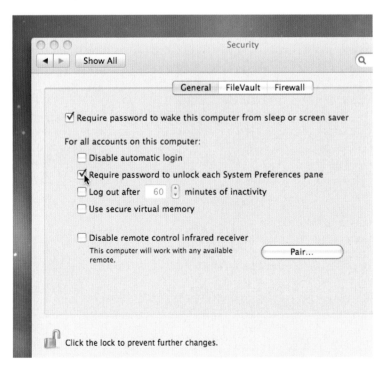

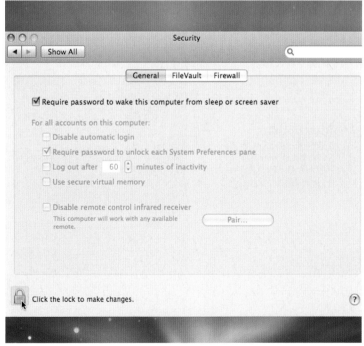

03 Preference panes

On the same window, click the 'Require password to unlock each System Preferences pane' box. This will ensure that none of your settings can be altered without a password.

04 Lock it up

Click the lock to prevent any immediate changes and to get the new commands running. You'll now have to type a password to make changes, which should prevent any tampering from unwanted users in future.

Build a screensaver with your snaps

One of the great features of Mac OS X is the way it can work in harmony with iLife. We show you how to throw up a screensaver of your most recent pictures from iPhoto…

There's nothing better than looking through your most recent pictures to marvel at the great times you're having and just how amazing your family and friends are. So why not be reminded of these great times every time your Mac becomes idle? All you have to do is create a smart screensaver. It's a lot simpler than it sounds; it's merely a combination of two very simple processes that you've probably done before, but when they're used in tandem they are very clever and brilliantly effective. This is certainly a better option than the generic screensavers that come loaded on your Mac. Although there's nothing wrong with the selection on offer, it's nice to have some shots that remind you of people or places you love while you're working.

The first step involves using iPhoto to create a Smart Album, and you then tell OS X to access that album when creating your screensaver. All you have to do is

"It's nice to have some shots that remind you of people or places you love"

let your Mac go idle and it will conjure a cool collage of your most recent snaps. Once you get the hang of the process you can then go ahead and create all kinds of super screensavers and activate them as and when you like. Soon you'll find yourself taking pictures when you're out and about, knowing that this will be a great shot for your screensaver collage.

Design your own screensaver

Use your personal images to brighten up your Mac

Pulling together
Having Mac OS X pull pictures from iPhoto means that there is never any need to have pictures duplicated across your system. They all get pulled from the same place

Plenty of options
System Preferences allows you to change all kinds of details about your screensaver. Just play around and see what suits you best

Knowledge base

Size matters
You may find that as you select the album in System Preferences your Mac slows down or the beachball icon appears. This will more than likely be to do with the fact that Mac OS X is processing a massive batch of pictures. Just be patient and it will soon spring back to life.

Plus it up
You can use the plus button to create a Smart Album without using file menus

Bigger preview
If you need a proper preview of how the screensaver will look just hit the Test button and your Mac will display the screensaver. Hit Escape to return

Step-by-step: Mac OS X Make a smart screensaver with iPhoto

01 iPhoto first

Begin by loading up iPhoto and heading into the File menu. Select New Smart Album. This will then bring up a contextual menu with a set of changeable values.

02 Name and specify

Name the album and then select the values: 'Date', 'is in the last', '3' and 'months'. Then click OK. When you get more accustomed to the system you can add any values you like.

03 Preferences

Now come out of iPhoto and load System Preferences. Once it's loaded head to the Desktop & Screen Saver option. This will load the settings for the screensaver.

04 Pick it, test it

Click the Screen Saver tab at the top then locate your newly created album on the left. Click on it to see it in the Preview window. You can then change the settings of the screensaver to suit your taste.

Combine Preferences with Exposé

The new features in OS X mean that minimised windows can be sent to the Dock. Combine this with the new Exposé and you've got great functionality…

One of the great things about Apple's fantastic OS X is that it's designed to be helpful. Whether you choose to use them or not, there are plenty of little tweaks and changes that can be made to improve your productivity and maintain your sanity when you are using your Mac, but sometimes you need to be shown how to get the most out of a number of these features.

As a busy Mac user you probably want to have a few applications running and a few app windows going too, but that doesn't mean that they should clutter your desktop or be a pain to retrieve as and when you need them. In this tutorial we'll show you how you can quickly send all minimised windows to an application on the Dock and retrieve them using the vastly improved Exposé

system. This means that rather than have the right-hand side of your Dock cluttered with different pages you can simply go to the application you want the page from and retrieve it. It's another one of those 'how did I live without it' features that you'll grow to love.

> ## "As a busy Mac user you probably want to have a few applications running"

Send open windows to icons on the Dock

Combine System Preferences with Exposé for great functionality

Knowledge base

Picking activation
Exposé can be activated in a number of ways. You can use hot corners, a dedicated key command or even a dedicated button on the mouse. These settings can be reached through System Preferences. The app can only be activated by clicking and holding on an icon in the Dock.

Thin white line
Exposé is divided into two sections; the windows above the white line are active and the ones below it have been minimised

One-click wonder
You can restore any window by clicking on it. This will take you into the app in question and out of Exposé

Blue highlight
As you wave your mouse over the available pages they will become highlighted with a blue line ready for you to click on them

Simplified signs
Each window has a nice little label underneath it so you can be sure which one you want

OS X Snow Leopard Send open windows to icons on your Dock

01 Head for the Dock

Begin by loading System Preferences from your Dock, the Apple menu or from the Applications folder. Now head to the Dock option under the Personal section.

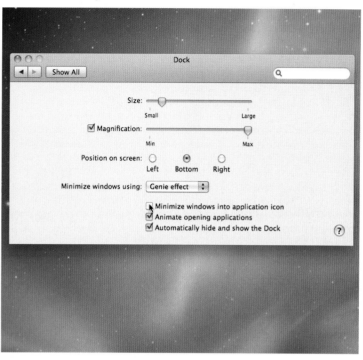

02 Tick it

In Dock preferences tick the 'Minimize windows into application icon' button. You can then leave System Preferences and load all the apps and windows you usually would.

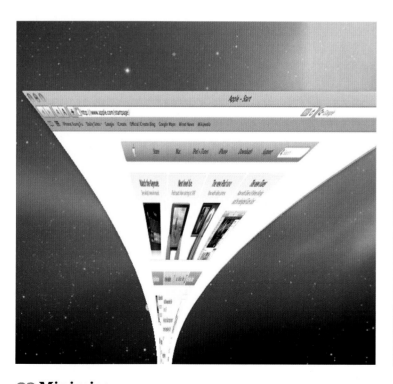

03 Minimise

Now, whenever you minimise your application windows they will be sent into the application's icon (for example, a Safari page will be sent to the blue Safari icon) where they will stay until you recall them.

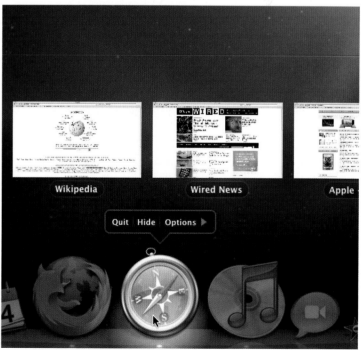

04 Total recall

Click and hold the mouse button on the application you have minimised windows to and you will see an app-specific Exposé window with all of the minimised items in it.

Create custom keyboard shortcuts

Is there a process in your favourite application that you use over and over?
Creating a custom keyboard command for it is easier than you think…

We think it's really important that everyone who uses a computer does so in order to enhance their lives. You probably already subscribe to this philosophy because you are a Mac user. There is little point in using a computer if it's going to frustrate, annoy or cost you time compared with a manual task. So, we fully understand how annoying it is when certain tasks that need to be done in any piece of software don't have a keyboard shortcut.

We also understand that software makers can't shortcut everything, but sometimes what they omit is shocking. Nevertheless, there is a way you can add your own, and in Snow Leopard the process has become much more organised and a hell of a lot easier. It means that you can create specific keyboard shortcuts for any task that you repeat so you can save yourself some valuable time.

"There is little point in using a computer if it's going to annoy or cost you time"

This is the beauty of owning a Mac, if you feel there is something missing that would enhance your user experience, you can add it yourself. The ability to speed up your workflow is invaluable, so learning how to master keyboard shortcuts is likely to pay dividends, and certainly save you from any occurrence of repetitive strain injury!

Save yourself time with keyboard shortcuts

Adding shortcuts is simpler than you might think

Edit
You can edit the existing shortcuts by selecting the application and editing what is already there. Use the Restore Defaults button to revert back to the old commands

Make them easy
Try to make the shortcuts you use as easy to remember and action as possible. It may even be worth noting them down until you learn them

Menu Title
If you are not sure what the exact command is, simply load the app in question and check the menu you use to complete the task/operation

Add and subtract
Use the plus and minus keys to add or remove more shortcuts. If you only need them for a limited time you can use the Restore Defaults button to go back

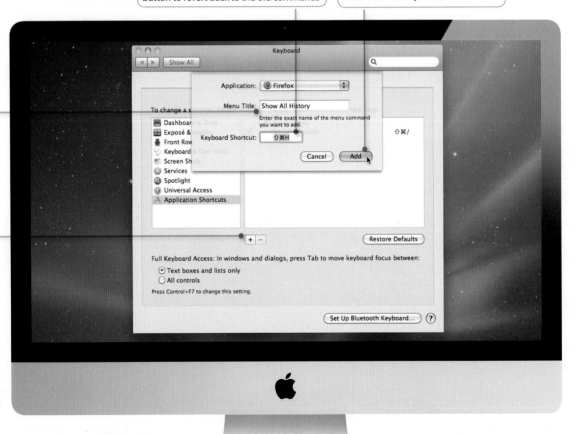

OS X Snow Leopard Customise your keyboard commands

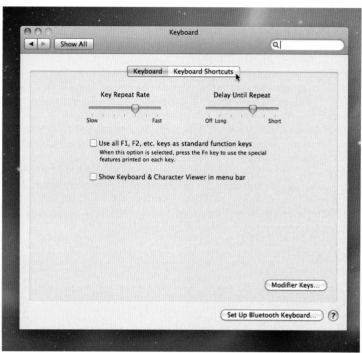

01 Open it up

Open System Preferences either from your Dock, Apple menu or Applications folder, and then simply click on the Keyboard option in the Hardware section.

02 Quick click

Click on the Keyboard shortcuts tab at the top of the newly loaded Keyboard Preference pane. This takes you to the screen with all the time-saving power.

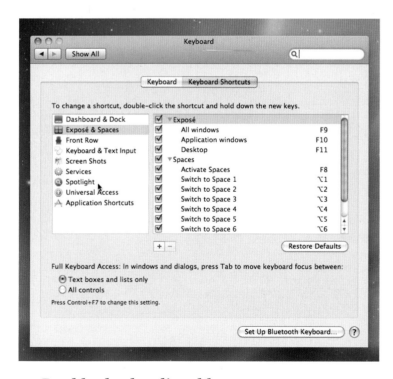

03 Double check, edit, add new

You can now see all of the shortcuts by application. Click on Application shortcuts and then use the plus button at the bottom of the window to add a new shortcut.

04 Drop down, type in

Use the drop-down menu to select the application you wish to make the shortcut for and then type the command you wish to shorten. Enter the shortcut you'd like to use and click Add.

Add applications to Spaces

Is your desktop often cluttered with running programs? If so discover how to add applications to Spaces…

We all know the troubles of a cluttered desktop; windows and applications begin to overlap, and before you know it the desktop background has vanished under a sea of Finder windows. It's especially a problem for those of us with smaller screens, such as those found on the 13-inch MacBooks. Screen real estate is often at a premium, so anything that can help tidy up your desktop and give your applications some room to breathe is most certainly welcome.

There are a few easy solutions, such as using Exposé or hiding applications as you go. There's also the obvious move of closing windows and applications as you go, but if you need to keep coming back to them then this can be both annoying and time consuming if you have to continually open and close numerous windows.

But with the introduction of Leopard came Spaces – a set of easily accessible virtual environments for you to use. It may sound rather complicated, but as with everything Apple introduces it's a doddle to use and another great addition to your Mac's abilities. Follow the nine-step tutorial as we find out how to add applications to Spaces.

"It's a doddle to use and another great addition to your Mac's abilities"

Use Spaces to its fullest

Every element of Spaces can be controlled from one window

Finder enabled
It's a good idea to click 'Show Spaces in menu bar', as this will enable you to quickly choose a particular Space from within the Finder

Activating Spaces
You can also modify which keys activate the Spaces preview from this window

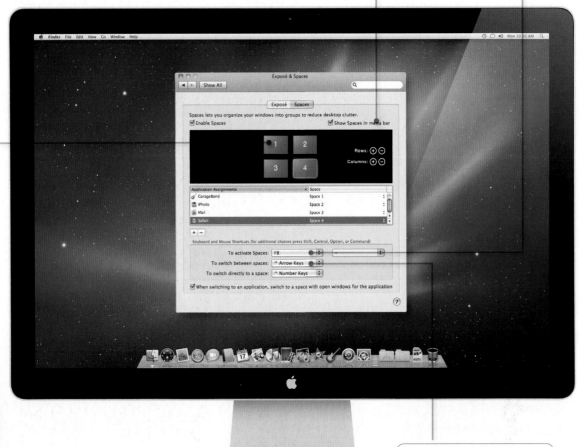

How many Spaces?
Choose how many rows and columns you need by clicking the plus and minus icons. We're sticking with the standard four Spaces

Changing Spaces
You can alter how Spaces are switched between from the lower portion of the Exposé & Spaces

Knowledge base

Memory hog
Spaces comes with four windows as default, but can be expanded to a total of 16. That might sound fantastic, but keep in mind each window eats memory for breakfast. To run the full 16 virtual windows, you'll need more than 12GB RAM – limiting the user-base to those with fully stocked Mac Pros.

Spaces   Add applications to Spaces with this easy guide

01 Load up Spaces
Open System Preferences, click on the Exposé & Spaces button, and select the Spaces tab. If Spaces isn't turned on, enable it.

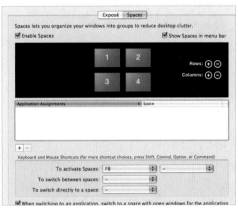

02 Assign a program
Click the + icon below Application Assignments to see a pop-up window displaying all the running applications. Choose one to add it.

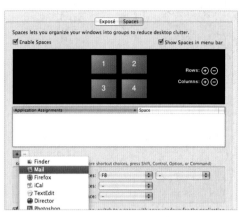

03 Choose a space
The application you choose will automatically be assigned to Space 1. You can choose a different Space using the drop-down menu to the right.

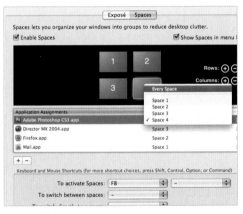

04 Add even more spaces
Add as many programs as you wish via Control Panel. By using the menu you can also choose to make an application appear in every Space.

05 Find a program
To add programs from your Applications folder, click the plus icon and select Other. You'll need to manually browse the Applications folder.

06 Drag-and-drop
It's also possible to drag-and-drop applications from one Space to another. Start by activating all Spaces (F8+mouse button 2 by default).

07 It saves time
Next, simply drag an application window from one Space to another. This is a great time saver for organising your programs.

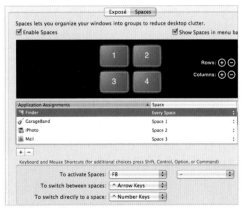

08 Always see the Finder
It's a good idea to set the Finder to appear in all Spaces, enabling you to easily access your files while keeping an application on the screen.

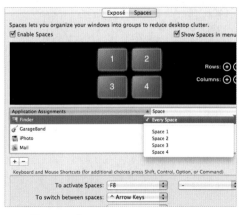

09 Every Space
To do this simply add the Finder to Spaces, and then choose Every Space under the drop-down menu. You'll now see the Finder in every Space.

Use Disk Utility to check the health of and repair your hard drive

Checking and improving the health of your hard drive is easier than you think. With a couple of clicks you can set your mind at rest…

It can become pretty scary when your Mac starts to show tell-tale signs of wear and tear. As well built as they are, like everything else on the planet they are susceptible to the pitfalls of ageing. Prolonged use and writing and re-writing of data can cause things to slow down, and in some cases cause errors.

Luckily Apple has made it very easy for people to check on the health of their hard drives. Using an application called Disk Utility, users can very easily check disks, repair damage and even erase free space to keep the volume healthy and happy. If used on a regular basis you can quite easily keep your hard drive from slowing down and retain that great snappy feeling you had when you first bought your Mac. You will also, with regular use, be able to spot any serious problems before they cause any devastating loss of data.

"Luckily Apple has made it very easy for people to check on the health of their hard drives"

Get a snappier drive with Disk Utility

Clearing free space on your drive can have a marked improvement on performance

Tab it up
Clicking here will take you to the Erase section. Be extra careful before you click anything here as you could wipe important files

Erase Free Space
This will only erase space that isn't being actively used; so if you've done some house keeping and cleared a lot of files out then this is a good way to get some performance back as a result of the change

Erase options
Here you can choose the level of erasing you wish to use. The 35 step is obviously the best, but it will take an incredibly long time. Pick whichever suits you best

Double check
Make sure you are making changes to the correct disk. Check and double check before starting actions in Disk Utility

Knowledge base
Serious problems
Disk Utility may not be able to repair serious problems, but it will definitely let you know if it spots anything untoward. Any serious problems will be highlighted in red and often there will be advice on the best course of action. In serious cases this will be to contact Apple or a reseller.

Mac OS X Use Disk Utility to repair your hard drive

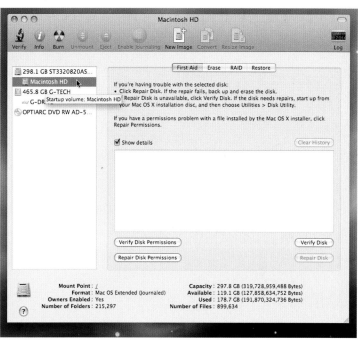

01 Load it

You can find Disk Utility by going to your Applications folder. Once you have navigated here, choose the Utilities folder and double-click on the Disk Utility option as shown in the screenshot above. This will then load the application.

02 Pick a drive

The utility will work on any connected drive, including your startup disk. These will be shown down the left-hand side. You just need to remember to click on the disk that you want to check before you start carrying out any specific actions.

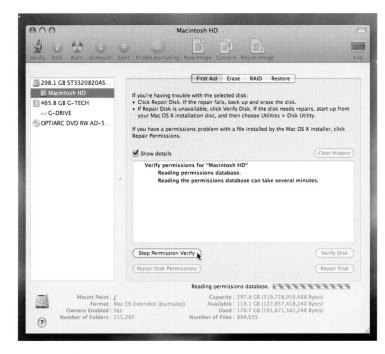

03 Verify Permissions

Click the Verify Permissions button and the utility will begin checking the disk for any errors. Depending on the size of the drive and the speed of your processor, this could take some time so why not go and make yourself a cup of tea while you wait?!

04 Repair Permissions

When the disk has been verified you should get a report detailing what it has found. If there are any warnings in there then you will need to click the Repair Permissions button. Again, this could take a while, so be patient. After that you're all done.

Discover the Activity Monitor utility

A lot of your computer functions take place behind the scenes. Activity Monitor helps you check and control these activities

Q uietly tucked away in your Utilities folder, Activity Monitor is one of those simple yet useful applications that is a crucial part of what makes a Mac great to work with. Firstly, it can give you a great deal of information on what is happening inside your computer and secondly, this very convivial software consists not only of an instructive tool for the beginner but also a troubleshooting powerhouse for the more experienced user.

Activity Monitor principally provides a flexible list of all the system and user processes taking place at any given moment inside your Mac. Additionally, it allows a quick look at your Mac's resource allocation and system performances. Let's see how to use this tool.

"It can give you a great deal of information on what is happening"

Understand processes

The inner workings of your Mac explained

View menu
Activity Monitor's View menu controls many aspects of the information displayed, from the type of Dock icon to the nature and number of columns in the main window, including the update frequency of the readings

Terminate a process
When a stalled process or the remains of a crashed software is found, it is possible to terminate it by selecting it in the list and clicking the red hexagonal Quit Process icon in the application toolbar

Process sorting or filtering
As column information can be sorted with a click on a header, the list can also be filtered by either typing a keyword in the toolbar search field or choosing a process from the drop-down list

Application icon
The default Activity Monitor Dock icon can be replaced with a number of alternative ones showing live information about your system. These can display CPU workload, disk activity and network activity as well as memory usage

Activity Monitor Inside the Activity Monitor utility

01 Locate and launch

Open a new Finder window in the sidebar, locate system Application, head to the Utilities subfolder and double-click on the Activity Monitor.

02 Activity Monitor's menus

The Activity Monitor menu has no Preferences menu item – its most relevant functionalities are located in the View and Window menus.

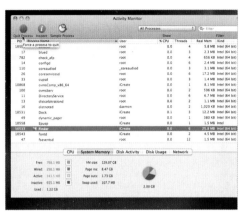

03 Toolbar

Many of AM's functions are accessible from its toolbar: terminating or inspecting processes and allowing the filtering and sorting of process data.

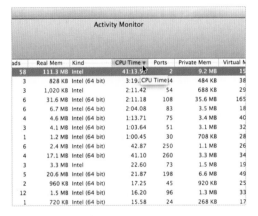

04 Process list

The main window is devoted to listing all the processes taking place on your computer. It's configurable and displays process information.

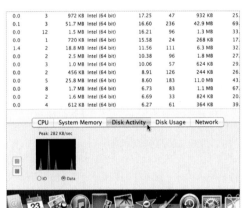

05 Monitoring tabs

Below the process list a row of monitoring tabs present info on CPU, System Memory, Disk and Network activity as well as performances.

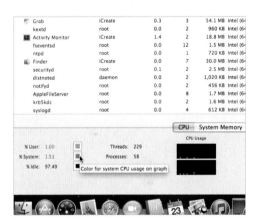

06 Monitoring CPU performances

Using a live display, this permits the monitoring of processor activity. It shows the amount of power used by User System and idle processes.

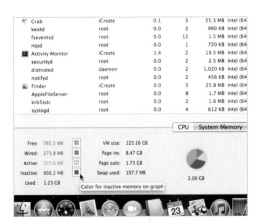

07 Monitoring System Memory

The System Memory tab interface is very detailed – the colour scheme used to list the amount of memory allocated can also be used in a pie chart.

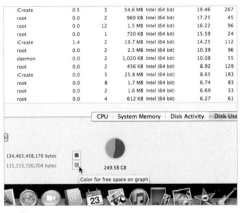

08 Disk Activity and Usage tabs

The Disk Activity and Usage tabs allow you to assess free and used space. They also give control of the amount of read/write operations occurring.

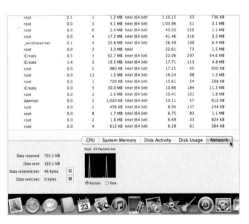

09 The Network monitoring tab

The protocol-level, network tab shows the number of sent and received data packets over your connection and a live view of traffic.

Learn about the Audio MIDI settings

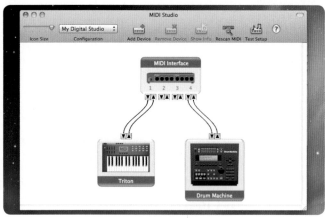

Macs are great tools for musicians and can easily be configured as a digital studio with Audio MIDI Setup

Macs are ideal for creative people, especially in the area of audio and musical creation, and at the centre of this market dominance lies Apple's Core Audio software suite and its Audio MIDI Setup (AMS) graphical interface.

Indeed, Macs are famous for having all the necessary features to interface with all levels and types of music-making or audio-editing and recording tools. Obviously, the powerful Core Audio set of drivers, which provides an extensively configurable environment for input and output audio and MIDI devices, is essential to this dominance. Not only because the convivial and clever AMS software is able to leverage all the functionalities available from Core Audio; but also because graphic interface greatly contributes to the success of Macs in the world of music making. Let us introduce you to the important points of how to configure your digital studio.

Configure MIDI settings

Allow your Mac to become a digital studio

Core Audio Info
The Core Audio Info pane lists all the built-in audio frameworks and components available on your system. This is very handy for checking all the properties of each part of the Core Audio bundle

Audio Devices window
This window is used to choose and configure input or output audio devices, to add new ones and to create aggregate audio devices from either input or output audio devices by regrouping several existing ones

MIDI device properties
Double-click on any MIDI device in your current configuration to open its Properties window and set its name, model and make and configure its MIDI ports and channels

MIDI Studio window
The MIDI Studio window allows you to set up MIDI configurations, add and extensively configure MIDI devices and reproduce and test the layout of your existing MIDI configuration

Knowledge base
What is MIDI?
Musical Instrument Digital Interface is a communication standard allowing MIDI-compatible instruments, sequencers, special effects pedals or lighting banks to talk to each other in order to play or record a track. A MIDI track is like a music score, but also includes the data to route info through your MIDI environment.

Knowledge base
What is a MIDI configuration?
A simple MIDI configuration consists of a USB keyboard plugged in your Mac and a digital studio, such as GarageBand. In more complex setups you will need to have MIDI cables, a MIDI interface with enough MIDI ports for all your synthesisers, sequencers, etc… and to set up a matching MIDI configuration in AMS.

Audio MIDI Setup Learn the Audio MIDI settings

01 Locate and launch
Open a Finder window and in your Applications folder, find the Utilities folder. Locate the Audio MIDI Setup software. Double-click to launch it.

02 AMS menus
The menu presented by AMS is the standard set for any application. The most relevant ones are the Audio MIDI Setup and Windows menus.

03 Preferences
The Audio MIDI Setup Preferences only offer three categories: General, Audio and Info. These settings and have little impact on operation.

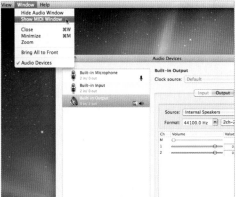

04 Window menu
The Window menu is used solely for the opening and closing of the two main application windows; namely, the Audio Devices and MIDI Studio.

05 Audio Devices window
On the left is a list of connected and powered-up audio devices and on the right, detailed info for the selected device.

06 Audio Device list
The microphone and speaker pictograms indicate the default input and output devices. The face indicates the default output for sound effects.

07 Audio Devices options
The Audio Device options panel displays info on the selected device, including if it is an input or output device and its hardware source.

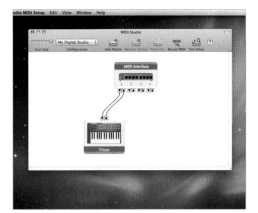

08 MIDI Studio window
This window displays MIDI devices that are powered-up, installed and connected to your Mac. It is useful to publish your configuration.

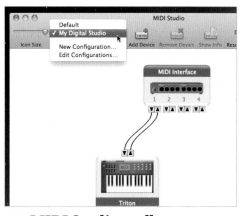

09 MIDI Studio toolbar
The MIDI Studio toolbar provides the basic tools to create MIDI configurations – from adding and configuring MIDI devices to testing.

Using iLife

Get creative with these iLife guides

Tip 1 Import photos

Tip 4 Make a podcast

"You will be able to create slick videos in no time at all"

Tip 2
Create events

Tip 3
Score a movie

Import & erase photos from your camera

Thanks to digital we can click, click and click away! But what do you do when your memory card is full? It's time to import your files…

Photography can be so wildly creative, but when it comes to the organisation it's a case of 'have to' rather than 'want to'. Thankfully, iPhoto makes importing and cataloguing faster and easier than ever before.

Simply connect your camera or iPhone to the Mac via the kit's USB cable, turn the device on and wait for your images to load into the app's Import screen. Make a selection of your top pics, or all of them if you are feeling less brave, and hit the relevant import controls. It's as easy as that! However, there are a few additional tricks and tips you can employ at the import stage that will save you bundles of time later on. Check out our four-step procedure to find out how to import your images and remove those that you've imported into iPhoto from your camera's memory card so you're free to head back out and snap without any fear of running out of space.

"Simply connect your camera to the Mac"

Step-by-step iPhoto Use the Import options to upload your photos

01 Import

Open iPhoto and connect the camera's USB cable to the Mac. Turn the camera on and follow any on-screen instructions. iPhoto will detect the device and log it in the Source pane. Once the preview frames appear, head to Event Name and Description where you can enter details to save time.

02 All or selected?

The great thing about iPhoto's Import function is that it allows you to decide whether to import all of the files on your camera or just selected ones. To make a selection hold down Command and opt for the frames you want to import. Hit the Import Selected button when you're ready.

Use iPhoto's Import options to upload snaps

Whether it's a camera or an iPhone, you'll need to know how to import

Event Name and Description
Entering your details here before you import will save oodles of time later

Import all/selected
These are the two Import buttons that are mentioned in step 2. Pick the button that suits you best

Knowledge base

Make Key Photo
Now that your set of images forms an Event in its own right you can scan over the thumbnails to run through your pictures. If you find an image which sums up the Event well or will act as the best reminder for the contents, simply Control-click and select Make Key Photo from the menu.

Autosplit events after importing
Be sure to check this helpful tick box; by doing so iPhoto will organise your photos better by date. If you'd rather they were kept together, leave the box blank

Hide photos already imported
This is an important box to tick, especially for iPhone users who only want to import their new photos and keep all the old ones on their phone

Device
Your device, whether it be iPhone or camera, will be logged here while the importing process is in session

03 Delete or keep?

Once you've selected Import All/Selected, iPhoto will start uploading and storing your files. You can watch as each one is processed. When the process is complete the app will ask you whether you want it to delete or keep the files on your camera or iPhone.

04 Finishing touch

iPhoto will turn this latest import into its own Event. To save time later why not add some additional details right away? Use the Info button to bring up a new window where you can add info about the people in the picture. You can also share the picture or create a slideshow, album, card or photobook.

Using the Find Faces feature

As our photo collections grow ever larger it can become difficult to find pictures of people that are not already tagged with names. Luckily, Faces is on hand to help

It's tempting to think that the Faces technology in iPhoto '11 might have originally been developed for some kind of hi-tech security scanning system, one that would be found in a James Bond movie instead of on your desk at home. Here, of course, it has far more benign uses, helping you to tag photos of people and make searching easier inside libraries that can run to hundreds or even thousands of photographs.

Pictures in iPhoto include metadata and you can organise them by date, location and event, but until now there has not been a way to search the actual content of a picture. Faces changes all that, letting you identify a person then automatically matching other pictures of them, even if they are not looking directly at the camera. It's a great way to search and group pictures, and will save you scrolling for hours to find all the photos you're looking for. It's also a great

feature if you want to compile an album as a gift for someone. Previously you would have had to manually search though entire photo collections for ones featuring a certain person, but Faces now allows you to quickly type in the name of the person you are looking for and it then does all the hard work. You've then got a great album of a friend or loved one to give as a gift.

"It's a great way to search and group pictures, and will save you scrolling for hours"

Getting to grips with Faces

Familiarise yourself with the interface

A Faces stack
In this view, all pictures of a person that have been identified, after naming by you, are displayed on the corkboard

The Info tab
Press to reveal the Info tab and you can see if there are any unconfirmed matches for that person – pictures that iPhoto thinks might be of them but isn't sure. You can confirm or reject these. The more pictures you correctly tag, the better it gets at guessing

Faces tab
As well as Events, Photos and Places, you can now search and group images using Faces as well. iPhoto automatically scans your library, picks out faces and matches them

The wall
Double-click the name of any person you have identified to change it. This will be updated in the rest of the images tagged of that person

Knowledge base

Use Faces with Facebook

You can use the Faces feature with Facebook. When you tag people's faces in iPhoto then upload those pictures to Facebook, the tags are carried across. If people's accounts are set up to allow it, they will be notified that a picture of them has been uploaded. When your friends add more tags they appear in your iPhoto library.

iPhoto Set up Faces in iPhoto '11

01 Open iPhoto

The first time you open iPhoto '11 it will automatically scan your library for faces. The bigger the library the longer this will take.

02 Click on Faces

Click on the Faces tab and you are taken to a corkboard where you can see identified faces. Click in the name fields to add a name to each.

03 Continue to Faces

Click Continue to Faces to go to the main wall. Click any person, looking at the bottom-left to see other possible photos of that person.

04 Confirm faces

Click on Confirm Additional Faces to review any faces and select those that are correct, or click again to reject incorrect matches.

05 Add more faces

From the toolbar at the bottom-right of iPhoto, click on Find Faces and any new or untagged pictures will be shown. Reject, or add names.

06 Quickly preview faces

From the main wall, move the mouse over any Face to see all pictures of that person. Hit space bar on any image to make that one topmost.

07 Manually add a face

If iPhoto has failed to identify a face, you can double-click the picture and hit the Info button. From the Faces tab on the right click Add A Face.

08 Tag the person

Drag the box over the person's face. Click to add their name in the name field. Hit return to tag. Click the arrow to see all pictures of that person.

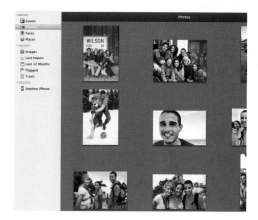

09 Search for faces

When you run a search, you can use a name to see all photos of that person, even if their name is not in the name of the image.

Position box around face **Done**

Add missing faces in iPhoto

iPhoto may not be able to recognise every face, so it pays to know how to add a missing face the manual way

So you love the new iPhoto and are thrilled to bits with its fantastic new feature Faces, but hate it when it misses certain images out from your portrait collection. These inconsistencies can seem quite minor but they can also be very annoying, especially if you are tracking down an image. You have it in your mind's eye, but then you dip into Faces to find it's not there, which can then make you start doubting your sanity, and that's never fun!

iPhoto is priceless in our eyes, but we know it's not perfect – sadly nothing is. Every now and then it just needs a little bit of extra help. The reason why some faces aren't recognised and grouped with others could be because the portrait is obscured with a hat or shades, or because it's a side-on view, or perhaps there's technical issues like the face being out of focus.

So, what can we do? Well, we can input the faces ourselves the good old-fashioned DIY way. Follow our quick four-step workshop to find out how.

> ## "The reason why some faces aren't recognised could be because the portrait is obscured"

iPhoto Add a missing face in Faces

Position box around face **Done**

Dave ⊙

Chad ⊙

01 Find a face

Isolate an image and hit the Name icon. If there is no name box around the subject, you will need to click Add Missing Face. Pull the box into position around the facial area, making sure you resize it to fit, and finalise this by hitting Done.

02 Give it a name

The next part of the process is to type in the name of the person – either their full name or just their forename – and hit Return. You may find that as you type iPhoto will suggest other names that begin with the letters you are typing. This will speed things along.

Add missing faces in Faces

Add a missing face the manual way in iPhoto

Arrow
By punching the arrow to the right of the nametag users can transport themselves into the Faces folder where other images of this person will be stored, as well as possible suggestions of new matches

Unknown face
Sometimes iPhoto will recognise that there is a face in the picture, but not be able to ascertain who it is. Simply add the name of the person into the space 'Unknown face'

Knowledge base
Click to confirm
Once you have input a fresh face into the Faces folder, iPhoto may suggest new matches. Simply click on the image and choose the Confirm Name icon. Then click the correct matches once and the incorrect matches twice. A coloured tag underneath the image will explain which you have actioned. Finalise the decision by opting for Done.

Suggestion
Once you start collecting Faces, iPhoto will be able to suggest people stored in your Faces folder who begin with the same letter as you type in a name

Add missing face
Hit this button to add missing faces to the image. A box will appear on screen and it will be your task to move it to fit around the subject's face and give it the correct name

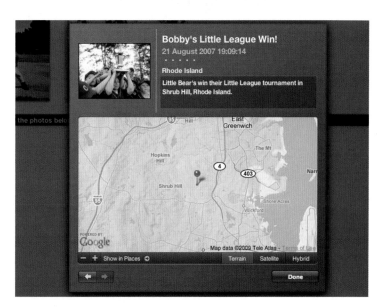

03 Faces collection
Look to the Source List and hit the Faces folder. On this corkboard all your Faces will lie in wait. Source your newly added face and hit it to see other images of the same person. Once you added the first name Faces will search through your other photos for the same person.

04 Add more information
Why not take this one step further and add the new Faces photo to Places? Simply spin the image around by actioning the 'i' button and then enter the relevant event, date and location details. Once you have completed all this choose Done.

Remove red eye in iPhoto

Thanks to the tweaks Apple has made in iPhoto, it can now automatically detect and correct red eye

Red eye is the result of several factors. First, the image would have been taken in an ambient level of light, causing the subject's pupils to open wider to allow more light into the retina. The younger the subject the wider the response. The light from the camera's flash then bounces off the subject's retinas because the human eye isn't quick enough to process the invasion of light and reflects this back to the camera lens. The closer the proximity of light bulb to lens on compact cameras, the greater the reflection angle of the flash, which will strengthen the effect as the light recoils back to the camera.

To stop this from happening when you take a shot read this tutorial's Knowledge Base over on the right-hand page, because if you can avoid this at the source then you should never need to edit your images to remove demon eyes. However, for a one-click fix check out iPhoto's new and improved Red-Eye removal feature, thanks to the app's new intuitive and innovative Face Detection technology.

"The eye isn't quick enough to process the invasion of light and reflects this back to the lens"

iPhoto Red eye removal

01 Ridding red eye

Start by selecting an image where the subjects appear to have red eyes. Activate the Red-Eye icon then hit the Auto button on the pop-up bar. The colour of the eyes in your frame should now be more normal. This is the quick and easy way to fix most of your images.

02 Close but no cigar

You can zoom into the image by keying 1 or 2 for greater magnification. By doing this you will notice that the application sometimes fails to cover the entire pupil. When this happens you will need to complete the process the old-fashioned way.

Detect and correct red eye in iPhoto

iPhoto can now automatically remove red eye in your snaps

Compare and contrast

To compare the results of the red eye adjustment hit Shift for an automatic comparison. For a more studied approach duplicate the image (Cmd+D) and transform one back to its original state then compare them in the Edit screen

Red eye at work

This is an example of red eye at work. The unsettling red eyes are not only demonic, but they distract the image as a whole. Make sure you banish them with iPhoto's one-click fix

Knowledge base

Photography tip

To avoid red eye in the first place set your camera's flash to the red-eye option (check your camera's manual to identify which setting this is). The camera will then fire a succession of flashes preparing the subject's pupils for when the shot is actually captured. Alternately, buy an external flash head and position this flash further from the lens.

Red-Eye icon

This is the icon you are looking for. Hit it once to retrieve the pop-up red eye bar. Use the Size slider to control the circumference of the brush

Auto

iPhoto's Face Detection technology will isolate and remove the problem when Auto is keyed

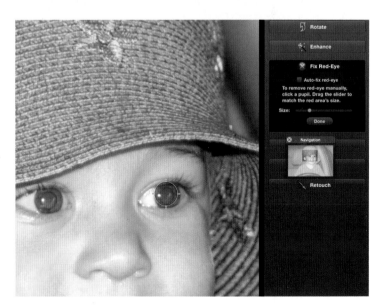

03 DIY red eye

To correct red eye manually by yourself, you will need to zoom in as close as possible to the frame and then select a brush size that will be large enough to cover the pupil. Hover over the iris to measure the circumference accurately.

04 Dot away

When you're happy with the size of the dot, simply click over the red pupil to apply it and hit Done to finish. If the results are unsatisfactory open the Photos menu and opt for Revert To Previous. You can then try again, and again… and again until you get it right!

Remove blemishes in iPhoto

Dust spots, moles, runny noses… there are a million reasons why you would need to use the Retouch tool

Just imagine getting home from a lovely holiday abroad and when you have loaded your images onto your Mac, you notice that your beautiful smooth shots are blighted with a random dappling of brown marks that distract from the lovely image you've taken. No doubt you're confused, and you hope it's just a one off, but as you scroll though you notice that the same marks are on every photo and in exactly the same spot. But what is it that's ruining your image collection? UFOs? No, it's dust spots.

When particles collect on the image sensor or when smears stain the lens these pesky pimples will pop up on your photos. In the long term you will need to invest in a gutsy lens spray, and consider having the sensor professionally cleaned. This should then solve the problem and nip it in the bud. In the short term there is hope in the form of iPhoto's Retouch tool, which gives you a one-click solution to rid frames from unsightly blots and banish dust particles from your photos for good.

However, this tool is also great for removing annoying little features you wish were never there in the first place. Whether that's a blurry object in the background or something much more subtle, help is at hand.

> ## "When particles collect on the image sensor these pimples will pop up on your photos"

iPhoto Remove unwanted spots and marks from your pictures

01 Pick a pic

Let's begin this tutorial by isolating a frame with an offending blemish you wish to remove. Select it from your Library, Event, Faces or Places.

02 Edit

Now Click on the Edit button at the bottom of the interface. This appears in the same place whether you are using full-screen mode or not.

03 Retouch tool

Click on the Retouch tool and the options will spring to life before your very eyes allowing you to make changes to the photo you have picked.

04 Pick the blemish

You now have to pick the blemish you wish to remove. In the case of this picture we are going to remove the blurred football in the background.

05 Click it

Just hover the Blemish tool over the offending item then click your mouse or trackpad to remove it. In a flash you'll see it has gone.

06 Zoom

If you need to get in much closer to a picture to remove a spot, you can use the zoom slider to increase the size of the picture being displayed.

Use the Retouch tool in iPhoto

Remove unwanted dust spots from your shots

In action

When the Retouch tool is in action a beige-brown mark will be seen. If you click once the blemish should be removed but, should it be larger than the size of the brush you chose, click and drag across the area to ensure it has completely vanished

Knowledge base

Dust spots

It's incredibly common, especially for images taken in dusty or sandy environments, for particles to collect on the camera's image sensor or for spots to cover the lens. When this happens spots like this can appear on your images. You may notice them in the same place in a series of images, especially when shown on an image with a block colour such as this. An easy and effective way to remove them in post processing is with a tool like the Retouch brush, but to cure the problem you'll need to have the sensor cleaned professionally and use a specific lens cleaner and cloth on the glass.

Navigate

Grab the clear rectangular portion of the Navigation box and drag it to the area of the image you want to see. To zoom in this close and have the panel pop up, hit 1 or 2 for greater detail. Select 0 to zoom all the way out

Drag me

Drag this slider to the left to decrease the size of the brush's circumference and the right to enlarge it

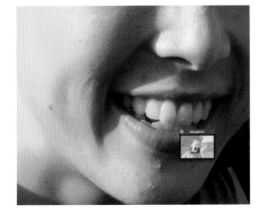

07 Position it

Use the positioning navigator to drag the area of focus around until you have the blemish in your sights. You can then make a detailed removal.

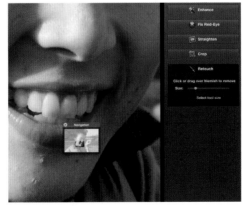

08 Tool Size

Use the slider to make the tool size appropriate for the size of the blemish. Keep the tool as close to the blemish size for a perfect removal.

09 Hit it

Now hit the button and then zoom out to admire your handy work. Repeat this process on all your snaps until you are happy.

Search your photos using Places

View your photos according to location by
using the Places feature

By using the Places feature in iPhoto, it's really easy to search and
browse through your photos according to the location where they
were taken. The majority of new cameras now have the ability to
automatically add GPS data to photographs, which means that when you import
your photos into iPhoto, the location data is automatically added for you. You
don't even have to have a GPS-enabled device, because it's so easy to add the
data yourself.

Combine this with the fact that we are increasingly on the move, and it
makes perfect sense to be able to search and browse your photos in reference
to the place they were taken. The number of pictures we take can often make
it difficult to remember where we were when we were snapping away, but by
recording them with the Places feature, no matter how far in the future you

"The number of pictures we take can often make it difficult to remember where we were"

browse through your images, you'll always remember where you were when
they were taken. With the improved Places feature in iPhoto, you can now refine
your searches quickly and easily on an interactive map. You can narrow the
search down to the exact spot those images were taken or you can search by
country, state or city – the choice is yours.

Move from place to place...

Navigate your map and see
where you took your photos

Zoom
To zoom in, slide the button to the right.
To zoom out, slide it left. If you have a
Magic mouse, slide your finger forward
to zoom in, back to zoom out

Alternative view
Click on any of these tabs to
change the view of the map to
satellite or hybrid

Move
Move around the map by holding
down the spacebar and dragging
the mouse

The red pin
Hover the mouse over the red pin
to see the name of the location. Tap
the arrow to view the photos taken
at that spot

Knowledge base

Smart Albums

The great thing about Smart
Albums is that once you've created
one, every time you add photos to
iPhoto that match the same criteria,
it will automatically add them to
the album. So in this instance, next
time we're lucky enough to visit
Paris, our photos will automatically
be added to this album, provided
the location data is there.

iPhoto Navigate photos according to location using Places

01 Places

Head to the Places icon on the left-hand menu and click. A world map appears, with places you have taken photos indicated by a red pin.

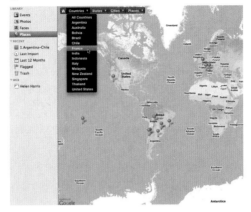

02 Countries

Browse photos by country by heading to the menu at the top of the map and selecting from the Countries drop-down menu.

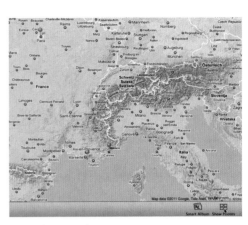

03 Show photos

The map will zoom in to that country. To view those photos, head to the bottom-left of the interface and select Show Photos.

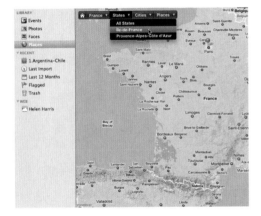

04 States

If you want to refine your search even further, go to the States drop-down menu and select the area you want to look at.

05 Cities

The map zooms into the selected state. Select the city you want to look at from the menu. If there is just one city, it'll be automatically selected.

06 Places

Search through your photos by selecting the very place they were taken from the Places menu. The map zooms into that place.

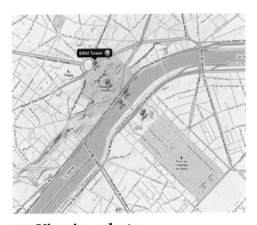

07 Viewing photos

To view the photo taken at that particular location, click the arrow (it will turn blue). To view all the photos in that area, simply repeat step 3.

08 Return to map

The photos are displayed in iPhoto as normal. To return to the previous map, just tap the Map arrow at the top of the interface.

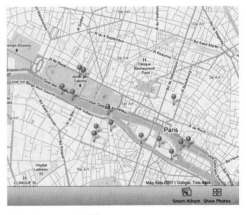

09 Smart Album

Head to the bottom-left of the interface and choose Smart Album. From this album, you can create a slideshow or share images.

Upload photos to Facebook

Gone are the days when you had to fiddle about with several steps to get pictures online. With iPhoto '11 it's a breeze…

As much as Apple would like everyone to use MobileMe for hosting online photo galleries, the reality is that Facebook, and to a slightly lesser extent Flickr, are where people do most of their day-to-day photo sharing. Of course, you have been able to export images from iPhoto to a folder for some time now, then log into Facebook and upload them to a new album, but this was a multi-step process that often felt more long-winded than it really needed to be. It seems Apple agreed and has kindly made the whole process much more straightforward.

iPhoto '11 makes it much easier to export images directly from iPhoto to your Facebook account, without ever leaving iPhoto. Just put a few details in before you start and the sizing, compression and exporting are all done for you. It couldn't be easier to get your albums online, and in an age where immediacy

rules all, you can have your friends and family viewing and commenting on your freshly taken photos in no time at all. Of course, it's also important to make sure only the people you want to see your photos have access to them, so within this tutorial we will also show you how to set the privacy settings, keeping unwanted visitors at bay!

> "iPhoto makes it easier to export images from iPhoto to your Facebook account"

iPhoto Upload an album to Facebook from iPhoto

01 Fire up iPhoto

Fire up iPhoto and go to an album that you have created. Make any edits that you like to the images, and give the album a name.

02 Open the Preferences

In the iPhoto menu, choose Preferences. Locate the section called Accounts and click 'plus' to add a new account. Choose Facebook from the list.

03 Enter your details

Enter the email and password you use for Facebook. This lets iPhoto interface with the site so you can upload straight from the application.

04 Verify the details

When you click OK, iPhoto will send the details to Facebook to check that they are correct. If they are, it will tell you your account is enabled.

05 Select your pictures

Exit Preferences. Choose an Event or album, or one or more pictures from one. Click the Share button, or click the Share menu in the menu bar.

06 Create an album

Click Facebook and a window will show any existing albums on your account. Choose one to add the photos to it, or click New Album.

Sharing your images

Exploring the upload options in iPhoto

Web feed
Click on the Facebook icon to display all photo albums that exist on your Facebook account directly within iPhoto. These include albums uploaded from iPhoto and from anywhere else, including mobile phones

Select images
Select one or more images or choose entire albums or Events and then select Share to upload them to Facebook, Flickr, MobileMe or embed them in an email. You can even order prints straight from iPhoto

Knowledge base
Edit online
By clicking the Facebook icon in the Web section of iPhoto's window, you can make edits to the images that make up your remote albums. Right-click to access edit features like rotate, cut or copy and it's even possible to drag and drop pictures from Facebook to your desktop or back into iPhoto.

Quick share
The quick share menu lets you send the selected images straight to the destination of your choice. iPhoto will make the necessary formatting changes to the pictures depending on where they are being sent

Full screen
iPhoto '11 encourages you to work in full-screen mode, which is less distracting and helps you focus on the images. You can send albums to Facebook while remaining in full-screen mode

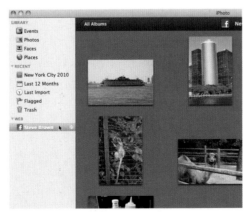

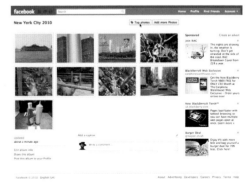

07 Set privacy
In the New Album window, give your album a name and set who will be able to view it – everyone, friends of friends, or friends only.

08 Publish the album
Hit the Publish button and iPhoto will optimise your pictures for online viewing and upload them based on the settings you have made.

09 Check the results
You can now log into Facebook in a browser and see the album is all there. iPhoto will have uploaded thumbnails as well as hi-res versions.

Publish to Flickr from iPhoto

Show off your best photography by sharing your shots
on the web using iPhoto's fantastic Flickr integration…

Taking amazing photos is so much more fun when you can share them with the world. Whether it's just so your friends and family can have access to your holiday snaps, or you want to show off to anyone who may be interested, there's nothing like sharing a picture you're particularly proud of, it would be a waste to have it sitting on your hard drive where no one can see it.

iPhoto helps you to do just that with seamless integration with Flickr, the world's most popular photographic website. Head to www.flickr.com and click the 'Create Your Account' button at the top of the page to get started. Signing up is quick, easy and free, and you will find that there's a thriving community of photo-enthusiasts who are happy to spur on your creativity with encouraging comments. Once you have created an account, it will only take a moment to tell iPhoto about it and then you'll be able to upload photos at the click of a button.

> "There's a thriving community of enthusiasts who are happy to spur on your creativity"

Every step of the process is explained in full, and if there's anything you're unhappy with or unsure about, the Flickr site will explain all the details in full. Sure, you may be wondering why bother posting to Flickr when your pictures are already on Facebook, but photos are the whole point of Flickr and it's also a great place for inspiration for new shots you can try.

View your Flickr sets in iPhoto

Manage your collections without having to open Safari

Pick the key photo
Scrolling your cursor over these thumbnail photos will scroll through a preview of every shot in the set. Click to set the one you want to act as a cover shot

Description
This pane (iPhoto '11 only), accessible by clicking the info icon at the bottom of the window shows the set's description, title and details. The description is only editable from the Flickr website

Shortcut to the web
Your photo set name is shown at the top of the window. Clicking the small arrow icon will open Safari and take you directly to the set on the Flickr website

Status bar
The thin grey bar that runs along the bottom of these photos tells you that the shot was downloaded from Flickr, not shared from this iPhoto library

Web list
Currently you have three ways to share your photos on the web from iPhoto: MobileMe, Flickr and Facebook. The galleries for each one are available here

Knowledge base

Photo resolution
If you have a free account with Flickr you won't be able to upload full-resolution copies of your photos. Upgrading to the Pro account will only cost you $24.95 a year and is a great idea for backing up your favourite photos to a safe place.

iPhoto　Connect with your Flickr account and publish photos

01 Share and share alike

Select a photo in iPhoto and click on the Share icon in the bottom-right corner of the screen. Choose Flickr from the pop-up menu.

02 It's a setup

As you've yet to connect iPhoto to you Flickr account, a dialog box will pop up asking you to access your account info. Click the Set Up button.

03 Sign in to Flickr

Safari will open and take you to the Flickr sign-in page. Enter your account details and click the yellow Sign In button to connect.

04 Better safe than sorry

As a security measure, the next page explains what is happening. As you asked iPhoto Uploader to connect, click the right-hand Next button.

05 Authorisation

The final Flickr page explains exactly what the iPhoto Uploader will be allowed to do. Click the 'OK, I'll Authorize It' button at the bottom.

06 All done

Close the Safari window and switch back to iPhoto. It will connect to Flickr, receive the authorisation and then you're good to go.

07 Try to share again

Now that you're all set up, head down to the Share icon, down in the bottom-right corner and give it another try. Choose Flickr from the list.

08 Sets appeal

You can choose to upload to your Photostream, or existing sets or you can create a new set from iPhoto by clicking the 'New Set' icon.

09 Publish

Photos will be uploaded to existing sets straight away. If you create a new set, you'll be asked to name it and set its privacy options.

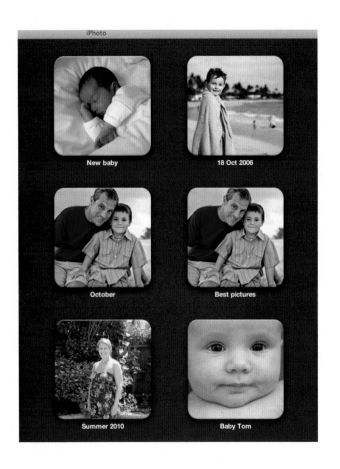

Create custom events in iPhoto

Learn how to duplicate your photos and create custom events while in iPhoto

Creating your own, custom-made event in iPhoto is the perfect way to organise your pictures. For example, the majority of us will take hundreds of snaps but only a few will actually be worth editing. How do you distinguish those images from the rest and what do you do if you edit them but then want to return to the original? In iPhoto it's incredibly easy to duplicate your selected photographs and collate the copies into custom-made events, while still retaining the originals.

Not only is this process very useful for organising photos for editing, this can also be a handy trick to learn if you're thinking of collecting images of a particular person or group of people for an impending project such as a Calendar, Slideshow or Book. By taking a few simple steps you can have the freedom to experiment with different photo effects and editing tools knowing that the original images will always be safe just in case anything goes horribly wrong and you need to revert back to the unedited copy to start over again…

> "You can have the freedom to experiment with different photo effects and editing tools"

iPhoto Duplicate photos and create custom events

01 Selecting images

Select the image you want to duplicate by clicking on it once. If you would like to select more than one image, simply hold down the Command key while clicking images. Once an image is selected, they will display a bold yellow outline.

02 Duplicate

Hold down the Control key and tap on an image to make a drop-down menu appear as shown in the screenshot above. Select the option 'Duplicate'. This will copy the selected images placing them next to the original in the window.

Duplicate photos and make a custom event

Create a custom event for specific images, while retaining the originals

Events drop-down
To change the crop on your selected image, either click on the image in the top panel; this will open it in the 'Editing' interface. Alternatively, click on the image and use the slider to change the size and the hand icon to move it around

All Events
Tap this button to go back to the original Events page. Or tap the Events icon at the top of the left-hand panel. The new event will sit next to the original

Knowledge base
Finish
Duplicating images will take up more space on your hard drive so if and when you have finished with your custom-made events, go back to the Events home page, click on the event once to highlight it and drag it into the trash. Or head up to the 'Photos' drop-down menu at the top of the interface and select 'Move to Trash'.

New Event
Your new event will sit underneath the original. Just type into the field to change the name

Zoom
Slide the button along the bar to make your pictures bigger or smaller. A great way to help you choose your best pictures

03 Create event
Select only one copy of your duplicated image and then head up to the 'Events' drop-down menu which can be found at the very top of the iPhoto interface in the toolbar. When you get here you'll need to select the first option, 'Create Event'.

04 Name
Your duplicated images will have been split into a brand new event. You can name the new event by typing into the blank field by placing the cursor in place and typing away. You're now free to edit your duplicated images without losing the originals.

Using iLife

Design a cool email collage

Apple has added a bit of sparkle to sharing pics via email,
to tempt you back from Facebook and Twitter

While social networking sites are undoubtedly a great way to share individual photos with your friends – and we've shown you how to do this in the tutorials on Facebook and Flickr – iPhoto '11 is bringing new features to tempt you back to your email. In the previous version of Apple's iLife suite, iPhoto's email capability was pretty limited – select photos, get taken to the Mail app, attach photos to your message. Email was overlooked in favour of Facebook integration, as Apple tapped into the growth of the most successful way of sharing ever known.

Now, iPhoto '11 is enticing users back to email by giving them completely customisable layouts, a choice of templates and a range of funky new fonts. The features are easy to use, and will help you make an incredible image to share in just a few minutes.

For example, the ability to create a collage of pictures from a particular event is a really nice touch that everyone will have a use for. Whether it's a holiday, wedding, birthday party or hen night, by designing an impressive collection of pictures you can easily share with others is a great feature that gives you an extra option other than having to post them onto a social networking site.

> "Now, iPhoto '11 is enticing users back to email by giving them customisable layouts"

Create a collage in iPhoto

Mark an event you want to remember
by designing your own classy collage

Full-screen mode
One new feature of iPhoto '11 is Full-screen mode. It clears the screen of any distractions and offers a minimalist interface, allowing you to concentrate fully

Templates
There are ten templates initially provided by Apple, and it is likely that a few more will be available in the future, either from Apple itself or from third-party developers. Watch this space!

Personalise your collage
iPhoto won't necessarily put your photos in the right place in the collage, but does allow you to move them around and resize them until it looks just as you want it

All-in-one
iPhoto automatically adds the individual photos in a .zip file, so that your email has both the collage and the photos in it. You can turn the option off, but it's a nice addition

Knowledge base

Attachment limits

One thing to consider when sending pictures through an email is the size of documents you attach. Different email providers have different limits, and it's important to check to ensure your email doesn't just bounce back to you. MobileMe accounts allow you up to 20MB of attachments, and the automatic file-zipping of photos should ensure you don't often reach this limit.

iPhoto   Show off an event with a cool collage

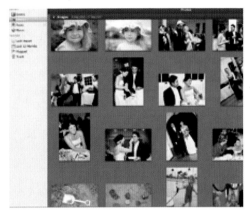

01 Open it up

First off you need to open up iPhoto '11 and, as it's a new feature, enter Full-screen mode to remove any other distractions from your view.

02 Choose your photos

Select the photos that you want to include, either by clicking and dragging, or choosing individual shots while holding the Command key.

03 Select email

Click on the Share button in the bottom-right corner of the screen to bring up a list of sharing options. Choose email from the list.

04 Address and subject

Add an email address and a subject to your message. If you have more than one account you can choose which one to send it from too.

05 Choose a style

iPhoto includes ten collage templates to help you add a different feel to your photo collections. Choose whichever one suits your style.

06 Send extra photos?

iPhoto will check the option to send the photos as a .zip file, but here you can uncheck it, or decide the size of the added photos.

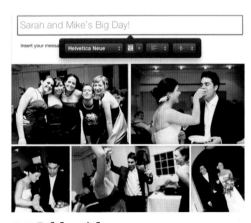

07 Add a title

As in Apple's iWork applications, you can click to edit the title and subtitle of the collage. Each style has a different setup, but all are customisable.

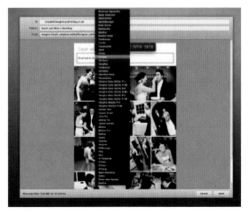

08 Change the font

There are a lot of fonts and sizes to choose from, and you can align your text from this tab. It also allows you to decrease line spacing, to fit more in.

09 Play with the images

Click on any image to bring up a slider. You can zoom in on the pictures and drag them around to get your collage looking just as you want it.

Using iLife

Compile a slideshow using Faces

Use iPhoto's Faces to create a personal slideshow that you can burn to DVD and send to friends

With the summer sunshine just around the corner, now is the time to start thinking about personalised gifts that you may want to give for birthdays or Christmas, and with wedding season on its way you're bound to have your camera out a lot. And what better way is there to start your creative juices flowing than by making a slideshow of your recipient's best pictures in iPhoto? With the addition of the Faces feature in iPhoto, this is made all the more easier.

If, like us, you have thousands of images at your disposal, it can be time-consuming to have to search through every event for the best shots, but using Faces means that you can refine your searches quickly and easily. iPhoto also offers some fun themes for slideshows, which are simple to add and edit but give your projects a slick, professional touch. Once you're happy with your final product, burn it to a DVD, print some labels, pop it in a case and wrap it up. So there you have it: a great and inexpensive personal gift that everyone will love – and a great reminder of a family wedding to treasure.

> "iPhoto also offers some fun themes for slideshows, which are simple to add and edit"

iPhoto Use Faces to create a personalised slideshow

01 Faces first

Once you have launched iPhoto, go to the Faces icon on the left-hand side of the interface and click. Select the person that you want to create a slideshow of, head up to 'File' and then select the option 'New Album From Selection'.

02 Choose the project

Select 'Slideshow', which is the fourth icon along the top, and enter a name for your project in the field that is provided. Ensure that it is something memorable that fits with your slideshow. Make sure that the box 'Use selected items in new slideshow' is ticked and press Create.

Use Faces to make a personal slideshow

Create a personalised slideshow for someone special using iPhoto

Changing the order
Change the sequence of images by dragging and dropping them around in this panel. It's usually best to start and end with the strongest images. For the opening shot, choose something fairly uncomplicated that will highlight the text

Themes
iPhoto's Slideshows option offers six different themes. Shatter offers cool transitions and typography while Scrapbook is reminiscent of a beautiful, antique album. Sliding Panels and Snapshots are slick while Classic and Ken Burns are more traditional

Editing your text
Just click on the text and highlight it to change it. If you want to change the font, colour or size then head up to the 'Edit' drop-down menu at the top of the interface and select 'Font'

Music
Slideshow themes will automatically add music. We like the tune that comes with the theme we selected but if you want to change it, hit this icon and you can choose anything from your iTunes library or even create a customised playlist

03 Select a theme
Hit the 'Themes' icon at the bottom centre of the interface to change the theme of your Slideshow (we like Shatter for its rather funky transitions). Click Choose, but don't worry if you don't like it: just hit 'Themes' again and select one you're happy with.

04 Preview and export
Select the Play button (situated on the bottom left) to preview your slideshow full-screen, or Preview to view within the interface. When you are satisfied with the results, hit the Export button (bottom right). Select the format and press 'Export'.

Create a travel journal in iPhoto

Chart your adventures using the iPhoto travel-themed books

I t's all too easy to come back from your holidays with good intentions of creating a beautiful album to show-off your photographs. The reality is, of course, that once you get back to the daily grind, your good intentions go out the window along with your tan and your pictures are resigned to your iPhoto Events, only to be looked at once in a while but never to see the light of day in the form of a book.

However, the iPhoto book options are so beautiful and easy to prepare that it really is worth investing a little bit of time to create a stylish keepsake that you can show your friends and family, and come back to time and again when you want to remember the fun you had in the sun. To make it even more interesting, the travel-themed book options allow you to add maps and text as well as images. So, to give you a bit more incentive, why not make it a 'Travel Journal'

combining maps that chart your journey, notes from your travels as well as your best images. This will not only act as a physical chart of the corners of the Earth you have visited – and show you where you have left to explore – but it will also remind you of where you were when you took specific photos and make them much more enjoyable to flick through.

> "The travel-themed book options in iPhoto allow you to add maps and text"

Compile your holiday snaps

Reminisce about exotic holidays the iPhoto way

Editing Maps
Use this black box to edit your maps. Use the slider to zoom in and out. Click the 'plus' sign to add a destination; as you type, Apple will automatically come up with suggestions – just click to add. To change the order of your itinerary click on a destination and drag and drop until you have the correct order and click the 'Show Lines' box to show the red line charting your journey

Change the background
Edit the template to give your book its own unique look and change the background by clicking on this icon

Layout
Click this icon to change your layout or to change a page to a 'Map Page'. There are layouts that have as little or as much text or pictures as you'd like – the options are endless

Photographs
Just drag and drop your pictures into the relevant boxes. A tick on the bottom corner will indicate if it's already been used. Clicking the 'Autofill' icon at the bottom will automatically drop images in

iPhoto   Chart your travels in iPhoto

01 Choose your photos

Create an album with the photos that you want to use in your photo book. When you're happy with your selection go to 'Edit' and 'Select all'.

02 New album

Select 'New Album From Selection' from the File menu. Click the book icon and give your project a name and choose a theme.

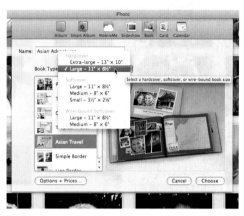

03 Book Type

From the 'Book Type' menu, select the book you want to make. Click the 'Options + Prices' button to go to the Apple website for more info.

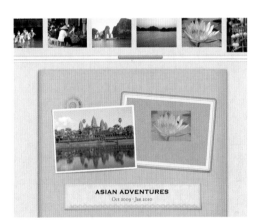

04 Drag and drop

Your book will load up with the selected photos running along the top. Simply drag them into the chosen field and give your book a title.

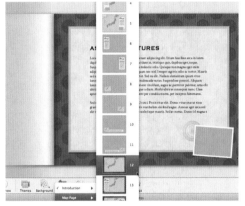

05 Intro

The 'Intro page' template contains a lot of text. If you find that too challenging, change the layout to a map page by clicking on 'Layout'.

06 Black box data

Use the black box to edit your map. Zoom in or out by sliding the top 'Zoom' button and move the map around by clicking on it and dragging.

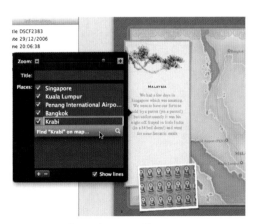

07 Destination unknown

To add a destination, click the '+' button. If Apple can't find the destination, click the blue box that gives you the option to find it on Google Maps.

08 Google Maps

Once your destination has been discovered, click done and it will add it to your map. If you want to add a 'Drop Pin' just click the button.

09 Continue on

You have all you need to finish your book. Now simply add as many maps, notes, captions, journal entries and pictures as you like.

Organise your movie clips

Use Smart Albums in iPhoto to organise your iPhone movie clips

While importing your pictures into iPhoto from your iPhone or digital camera is a great way to back up and organise your photos, it can also be frustrating that it will import all of your video footage as well – especially if you plan to edit the footage in iMovie at a later date. Unfortunately iPhoto won't automatically organise the video footage from the photos, which is annoying if you would rather keep them separate and export in bulk later.

By simply setting up a Smart Album and setting some basic conditions that you can tailor to your individual needs, you can easily get iPhoto to recognise movie clips and distinguish them from your photos, saving you all the aforementioned hassle and headache. This simple four-step tutorial shows you just how easy it is to set up a new album and set the preferences, so that when you import video footage iPhoto will automatically save it into the appropriate album. This album will keep all your videos in one place, making them easy to locate and they will then be sat there ready to be burnt onto a disc, exported to iDVD or iWeb, or exported to MobileMe, Facebook or Flickr – the choice is yours.

"iPhoto will automatically save it into the appropriate album"

Organise video footage using Smart Albums

Create a Smart Album to automatically separate video footage from photos

New Album
If you select New Album instead of New Smart Album, you still have the option of creating one. Simply select the second icon from the left

Set conditions
By clicking on the plus button, you can specify more conditions to organise your media. Instead of using 'Any Text' you can use the date, file name or even specify the camera model

Contains
Use this drop-down menu to change the conditions. For example, you can change it to 'does not contain', 'starts with' or 'ends with'

Editing Smart Albums
If you want to change the conditions of your Smart Album, or if you want to delete it, Control-click on the album and select Edit Smart Album

Knowledge base

Exporting
To batch-export your video footage, click on your Smart Album, head to the Edit menu at the top of the interface and click Select All. Then select either Export from the File menu or – if you want to export to iDVD, iWeb, or if you want to burn them straight to a disc – go to the Share menu and select your favoured option.

iPhoto   Use Smart Albums to organise movie footage

01 New Smart Album

Head to the File menu at the top of the interface and select New Smart Album from the drop-down menu. Alternatively, you can select New Album and then Smart Album, or use the keyboard shortcut Alt+Cmd+N if you want to save a little bit of time.

02 Set the conditions

Choose a name for your Smart Album and type it into the 'Smart Album name' field, making sure it's something fitting for the content. From the Album drop-down menu, select the Any Text option. Leave the 'contains' menu as it is.

03 Finishing off

In the end field type '.MOV', which is the common ending for a movie file. If you're importing from a digital camera or a video camera, you may need to change this to '.MPG'. You will need to check this first, either in your camera's instruction book or via the internet.

04 Import

When you're ready to go, the final step is to actually import your media. The movie footage will automatically be organised into the Smart Album. From there you can batch export to iDVD, iWeb or burn them straight to disc if you wish to keep a hard copy for yourself.

Edit in iMovie part 1

Get to grips with the powerful editing tools in iMovie by importing, editing and adding transitions

Let's dive straight in and use iMovie to edit some raw holiday footage into a slick video souvenir that can be shared with friends and family, and make a nice souvenir of your trip for you to keep.

iMovie is a fantastic piece of kit that every Mac owner should learn to get to grips with. If you have dreams of becoming the next Hitchcock, Tarantino or Eastwood, then this is a good place to start. By familiarising yourself with the basic editing functions of iMovie, you will be able to create slick, professional videos in no time at all. These foundations will then help you progress to more complex editing features, but it's always essential to master the basics before you get ahead of yourself.

In part one of this iMovie editing tutorial you'll test-drive some of the enhanced editing tools and add a transition to give your video more

professional-looking production values. You will even be able to salvage shots that you may think have been ruined by a shaking camera thanks to the exciting new Image Stabilization feature. In part two – which is over the page – you will then enhance the video with graphics, music and themes, taking your video to a whole new level.

> ## "You will be able to create slick, professional videos in no time at all"

iMovie   Import footage, stabilise it then edit and add transitions

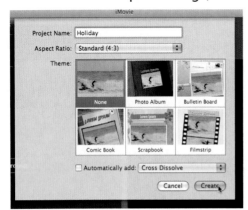

01 Create new project
Go to File>New Project and label it Holiday. Choose Standard 4:3 as the Aspect Ratio. Leave the Theme option set to None. Now click Create.

02 Import footage
Choose File>Import>Movies. Tick Create New Event and label it Holiday. Browse to your raw footage folder and then click OK.

03 Analyse camera shake
In this footage some shots shake. You can select the clip's Gear icon and choose Clip Adjustments to open the Inspector. Click Analyze Entire Clip.

04 Stabilise footage
Click Done when the camera shake has been analysed. Drag the clip into the Project window to view the dramatically stabilised version.

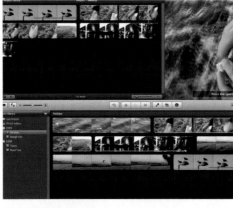

05 Add clips
We've added a clip of hands breaking up bread into the Project window. Then we add the wide shot of the girl throwing bread for continuity.

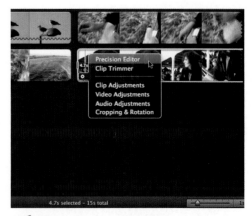

06 Fine-tune the edit
By cutting on repetitive movements you can make the action flow smoothly. Click on the last clip's Gear icon and open the Precision Editor.

Add smooth transitions in iMovie

The first steps to editing your movie into a masterpiece

Steady cam
iMovie's Image Stabilizer can rescue the wobbliest of shots, enabling you to shoot a steady image even at full zoom. A red wavy line indicates that a shot's undergone stabilisation

Tweak transitions
For a longer dissolve between clips click on the Gear icon below a transition and choose Transition Adjustments. A longer duration creates a gentle jump forward in time from a static seagull to the birds in flight

Precision editing
The iMovie Precision Editor enables you to fine-tune where one clip ends and the next begins, letting you match repetitive actions and produce smooth flowing cuts from one shot to the next

Thin blue line
The blue line indicates the point where we cut from the previous clip to the next clip. Click on the grey bar between the top and bottom clips and hit the Spacebar to preview the cut in the main Viewer

07 Precision editing
We've dragged the top clip so that the arm begins to fall. Drag the bottom clip to place the arm in the same position. Click Done.

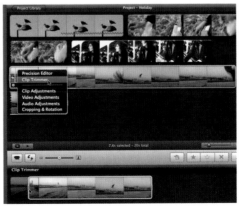

08 Quick trim
Add another clip. Click its Gear icon and choose Clip Trimmer. Drag the trim handle so the clip starts with the last clip's final action.

09 Transitions
Place a fresh shot before your first shot, click the Transitions browser icon and drag a Cross Dissolve between the first two clips.

Edit in iMovie part 2

In part two of our iMovie editing double-bill you'll create a more polished production by adding music, captions and even slick animated graphics courtesy of iMovie's Themes browser

Once you've used tools like the new Precision Editor to cut a slick sequence together you can raid iMovie's large selection of post-production assets to add the icing to your cake! In the previous tutorial we took you through some of the basic features of iMovie that are essential to master when you are just starting out. However, when watching professionally produced programmes and films we take it for granted that they'll have a title sequence designed to hook the viewer into watching the show or movie, as well as the usual bells and whistles like captions and music to grab the viewer's interest and make sure they carry on watching.

The iMovie Themes browser enables us to 'top and tail' our video sequence with animated graphics that we can personalise to introduce our edited video in a more professional-looking way. There are also a number of other excellent tricks iMovie has up its sleeve to help make your sequence the best it can be. By adding simple things like music, your film can be transformed from a dull and lifeless sequence of images to a movie that keeps you entertained. These are all great editing tips that will help you master the basics of iMovie, and some will be covered in much more detail in the following tutorials

"The iMovie Themes browser enables us to 'top and tail' our video sequence"

Polish off your iMovie masterpiece

Take your movie to the next level with music and more

Terrific titles
iMovie is packed to the gunnels with a selection of customisable animated titles that can give your movie sophisticated production values with the minimum amount of time and effort

Choose a theme
Once you've chosen a specific theme (like Photo Album) the Theme browser provides you with a range of animated graphics and titles that you can drag to the clips in the Edit Project window

Change duration
There are two ways to change the length of a title. You could click on the start or end point of a graphic bar and drag the cursor to extend it. Or double-click on the title bar and type a new duration into the Inspector

Marvellous music
Music makes a video more entertaining to watch and helps link all the separate shots together in a seamless flowing narrative. The green backdrop indicates that music has been added

Knowledge base

Director's cut
RSS feeds are simply a standard form of stripped down summaries of the posts made to a website. Using the RSS widget in iWeb, you can embed the feed into your site so that all the updates posted to the original site also appear on your page. Clicking an entry takes you to the original post.

iMovie
Add music, captions and animated titles to add polish to your production

01 Choose a theme
Click on the Titles browser. Click Set Theme and choose Photo Album. Untick 'Automatically add transitions and titles'. Click OK.

02 Add opening title graphic
Drag the Photo Album title to the first shot in the Edit Project window. Extend the title to a length that suits and type text into the text field.

03 Add an animated caption
In the Titles browser scroll down and drag Lower Third 1 to your second shot in the Edit Project window. Extend it and type in some text.

04 Add more graphics
Add Upper Third to the third shot and place Lower Third 2 at the start of the final shot. The captions fly in and out of the screen.

05 Closing titles
Pop Credits 1 over the end of the last shot and type in the name of your movie's star. The video will shrink to fit inside the animated graphic.

06 Test your titles
Drag the cursor to the start of the movie and hit the Spacebar to play the footage. Fine-tune the duration of the graphics if necessary.

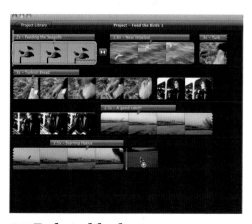

07 Fade to black
In the Transitions browser scroll down to Fade To Black and drag it over the end of the movie. Shorten the Credits 1 bar so it doesn't overlap.

08 Create closing credits
Place the Centered title after the last clip. You could use a colourful background, but a classy black backdrop should suffice on this occasion.

09 Finishing touch
Click on the Music browser icon and navigate to Jingles. Drag a music track onto the project's grey background to add music to the programme.

Use the Analyze Video tool

iMovie has some clever features you may not know about that can analyse your video clips in different ways to help you get better results and for easier searching…

Photo has been able to analyse still images for a little while, with the principal function to identify faces. And while iMovie cannot actually recognise individuals just yet, it can tell if there are actually any people in the shot. This is particularly useful for quickly finding footage of people as opposed to trawling through endless establishing shots, seascapes and other kinds of footage.

Perhaps even more usefully for the casual or intermediate film maker, iMovie is also able to analyse footage for stabilisation, either during or after the actual import of the footage. Modern handheld camcorders – and indeed iPhones – are small, light and notoriously difficult to hold still so many people find that their footage invariably suffers from camera shake. This can lead to huge disappointment when you've done some filming and upon upload you notice

that none of it is usable for your projects, or the memory is now lost forever due to extreme shaking. The way that iMovie corrects this is to zoom in and crop the video to eliminate the areas that move around. This technique may not always produce the exact results you want but in a lot of cases it can really save your bacon…

> **"iMovie is also able to analyse footage for stabilisation, either during or after the import"**

iMovie Use iMovie's Analyze tool

01 Analyse during import

Choose your footage in the Import window, and in the After Import menu select to analyse the video for stabilisation, people or both.

02 Wait for analysis

Analysing video can take a while and the longer the footage the longer it will take. For longer clips on older machines be prepared to wait a while.

03 Analyse after import

You may have imported footage but later decide that a clip is too shaky. Locate it in the Event Library, right-click and go to the Analyze menu.

04 Choose analysis type

Select whether you want to analyse for people, stabilisation or both. Select multiple clips and perform analysis to save repeated key presses.

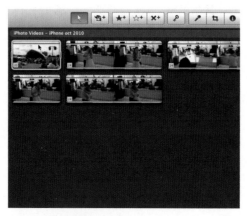

05 Filter the view

Press the small people icon at the bottom of iMovie's window and you will see only the analysed footage containing people.

06 Repeat for stabilisation

If a clip needs stabilising, repeat the command, which can be found in Edit. Stabilisation zooms in and crops a clip but can be undone.

Let iMovie do the analysing

The Analyze tool can recognise faces and stabilise your shots

Analysed footage

Footage that has been analysed is displayed with a coloured marker to denote the kind of analysis that has taken place. This makes it easy to see at a glance what you are working with

Analyze menu

Available from the contextual menu or the File menu, the Analyze Video sub menu contains a number of commands. Analysed footage can have its zoom settings modified only once it has been dropped into a project

Filter the view

By using the two buttons at the bottom you can choose to filter your library view to show only footage that contains people or only footage that has been stabilised, making searches quicker and easier

Analysis types

You can choose to analyse footage for stabilisation, which will correct shaky footage, or people, which can identify when people feature in a clip, or both at once which takes longer. You can also choose to show using markers where camera pans occur

07 Disable stabilisation

When a clip has been analysed, add it to a project and double-click to open its Inspector. Here you can specify if clip smoothing should be on or off.

08 Set zoom level

Using the Maximum Zoom slider, you can alter the amount of zooming to stabilise shaky footage. Try to find a happy medium.

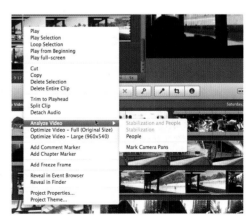

09 Mark camera pans

Activate Mark Camera Pans and iMovie will display a blue line wherever the clip contains camera movement, making it easier to identify.

Create better titles in iMovie '11

With a little exploration of the font panel and a touch of creativity, you can completely customise text in iMovie

Adding text is an important element of the movie-making process, whether it's adding a credit to the end of the show, adding subtitles to speech or just giving your audience a little heads-up on what's happening on screen. On the face of things, the text-editing abilities of iMovie are a little limiting but, if you know your font panel well enough, you can easily make much more of the templated titles at your disposal. In this tutorial we'll show you how to use colour and outline to make ordinarily tough-to-view text easy to see. Experimentation should always be part of your creative process, and there is no reason why text should be any different.

> "You can easily make much more of the templated titles at your disposal"

Step-by-step iMovie '11
Make text easier to see with creative use of styles and colour

01 Show or hide
Once you have a clip in your project you'd like to add a title to, click this Title browser button to show available titles. Look through, and pick one.

02 What a drag
Drag and drop the title onto the clip. The entire clip will then be highlighted, and the title and clip will be the same length. Now edit the title.

03 Standard fonts
The standard fonts are great for making quick changes. To make more adjustments to the type face you want to use, click System Font Panel.

04 Familiar face
The Fonts panel is the same one that you use in a number of other apps, including iWork. You should be able to negotiate the interface easily.

05 Select text
Select the text you want to apply changes to; you can tell when the text is highlighted. You can then return to the font panel to make changes.

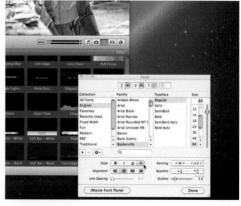

06 Outline
Using the Outline button is a good way to add immediate impact to text, no matter what the font. As you can see here, the difference is huge.

Highlighting the text editing interface

A quick look at some of the tools at your disposal

Live preview
See your changes taking shape in the viewer in this window. Experimentation is the key here, as you will know when your changes are for the best

Colour
Using the right colours is as important as having writing at all. You need to be able to clearly see and read the text you are adding

Good starting point
There are a great range of titles in iMovie, but you can soon become bored of them. Customising your text is a good way to shake up a tired title

Flipping panels
Easily switch between panels with this button. You can make use of quick editing by combining the easiest elements of both

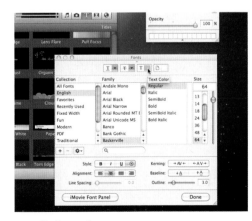

07 Colouring
Hit the Text Color button and the Colour palette will spring to life. You can then use the slider to get the perfect tone for the inside of your text.

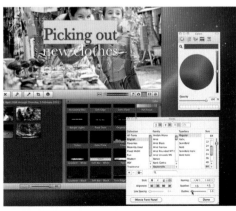

08 Outline again
Use the Outline slider to reduce the weight of the outline on the text. You don't need a really thick line to add plenty of impact.

09 Others
Use as many of the other elements on the Fonts panel as you like – we also used the Bold setting and changed the colour of the outline of the text.

Create a better soundtrack

The key to a good movie is getting the sound as well as
the visuals right. iMovie '11 now has all the tools you need

While visuals for movies are obviously very important, poor
sound can make a project seem less professional. The
biggest culprit is uneven sound; sound that jumps wildly
from one scene to another. In one it might be really quiet and in the next
really loud, creating a jarring crossover that is unpleasant for the viewer.
In one scene you might have a lot of deep rumble in the sound from an
air conditioner or road noise but in the next, no background noise at all.
Of course, it would be unnatural to mess with the sound too much, but
there's a happy medium where you edit just enough to give a smooth
and polished feel to the overall sound. We'll show you how it works…

> "There's a happy
> medium where
> you edit just
> enough to give a
> polished feel"

Step-by-step iMovie '11 Editing sound for better results

01 Select a clip

Find a clip with 'problem' sound, eg one louder
than those next to it. Double-click to open the
Inspector window. Click on the Audio tab.

02 Change the volume

Here you can change the overall volume of the
audio. This is the quickest way to deal with a clip
being too loud or too short.

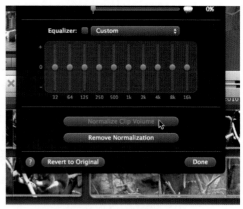

03 Normalise the volume

If a clip is too quiet, use the Normalize button to
have it analysed and raise its volume. This action
can easily be undone if it's not right.

04 Reduce background noise

If a clip has too much background noise, hit
Enhance and use the slider to determine how
much noise is removed.

05 Use EQ

Equalisation is a useful tool. Activate it then
choose a preset like Hum Reduction. Play back to
see if they fix the sound to your liking.

06 Set EQ manually

To tweak an EQ preset, move the sliders. They run
from lowest frequency on the left to highest on
the right. Raise or lower one to boost or cut levels.

Editing audio in movie clips

The tools and tricks you need for more professional sound

Equalisation
EQ is really handy as it lets you cut or boost ten bands, in this case, of frequencies. If a clip is too bassy, knock off some of the bottom end. To enhance voices, try pulling up the mid-range. To get rid of hiss, knock down the very top end

Level meters
Keep an eye on the level meters to see how the overall sound levels are looking. These give you a better representation than simply believing your speakers, because they may be turned up or down too far and so give you an inaccurate reading

Knowledge base
Split it off
iMovie '11 now allows you to detach the audio from one or more clips and treat it separately. It can then be moved around or even deleted, leaving the video in its original place. This is handy for more creative editing, for example layering the sound from one clip over another.

Volume slider
The most fundamental control you have to work with audio, this controls the overall volume of the clip. Match volume relative to other clips

Knowledge base
Voice-over
By clicking on the microphone button in iMovie's toolbar you can access the voice-over tool. This allows you to use your Mac's built-in mic or an external mic to record voice-over directly into a project and associate it with a clip if you like. It's great for narrating holiday or even corporate videos.

Enhance
You can choose to reduce the background noise in a clip using a variable amount slider. This is good for getting rid of road noise or hiss, but be careful not to knock out sounds you wanted to keep

07 Use effects
Go to the Clip menu and you can add an audio effect to the clip. Choose from the presets and hover over one to hear the sound played.

08 Use fades
In the Audio menu, you can add manual fade-ins/ outs to a clip, independent of transitions – handy at the start and end or when you need silence.

09 Cut and paste settings
Select a clip you've edited and Edit>Copy. Choose other clips and Edit>Paste Adjustments>Audio to apply the same settings to those clips.

Edit with precision

Use the power of the Clip Trimmer and the Precision Editor to make action flow smoothly

A skilled video maker can shoot a variety of clips and then cut them together so that they appear to unfold in real-time, even though minutes or even days may have elapsed between each clip. We filmed a horse jumping a fence twice – first in a wide establishing shot and then in a dramatic close-up. Because the shot size changes, we can cut between the clips, making it look like we shot the action with two cameras. This change of shot size also adds variety to the edited production. For the action to flow smoothly it's essential that the position of the horse is the same in both clips, as we cut from one to the other. The Clip Trimmer and the Precision Editor enable us to fine-tune the cut to perfection…

Fine-tune your editing

Use the tools iMovie has on offer to edit your movies

Clear cut
The edit that you're fine-tuning with the Precision Editor is marked with a blue bar, so you can clearly see which cut you're working on in the Project window

Edit point
This blue dot indicates the point at which you cut from the clip in the top bar to the clip in the bottom. Change the edit point by dragging this blue dot left or right

Next please!
You can use the Precision Editor to fine-tune multiple cuts with ease. Simply click here to jump to the next edit point

Back and forth
To rewind a clip, click on it and drag it right. This will make the action start earlier. To make the action start later in the shot, drag the clip to the left

Knowledge base

Sound bridge

When cutting between two shots, you may get the continuity spot-on, so the action will flow perfectly. However, a jarring jump in audio content can spoil the cut. This is why we muted the sound in our second clip and extended the sound from the first clip over the cut. As the sound flows between the two clips it helps bridge the cut and helps things flow a little more effectively.

iMovie Fine-tune your cuts with the Precision Editor

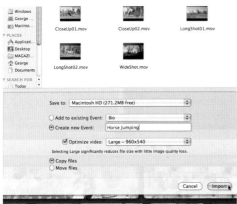

01 Get started

Go to File>New Project. Choose a ratio of 16:9. Click 'Create'. Go to File>Import Movies. Browse to the footage on the disc and click Import.

02 Quick trim

Drag the first two clips into the Project window. Click on the first clip and Window>Clip Trimmer. Drag the yellow handle to make it end at 2:21.

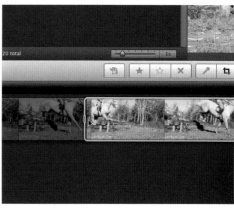

03 In sync

Use Clip Trimmer to make the second clip begin as the horse lands at 1:10. Play the sequence. It flows smoothly, but the second clip is too short.

04 Precision Editor

Go to Window>Precision Editor. Drag the blue dot left to start the cut nine frames earlier. Slide the cursor along the grey bar to preview.

05 Maintain continuity

The horse doesn't jump as high in the second clip, so his legs are behind the fence. Drag the second clip two frames left to reveal his hooves.

06 Sound bridge

Click the second clip. Go to Edit>Mute Clip. Click the first clip. Choose Edit>Detach Audio. Drag the audio clip to extend it over the second shot.

07 Offset cut

Add clips three and four. Go to the Precision Editor. Drag the bottom clip left by 1:08 seconds and the top right by -2:03. Click 'Done'.

08 Detach audio

Use the technique in step 6 to mute the fourth clip's audio, then detach and extend the sound from the third clip over the fourth.

09 Cross the line

Add the last clip. In the previous shot the horse moves from left to right. To make it flow in the same direction, use the Flipped Video effect.

Add slo-mo special effects in iMovie '11

With iMovie '11 add interest and character to your projects by using slow motion and other speed effects

Manipulating speed is made much easier by the technology behind digital video. When working with analogue tape, slowing the speed of playback could cause unwanted side effects like wobble and jitter. With digital source material, however, the computer can easily alter the number of frames per second. Slow motion in movies is often used in action scenes to show things that happen very quickly in more detail, which enhances the dramatic tension. For home movies it can also be useful for changing the pace of a scene, or simply to make a short clip last a bit longer than its original duration for the purposes of filling out some time.

Movie '11   Using slow motion

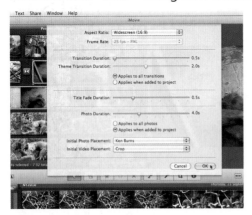

01 Import your footage

Import your footage. It's likely to be a high frame rate (25 or 30fps). To check the project frame rate, go to File>Project Properties.

02 Open the Inspector

Select a clip in the project, but not in the source bin. Only when a clip exists in a project can you modify its speed.

03 Open the Inspector

Click the 'I' button in the toolbar or choose Window>Clip Adjustments. This is contextual and will show properties for whichever clip you select.

04 Convert the clip

Before clip speed can be changed, the clip must be analysed. Click the button marked 'Convert Entire Clip' in the Speed section to do this.

05 Change the speed

Use the Speed slider to change the speed, or enter a numerical value for a percentage of the original speed or a new value in seconds.

06 See the results

You should see the clip extend itself on the timeline. Try playing it back. It may look a little more jerky but it should be slower.

Find your way around the Inspector panel

Discover the flexibility of editing your clips in iMovie '11

Numerical boxes
Instead of the slider you can enter a more precise value here, either a percentage of the original speed or an exact duration in minutes and seconds

Speed slider
Change a clip's speed by using this slider. Left for slower and right for faster. Use the Reverse button to play it backwards

Knowledge base

Slow sound
If you want to slow a clip's sound down independently of the video, right-click on a clip then select Detach Audio. Then use the Inspector panel to independently change the speed of the audio using controls similar to those for video. Once audio is separated like this, you can move it around a project independently, for greater flexibility.

Knowledge base

Export video
When video is inside iMovie it remains flexible and can be manipulated, and its speed returned to normal. If, however, you want to export a slowed-down clip for use elsewhere, simply drag the clip to a new project, perform the speed changes and then use the Share>Export Movie command to output a version to the hard drive with the speed changes 'glued down' as part of the file.

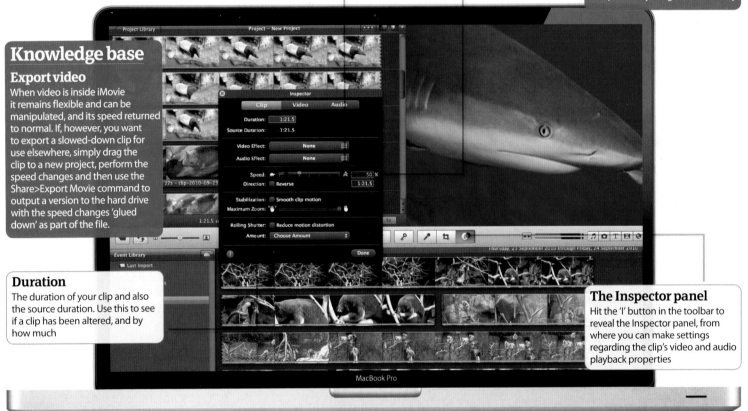

Duration
The duration of your clip and also the source duration. Use this to see if a clip has been altered, and by how much

The Inspector panel
Hit the 'I' button in the toolbar to reveal the Inspector panel, from where you can make settings regarding the clip's video and audio playback properties

07 Try a new value
For extreme slowness, choose a low value. Go to the Clip menu and choose Clip>Slow Motion and then use a preset value of 50, 25 or 10%.

08 Save the sound
The sound is also slowed down. To avoid this, right-click on it and choose Detach Audio. Then perform the slow motion on the video.

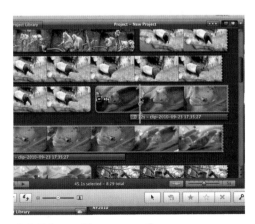

09 Move the sound
The video may be slower but the sound is the same speed, pitch and length but doesn't cover the length of the clip. Add sound to fill the gaps.

Turn iPhone clips into video sequences

Package your iPhone holiday clips into a 'memory lane' style video sequence using iMovie's slick post-production tools

We may have fond memories of seemingly endless childhood summer holidays, but with only a handful of photos to jog our recollections. Thanks to our ever-present iPhone we can return from more recent family holidays with hours of footage, giving us the problem of sharing it. Thanks to iMovie's tools we can present our modern holiday footage in a 'trip down memory lane' inspired sequence. To evoke the hazy childhood memories we'll show you how to add gentle blur effects to the edge of the shot. As time can seem to slow down in childhood memories, we'll re-time certain clips to dwell on a cherished moment.

> "We can present our holiday footage in a 'trip down memory lane' sequence"

iMovie   Add themes, titles and effects to enhance favourite holiday memories

01 Create a new project

Go to File New Project. Choose a 4:3 Aspect Ratio to suit the iPhone footage. Set Theme to None to avoid adding titles and transitions automatically.

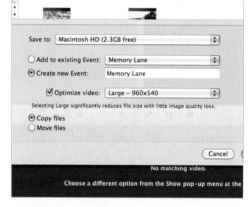

02 Import clips

Go to File>Import Movies. Browse to Memory Source Clips folder (from the disc). Press Cmd+A to select shots. Create a new Event. Click Import.

03 Add clips

We've trimmed the clips and ordered them so they don't need much editing. Drag the clips from the Events Browser into the Project Window.

04 Add the memory effect

Press Cmd+A to select all the project's clips, then press I to open the Inspector. Click Video Effect, then Romantic to blur the frame edge.

05 Play with time

Click in a grey area to deselect the clips, then click on shot 4. Press I to open the Inspector. Set Speed to 50% to slow down the spinning boy.

06 Choose a theme

To enhance our video memories, click on the Titles browser. Set Theme to Scrapbook. Untick Automatically add transitions and titles. Click OK.

Enhance your holiday clips

Add those extra touches only iMovie can provide...

Music
The Elysium track has a light optimistic feel that complements the childhood memory footage. Music also helps link our separate clips into a coherent whole

Effects
By using iMovie's Effects to blur the edges of each shot you can evoke a sense of reliving the holiday as a childhood memory

Animated captions
Captions answer the viewers' 'who', 'where' and 'when' questions, and give your sequence an attractive and professional looking production value

Transitions
If you let iMovie apply transitions and titles automatically there can be too much 'icing' on your 'cake'! Drop in a couple of transitions and titles to keep a more restrained, professional feel

07 Add a title
Drag the Scrapbook title onto shot 1. Click in the text field and type 'Down Memory Lane'. Click Done and play the clip to see the animated title.

08 Add a caption
Drag Upper Third onto shot 2 and add a caption. Drag the edge of the caption bar to extend it over the start of shot 3. This knits the clips together.

09 Edit the transition
In the Transitions browser, drag Scrapbook 4 between the last two shots. Click the Transition icon. Drag the numbers onto clips you want.

Creative Ken Burns effects

Use iMovie's Ken Burns effects to enhance your still images by panning and zooming to specific areas

Professional documentary makers add extra content to their programmes by dropping the odd photo into the mix. This technique enables them to illustrate topics that maybe aren't covered by existing video clips, and enhances the overall feel of a project.

Thanks to iMovie's full integration with iPhoto it is very simple to sprinkle a few stills into your own iMovie projects to give them that professional look, and add the odd segue if necessary. To make the stills look a little more interesting, iMovie automatically adds a camera move – which is commonly known as the Ken Burns effect – to them.

This technique is named after the American documentary maker Ken Burns, who is known for his panning and zooming effects. This move in iMovie may include a zoom, a pan, or possibly both. By taking control over the Ken Burns virtual camera, you can draw attention to a specific object in the photo using a variety of camera moves, enabling you to add valuable extra content to your productions and tell stories from your stills.

"It is very simple to sprinkle a few photo stills into your own iMovie projects"

iMovie   Add creative Ken Burns effects

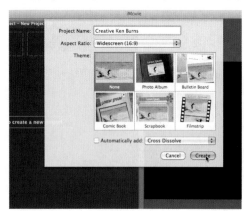

01 Create new project
Go to File>New Project. As most digital stills have a larger resolution than video footage, choose a large Aspect Ratio of 16:9. Click Create.

02 Import images
You'll find a folder of source images on your CD (Ken Burns Sources). Drag Zoom.JPG onto the grey project window to add it to the project.

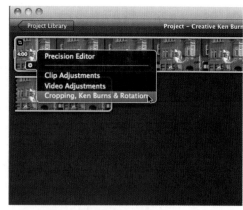

03 Take control
iMovie adds a camera move that may not suit its contents. To change this move, click the Gear icon and choose Cropping, Ken Burns & Rotation.

04 Start and finish
Resize the Start and End windows so that they are as small as they can be. Place Start over the lower left cup. Place End over the girl's face. Click Done.

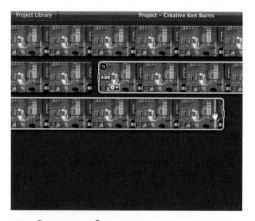

05 Copy and paste
Play the clip. The shot pans from the cup to reveal the juggler's face. Click the clip to select it. Choose Edit>Copy, then Edit Paste.

06 Swap
The copied clip has the same moves. To make the clip's move start where the first clip's move ended, click the red End box's little swap arrow.

Learn to shoot and edit like a pro in iMovie

Combine professional shooting tricks with editing techniques

Multiple moves
You can add multiple moves to a single photo by copying and pasting it, then editing the copied picture's Ken Burns settings

Pan and Zoom
Drag the corners of the Start and End windows to choose a specific shot size, then drag inside the windows to position the camera. iMovie will then add movement between the two positions

iPhoto browser
Use the iPhoto browser to search for suitable stills to add to your video project. Once you find an image you like, simply drop it onto the grey project window

Get in gear
To edit the random camera moves that have been added to your stills, click the Gear icon and choose Cropping, Ken Burns & Rotation

07 Zoom out

To get the Ken Burns camera to zoom out and reveal the girl and her three juggling cups in a single shot, enlarge the End window. Click Done.

08 Pan down

Add Pan.JPG to the project. Resize and re-position the Start and End windows so that we start on the man, then pan down to the girl.

09 Change duration

By default all stills have a duration of four seconds. Click the second clip, press 'I' to open the Inspector. Set the duration to 2:00 seconds.

Manage files on multiple hard drives

If your Mac is bulging with videos, spread the weight by shifting iMovie Projects to external hard drives

Rewind a few years and most camcorders captured footage onto tape-based formats like MiniDV. When you wanted to edit the footage, you copied the best bits to your Mac, and the outtakes stayed on tape. Camcorders were often only dusted off to shoot special occasions, and this kept your Mac's hard drive relatively free of video clips.

In these digital days we carry a video-recording iPhone or smartphone with us at all times, so we're more likely to shoot everyday events. To free up space on our phone we need to download clips onto our Mac, and we therefore have much more footage to store. Other gadgets like digital SLR cameras produce huge HD video files that fill our poor Mac's hard drive.

You can solve all of your storage problems by investing in an external hard drive. iMovie then enables you to store and manage clips on multiple external drives, allowing you to free up the Mac's disk space.

"Other gadgets like digital SLR cameras produce huge HD video files"

iMovie Organise files on external hard drives

01 Attach external hard drive

Plug in an external hard drive to your trusty Mac. For it to work with iMovie you will need to format it as a Mac OS Extended disk. You can partition it as several disks and dedicate one of them to storing your iMovie Projects and iMovie Events.

02 Group by Disk

Open up iMovie. By default video footage is stored on your Mac's hard disk in the Event Library. Go to the Event Library panel. Click on the 'Group Events by Disk' icon at the top of the sidebar. You'll now see any attached hard drives appear.

Working from external drives

Manage clips on multiple disks to save hard drive space

Breathing room
By dividing an external hard disk into partitions you can create a huge chunk of space for iMovie to store video and Projects. This will free up valuable disk space on your Mac

Portable Projects
You can also store Projects and all associated clips on external hard drives. This enables you to plug the external drive into another Mac and edit your Projects on that

Knowledge base

Move or copy?
If you drag an Event to an external drive while holding down the Command key, any iMovie Projects that use that Event will refer to the clips in their new location. If you drag an Event to an external drive without holding the Command key, then you are simply making a copy. iMovie will still refer to the version on your Mac's hard disk.

Different disks
Click on this 'Group Events by Disk' icon to see any external hard drives attached to your Mac. The hard drives will appear

Transfer Events
Drag an Event containing video clips from the Macintosh hard disk onto an external disk's icon. The transferred Event will show up when you click on the drop-down arrow next to the appropriate disk icon

03 Move an Event
To move clips from the Macintosh HD to an external disk, hold the Command key and drag the relevant Event to the external disk's icon. Depending on the size of the clips this may take a few minutes. The Event will appear under the relevant disk.

04 Copy Projects
If you would like to edit existing Projects using iMovie on another Mac, drag it from the Edit Project window onto an external hard drive. You will then be given the option of transferring any other relevant Event clips at the same time.

Use iMovie's advanced editing tools

Enjoy extra editing features like split screen effects and blue screen compositing

i Movie's basic editing tools already provide a fast way to edit. You can select the best bits of footage in an Event by scrubbing the cursor across a clip, and then dragging the selection into your project without having to play each clip in real-time. You can speed up the editing process even more by accessing advanced tools like the dual-mode toolbar. This lets you select and add a clip to the project in one timesaving swipe. iMovie's advanced tools also enable you to add extra post-production effects like Side by Side (or split screen), and drop in chapter markers for burning the project to disc. You can even replace one background with another. So, here's how to advance your editing and organising skills…

iMovie '11 Take iMovie's advanced editing tools for a test drive

01 Advanced tools

For advanced tools go to iMovie>Preferences. In the General section tick Show Advanced tools. The toolbar will expand to include new icons.

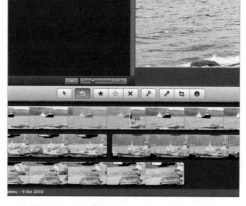

02 Faster editing

Click on the Edit tool icon. Click and drag an orange bar to select part of a clip. The selection will be added to the project window.

03 Faster favouriting

You can also favourite clips quicker using the advanced toolbar. Click on the Favorite tool icon, then scrub the green-star icon over the best bits.

04 Hide and seek

Favourited clips will feature a green bar along the top. To show favourited clips (and hide everything else) set Show to Favorites only.

05 Back to basics

To return from Advanced to Basic editing mode click the arrow icon (or hit Escape). Now any clips you click on will be selected with the yellow bar.

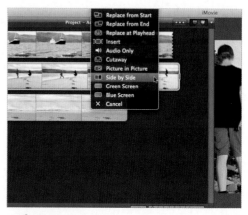

06 Split screen

Drag a clip onto a shot in the project window. The advanced menu features new options like Side by Side. This creates a split screen effect.

Use iMovie's advanced tools

Activate and enjoy iMovie's collection of advanced tools

Assign keywords to clips
Once you've chosen the keywords that you want to assign, click and drag the mouse over part of a clip. A blue bar indicates the keyworded section of the footage

Chapter markers
To find specific sections in a long project add chapter markers and comments. You can then instantly jump to a particular comment or marker using the fly-out menu

New toys
The context-sensitive pop-up menu boasts new features. Side by Side lets you place two clips on the same screen. You can also replace blue backgrounds with video footage using Blue Screen

Faster editing
In Advanced mode the Edit tool works much more quickly. Simply scrub over part of a clip in the Events browser and the selection will be instantly added to the Project

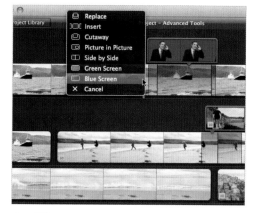

07 Blue screen
Shoot against coloured backdrops, drag the clip onto an existing clip and choose Blue (or Green) Screen. The coloured background will vanish.

08 Keywords
To find specific clips click the Keyword icon. Tick to add preset keywords to a clip, or Add to create your own. Drag across a clip to add the keywords.

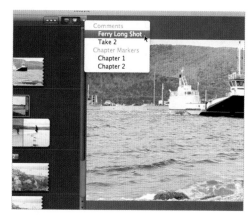

09 Quick comment
Use the Advanced mode to drag a comment icon onto project clips. You can then jump to specific comments with the fly-out menu.

Create a seamless multi-camera sequence

Edit with iMovie's cutaway-inserting and clip-trimming tools

When we watch a stage play, we see the action unfold as a single 'shot'. However, one long wide shot would make a boring video. When viewing video, the shots' different durations, angles and sizes help to tell the story. You could shoot with multiple cameras to capture different angles of a single take, however, as you probably only have one camera, it makes more sense to emulate Hollywood filmmakers. They tend to shoot with one camera and then repeat the action while filming from another angle. We filmed a man feeding horses. As his actions were repetitive we were able to capture different shot sizes and angles. We'll show you how to cut the footage together as if there were several camera operators recording the action.

> "As you only have one camera, it makes sense to emulate Hollywood filmmakers"

iMovie Edit different shots and angles to create a sequence

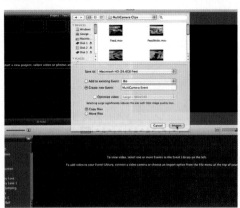

01 Import assets

Create a new 16:9 project. Choose File>Import> Movies. Import a series of clips and add them to a new Event. Choose View>Playhead Info.

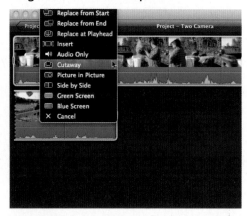

02 Add a cutaway

Drag the first shot into the project window. Drag the second shot onto the first clip at 1:26. Choose Cutaway. The clips will run parallel.

03 Trim the cutaway

Click the cutaway clip's gear icon. Choose Clip Trimmer. Drag the clip's end so its duration is 2:08. Slide the cutaway five frames right.

04 New cutaway

Select the last second of the third clip in the Event browser and add it as a Cutaway at 5:00. Trim the first clip to end at 6:00.

05 Split and trim

Add clip four to the project. Scrub to 7:27. Right-click. Choose Split Clip. Drag the last clip's yellow selection handle to 10:10 and choose Trim.

06 Playback

Play the sequence. We've turned four source clips into six flowing shots. We've removed a wobbly zoom and the man looking at the camera.

Create cutaway shots

Shoot and edit to create a multi-camera sequence

Playhead Info
By pressing Command+Y you can activate the Playhead Info banner. This gives you precise timecode information as you slide the cursor along the timeline

Timeline view
By clicking here you can view the project as a horizontal timeline (instead of the default vertical timeline). This gives you extra information like the timecode starting point of each clip

Bigger thumbnails
To get a large preview of a clip's thumbnail, drag this slider to the right. This will help you identify a clip's content without having to play it

Cool cutaways
Cutaway clips run parallel with the main action. You can drag their start or end points to fine-tune their duration. Drag within a cutaway to make it start or end at a different point in the sequence

07 Different angles
Add clips five, six and seven. These show the horses eating from different angles, as if we had three camera operators filming the action.

08 Add last clip
Add the last low-angle clip, which pans from the horses to the man. This contrasts from the previous view of the feeding horses.

09 Musical merge
The action flows, but we can knit the shots together using music. Add Tour Bus Medium from the iLife Sound Effects Jingles folder.

Switch scenes with terrific transitions

iMovie has a rich vein of post-production effects for you
to plunder to enrich your video productions

Since cinema's earliest days, moviemakers have used transitions to demonstrate a change of location or mark the passing of time. Optical film processing techniques limited transitions to simple wipes or dissolves from one scene to another. When tape-to-tape video-editing became popular in the Eighties you needed two players, a video recorder and a vision mixer, to create a simple transition. This meant that transitions were difficult and expensive to do, and often when they were included they didn't add a huge amount of professionalism to the overall piece.

iMovie's Transition browser can mimic traditional optical effects (see the classic Cross Dissolve for an example), but as it uses digital technology we can also have more creative-looking transitions that will add a little sparkle to your movie. You can drop in as many transitions as you like without the constraints faced by film and video editors of old, and it's a doddle to fine-tune the duration and position

> ## "We can have more creative-looking transitions that will add a sparkle to your movie"

of a transition, as you'll see. There's a chance you may get carried away with all the new options available to you though, so try not to overdo it…

Transitions in iMovie

Get to know these
valuable editing tools

Perfect preview
To see how a transition will behave before you add it, simply let the mouse hover over its icon in the Transitions browser. You'll see an animated preview from shot A to B (or a blue graphic to an orange one)

Informative icons
Drag a transition from the Transitions browser between two clips in the Project window. Each transition has its own icon to help you quickly recognise it in the timeline

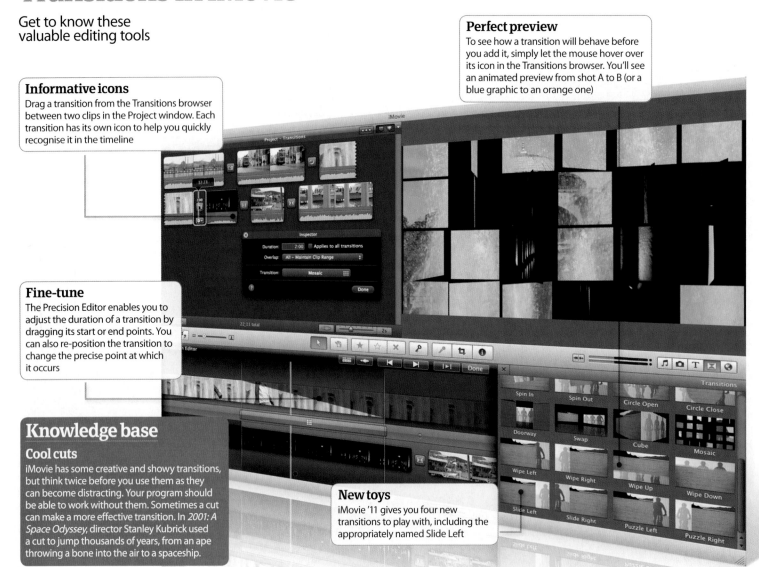

Fine-tune
The Precision Editor enables you to adjust the duration of a transition by dragging its start or end points. You can also re-position the transition to change the precise point at which it occurs

Knowledge base

Cool cuts
iMovie has some creative and showy transitions, but think twice before you use them as they can become distracting. Your program should be able to work without them. Sometimes a cut can make a more effective transition. In *2001: A Space Odyssey*, director Stanley Kubrick used a cut to jump thousands of years, from an ape throwing a bone into the air to a spaceship.

New toys
iMovie '11 gives you four new transitions to play with, including the appropriately named Slide Left

iMovie Use transitions to add meaning and enhance your edits

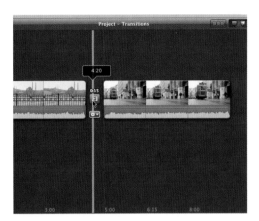

01 Classic wipe

Import 'Wipe01.mov' and 'Wipe02.mov' and place them in a project. Place Wipe Right from the Transitions browser between the two clips.

02 Change of pace

The wipe follows the movement of the men, but it's too fast. Double-click on the transition's icon. Type a duration of 1:19 to slow it down.

03 Ripple effect

Add 'Fountain.mov' and a Ripple transition. The Overlap is set to All – Maintain Clip Range. This shortens it by the duration of the transition.

04 Change Overlap

If you want to keep a duration, set Overlap to Half – Maintain Project Duration. The transition borrows a few frames from the start and end.

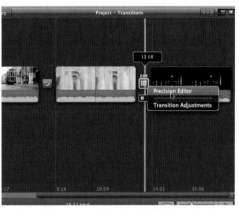

05 Fine-tune transition

Add 'Cistern.mov' and drop in a Mosaic transition. Click the gear icon and choose Precision Editor to drag the transition to where it should start.

06 Open door

Use Doorway transition to move from 'Cistern. mov' to 'Boat.mov'. Give it a duration of 2:00. This is a great way to introduce a new location.

07 Cross Blur

Add 'Disembark.mov' and drop in a Cross Blur. Like Cross Dissolve it mixes clips, but it also defocuses the first clip before refocusing on the second.

08 Quick change

Click a transition's icon in the window. Press 'i'. Click the transition's name for a window featuring all transitions. Preview, then click to choose one.

09 Natural transition

You can create a transition using a cut. Trim the clip so it ends as people walk into shot and block the frame, then cut to a new shot.

Create a comic book-style movie

Use post-production tools like titles and animated transitions to turn your footage into a comic book!

Comic books (or graphic novels) have been popular for decades, and graphic novels in particular have been making a massive comeback over the last few years. Indeed, a number of popular Hollywood movies have been based on graphic novels, and comic-book movies are bigger than ever. One factor in their success is perhaps their interesting presentation of information, with the arrangement of panels on each page enabling the reader to focus on key story points.

This panel-based layout is a terrific template to present your video footage in, as you can make a few clips look much more interesting than they would if you simply cut them together. iMovie's Comic Book theme pops your clips into comic-style panels, adding an extra level of colour to your productions. The

animated, rostrum camera-style transitions add extra movement as they pan from one panel to another. You can even add comic book-style captions to help tell your tale! So why not try out this cool technique next time you're putting a movie together, and see if it brings your movie to life!

> ## "This panel-based layout is a terrific template to present your video footage in"

Create a comic book movie

Use the tools on offer to add some extra pizzazz to your footage

Change panel order
By clicking on an animated transition you can see which clips will be inputted into which comic book panel. Drag the numbers in the project window to a new clip to change each panel's contents

Transitions
When you choose a Comic Book theme for your project you'll find a suitable selection of comic book-style transitions by clicking here

Animated titles
These comic-themed animated titles enable you to add useful information, like the star and director of your video. You also have access to themed captions to maintain the comic book look

Change graphic timing
You can make an animated caption pop up at a particular point by trimming its start point. Make sure that the title bars don't overlap the transitions, or the transitions won't be visible

Knowledge base

Less is more
Feel free to drag the start and end points of your comic book title bars to shorten them. This enables you to see a bit more of your footage before the title or credit starts appearing. The animated titles shouldn't distract the viewer from the actual content of your film!

iMovie Create a comic book project

01 Create new project

Go to File>New Project. Click the Comic Book theme. Untick Auto add transitions. Click Create. The Themes panel will show graphics and titles.

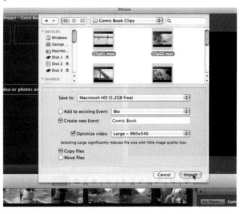

02 Import assets

Choose File>Import>Movies and add clips 01-08 from the disc into a new event. Drag the clips from the Event browser into the Project window.

03 Add title graphic

Drag the Comic Book title onto the first clip. Type in the title. Click Done. Trim the end point of the title so that it runs for two seconds.

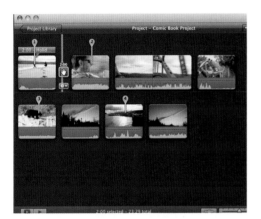

04 Add comic transition

Drag Comic Book 1 from the Transitions browser between the first and second clip. Click on the transition's icon. Drag the numbers onto clips.

05 Add new credit

Drag Credits 1 onto the second clip. Extend the title to overlap clips 2 and 3. Edit the text to add the name of your 'star' to the animated title!

06 Title and transitions

From the Transitions browser place Comic Book 3 between clips 3 and 4. Pop a Lower Third 2 title over clip 4 and edit the text to name the co-star.

07 Add comic captions

Use the Comic Book 2 transition to move from the shot of the horse to the bear. Pop an Upper Third over the bear and edit the text. Click Done.

08 Link clips

Insert Comic Book 4 between clips 5 and 6. Extend the Lower Third 1 title over clips 6 and 7. This connects the two clips.

09 Musical finish

The comic book titles and animated transitions are snappy. Add a track from the Music browser to help join the clips and graphics together.

Create a track from loops in GarageBand

Use GarageBand's expansive Apple Loop library to create your own royalty-free music track

GarageBand has the ability to turn the most non-musical of us into composers, and a lot of that is thanks to the large library of Apple Loop audio samples it ships with. Not only that, but the GarageBand licence actually allows tracks that have been created with these loops to be used for any purpose without recompense, making this a great way to provide a royalty-free soundtrack to a movie, DVD or podcast that you may have created yourself.

Putting a selection of loops together into a coherent musical piece is made easier by the loop families feature, which groups similar-sounding variations of the same loop into families, and makes them selectable from existing regions in the Arrange window. To see how this is done, and to get an idea of how to construct a track from loops alone from start to finish, just follow the steps outlined on these pages and in no time at all you'll be thanking Apple for ever creating those magical loops…

> "Putting a selection of loops together is made easier by the loop families feature"

GarageBand Program a tune from scratch with Apple Loops

01 Launch!
Open GarageBand and select the Loops option in the New Project intro screen. Now click the Choose button to continue.

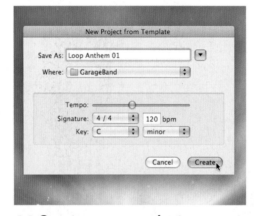

02 Create a new project
Type a title and choose a time signature, tempo, key and save location for your project, then click the Create button.

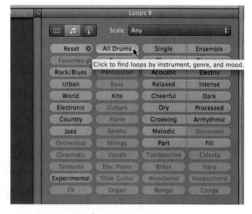

03 Browse loops
The project should now open with the Apple Loop browser already open. Click the All Drums tab to bring up a list of drum loops.

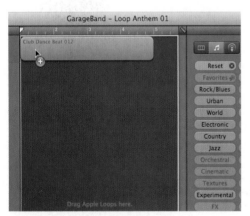

04 Drag and drop
Click on any loop in the list to audition it. When you find a loop you like the sound of, drag it from the browser into the Arrange window.

05 Cycle
Turn on Cycle mode and set the cycle region length so it matches the length of your Apple Loop region. Press Play to start the track looping.

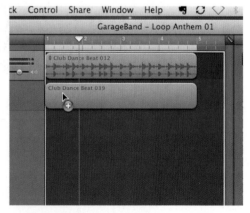

06 Find more loops
Click additional loops in the browser to audition them alongside the first loop. Drag them onto a new track using the same method.

Construct your own track

Master Apple Loops to build your own music

Loop colours
Blue loops are audio recordings, whereas green loops are MIDI sequences. MIDI loops have the advantage that the parts can be edited or transposed freely without affecting the quality of the sound

Narrow it down
Further narrow down your search by selecting more specific categories and mood descriptors from the panel on the right. These help to determine the style of loop you're looking for

Knowledge base
Mix it up
Use the individual track volume faders to balance the levels of each track. If a track's meters go into the red, pull its volume fader to the left to reduce the level. If the output level of the master track goes into the red, try placing a limiter plug-in across the Master track's Effects slots.

Balance it out
While auditioning loops in the Loop browser, they can often be too loud against your existing track. Alter the playback volume if necessary with this volume slider

Spotlight it
If you know the name or part of the name of the loop you're searching for, you can enter it into the Spotlight search window

07 Start new search
Click the Reset tab, then click Bass to access all the bass loops. Leave the drums cycling to hear how each loop works with your drum track.

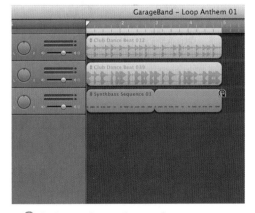

08 Adjust loop length
If any loops are too short, grab the top-right corner and the cursor should change to the Loop tool. Click and drag the loop to the correct length.

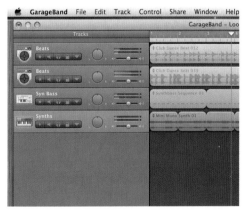

09 Build it up
Continue to audition and add new parts. After the bass, try adding synths etc. For best results, aim for loops that are in the same key.

Using iLife

10 Arrange rover

Once you have a few parts layered that work together, you can begin to arrange your song. Select Show Arrange Track from the Track menu.

11 Create arrange region

Click the small grey '+' button to create your first arrange region, then drag the right edge to match its size to your region.

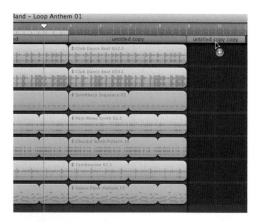

12 Copy sections

Hold down Alt and drag your arrange region to the right to copy it, and all the tracks, to the next few bars. Repeat this to make several copies.

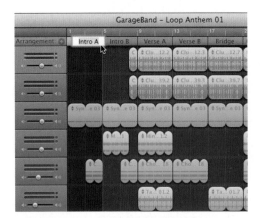

13 Arrange and rename

Select and delete regions so that each arrange region contains a different combination of parts. Rename each region by clicking on its name.

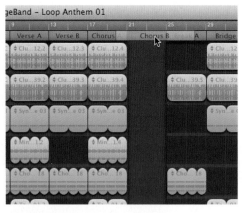

14 Re-arrange regions

Drag arrange window regions around to re-arrange your track. This method makes it easier to move whole sections of your song.

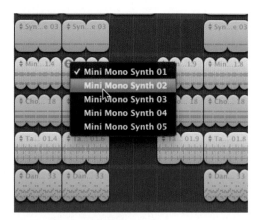

15 Family affair

Similar Loops are grouped together in families. To replace a part with a different one from the same family, click these arrows and pick a new version.

16 Select master preset

Open the Track Info pane and select Master Track. Choose a suitable genre and flick through the presets to find one that sounds good.

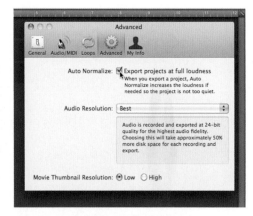

17 Set export preferences

Open the Advanced tab and tick Auto Normalize for maximum loudness when you export your track, and Best Quality for 24-bit audio quality.

18 Export to iTunes

Check that the song end marker is in the right position and export your song to iTunes using Send Song To iTunes from the Share menu.

Extend loops in GarageBand

When inspiration hits you, you'll want to get your ideas down as quickly as possible, which is where this cool tip comes into play…

One of the things about being creative is that it can strike at any time. When that magical moment does arrive, you need to be able to get those ideas down into a tangible format as soon as possible. It's one of the reasons that the majority of Mac users are creative. GarageBand users will know all too well that inspirational ideas can still be hampered by a users' ability to convert the idea into a finished product in time with the quick processes of the mind. This tip should help with this problem and it's very simple.

By hovering your mouse over the top right-hand corner of a loop or clip you can quickly drag it to the right to extend the time frame of the loop or clip in question. So, when making an arrangement you need only drag one loop over to the main browser and extend it as long as you need it to be. There's no need for copying and pasting or fussing with the playhead.

"The majority of Mac users are creative"

GarageBand   Drag and extend loops

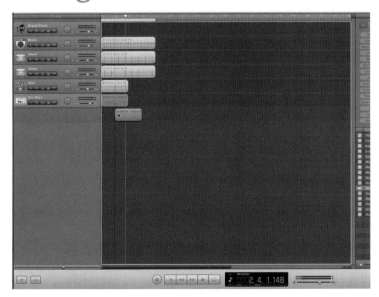

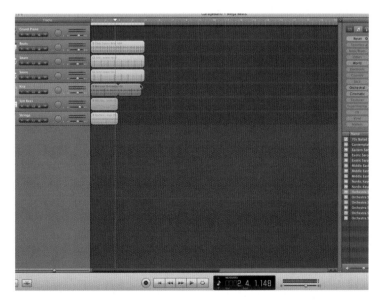

01 Drag and drop

To begin your project, you simply need to drag and drop the basics of your track into place on the GarageBand interface as shown in the screenshot above, until you have the groove you want in its most basic form. You are now ready for the next step…

02 Circular arrow

Place your cursor in the top right-hand corner of a loop and it will change to a circular arrow. When this happens you can simply click and drag the loop to the right to extend it. It's as simple as that, but it is definitely something worth knowing and you may use a lot.

Whirly

Record and edit Magic GarageBand tracks

Not only is it possible to play along with Magic GarageBand, but you can edit the tracks too

If you are any kind of musician then you'll know that practice makes perfect. It's a universal rule and one that, if kept to, can improve your skills dramatically – even over a short period of time. As a Mac user you have a fantastic practice tool at your disposal in the form of GarageBand. The free music suite that comes pre-loaded on all new Macs is a total powerhouse, and one of the many unsung features is Magic GarageBand. Often regarded as a bit of a gimmick, Magic GarageBand actually has the power to be incredibly useful for musicians wishing to practice in a live situation without inviting the band or orchestra round to rehearse. It comes pre-loaded with nine styles for you to play along with and, as an added bonus, you can delve into any of these and edit them so they are tailored to suit your needs. As you would expect, the process is simplicity itself. Users of older Macs may find that Magic GarageBand takes a few minutes to load, but just be patient as the system is a little heavy on the processors.

"Magic GarageBand has the power to be very useful for musicians"

GarageBand Edit Magic tracks

01 Lock and load

Launch GarageBand form your Dock or Applications folder. A window of options will appear. Click the Magic GarageBand option in the left-hand sidebar to be presented with your nine genres. Pick the one you want to play and then hit Choose.

02 Visualiser

In order to appear slightly more simplistic, the Magic GarageBand system uses a visual system to show you the song. You can then edit your own and all the other instruments directly from here; simply click on an instrument to edit it.

Edit a Magic GarageBand jam

Add the professional touches to a great rehearsal

Tweak the backing
If your lead solo was drowned out by the rest of the band, you can easily automate a ducking of their sound so your super shredding or quick keys stand out the right amount

Your part
Once you've recorded your part, you can edit all the facets of its sound – including the panning and automation – from here

Knowledge base

Replace too
You don't have to stick with the Magic GarageBand templates if you don't want to. You can easily drop other loops in and out in all of the other parts so that the song has the features you need to rehearse properly. Just remember to save the project…

Record it all
With GarageBand you can keep on recording over and over again, and then choose the best take and use it in the final mix

Share it, learn it
From here you can Share your song to disk and load it onto your iPod or iPhone so you get to know the song and can mentally practice when away from your instrument

03 Ready to edit
Once you have played around with the settings and got them to the level you desire, warmed up using your own instrument and are ready to edit, click the 'Open in GarageBand' button in the bottom right-hand corner of the screen.

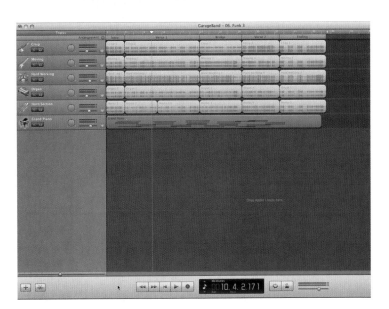

04 Familiar interface
The song you have been playing will now be loaded up and you can edit all the elements in the same way you would do for any other song. You can also record your own part, adding effects and automation as you see fit.

Prepare a movie for scoring in GarageBand

Creating a musical backdrop to your iMovie projects is probably easier than you think. Here we demonstrate how to set it up…

There's something intrinsically satisfying about adding your own soundtrack to your movie, knowing that what you're both seeing and hearing is all your own work. Traditionally, when writing music for movies, the work is broken down into cues that go with each scene. But for projects that are only a few minutes in length, the whole movie can often be scored in one GarageBand project. It's actually very easy to do, not to mention great fun.

Although iMovie has a wide range of options for editing backing tracks, if you want to assemble your own audio backdrop from a variety of elements then it's

much easier to import the video file into GarageBand so that you can make full use of its audio-editing capabilities. We'll show you how to import your movie into GarageBand so that you can view it as you compose the score.

"For projects only minutes long, the movie can be scored in one GarageBand project"

Start the prep

Do the groundwork in preparation for adding a score

Display modes
Click on the clock icon in the LCD display to switch between the available display modes. Measures is usually the best choice for sequenced tracks

Knowledge base

Chapter markers
If your iMovie project contains chapter markers marking out the scenes, these too will be imported into GarageBand, so you can easily identify specific passages in the movie should they require different soundtrack styles. These markers will not be carried over if you export the soundtrack merely as an audio file as shown.

Audio track
If your movie has existing audio, this will also be imported and placed on its own track beneath the movie track, where it can be panned or muted as required

Thumbnails
When you import your movie, GarageBand generates a series of thumbnails to display on the movie track. These give a rough visual idea of the timing of your clip

Knowledge base

Movie preview
You can preview movies in the Media Browser before you add them to your project. Browse to the location of the movie you want to preview. Select the movie in the Media list, then either double-click the movie or click the Play button in the lower-left corner to preview it. The movie icon changes to show a miniature preview of the movie.

Media Browser
Use this button to close the Media Browser pane when it's not required. This will give you more room on screen to create your score

GarageBand Set up iMovie projects for scoring

01 Open iMovie

Launch iMovie and click the Project Library tab in the top-left corner to display the list of projects that are on your system.

02 Load project

Choose the project that you want to add a soundtrack to from the list. Now double-click it to load it into the Project editor.

03 Prepare to share

Select the Media Browser option from the Share menu. This option will ensure that your movie is visible within GarageBand's Media Browser.

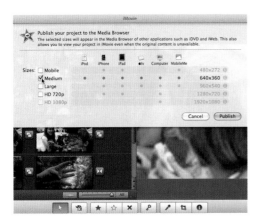

04 Select file size

As it's only a guide for scoring in GarageBand, choose a small size. This will free up power, allowing you to create a complex soundtrack.

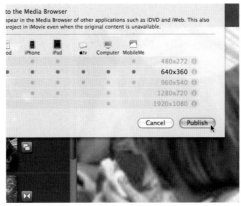

05 Publish

Click the Publish button and put the kettle on while iMovie renders your project. Smaller file sizes shouldn't take more than a few minutes.

06 Launch GarageBand

Now quit iMovie and launch GarageBand. At the New Project intro screen, scroll down to reveal the hidden Movie option and double-click it.

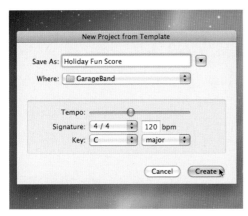

07 Name project

Give your project a name and choose a save location. You can enter key and tempo info here if you know it. If not then you can change it later.

08 Select target movie

The Movies tab of the Media Browser should open automatically. In the list of available movies should be the one you just shared from iMovie.

09 Drag movie

Select your movie and drag it onto the Movie Track in the Arrange window. Release it on 'Drag Movie Here'. You're now ready to begin scoring!

Score a movie in GarageBand

Having imported your movie into GarageBand, the next step is to create some music to go with it

So now you've got your movie into position in GarageBand by following the previous tutorial, it's time to get creative and take full advantage of its ability to play back movie files in sync with the project on its special Movie Track. This can be used as a timing guide so that you can add software instrument parts, Apple Loops and recorded elements to create a unique soundtrack to go with the visuals. Once you've composed your backing track, there are options to export the whole movie (together with its newly programmed soundtrack) as a podcast straight to iWeb, or as a QuickTime movie file to iTunes.

"Create a unique soundtrack to go with the visuals"

GarageBand Score a movie with GarageBand

01 Create new track

Select the New Track option from the Track menu. In the subsequent option screen, select a new Software Instrument track and click Create.

02 Strings attached

The Track Info pane should open on the right, containing a list of preset instruments. Select Orchestral Strings from the Strings category.

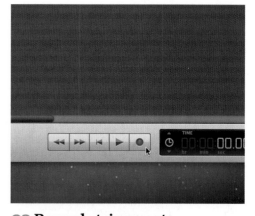

03 Record string part

Click the record button and play along with the visuals to record your string part. If you go wrong, simply undo the recording by hitting Cmd+Z.

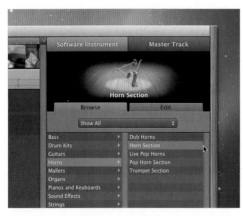

04 Add brass

When you're happy with the strings, create another new track and this time select a brass Software Instrument from the Horns section.

05 Record horns

Now, using the same method as before (see step 3), record your brass parts. Remember to use Cmd+Z if you go wrong.

06 Balance

Once all the parts are right, use the volume sliders in the track headers to balance the volume of each track against each other.

Create a soundtrack in GarageBand

Use GarageBand's capabilities to full effect

Automation station
Click the small triangles in the track headers to reveal the volume automation curves. These can be used to help highlight key moments in your movie

Size matters
If the movie file is very large, consider reducing its file size before importing it into GB, as a smaller file will free up some CPU power for more instruments

Knowledge base
Quality control
You do, of course, have the option to leave the movie track open and export the GarageBand project as a movie with incorporated soundtrack attached. However, if you were using a reduced quality copy of the original movie to score to, it makes more sense to export the audio back into iMovie, as this will preserve the original quality of your video.

Turn off movie audio
Hiding the Movie Track does not mute the movie's original audio track, so if you don't want to include it you'll need to mute it by clicking its mute button

Through the window
So you can really see what you're doing, double-click the thumbnail in the Movie Track header to view your movie in a floating resizable window

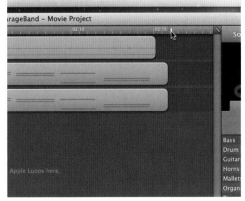

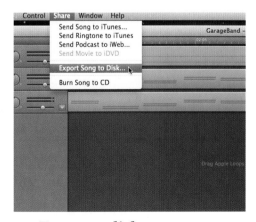

07 Hide Movie Track
We want to export just an audio file rather than the whole movie, so you'll need to select Hide Movie Track from the Track menu.

08 Magic marker
The song-end marker, a purple triangle, is usually found at bar 200 by default. Drag it back to the point where you want the audio file to end.

09 Export to disk
The Share menu will now list options for exporting the project as a song rather than a movie. Choose the Export Song to Disk option.

Make amazing podcasts in GarageBand

Podcasts are now a well-established part of the iTunes experience, but how can you create your own?

A podcast is a kind of pre-recorded radio show that you record on your Mac and then distribute either by uploading it onto the internet via iTunes or iWeb, or by exporting it on your hard disk. The subject matter can be anything, so if you've ever felt the need to commit your daily musings to audio for the world to hear, podcasting is the perfect medium.

In terms of the equipment required, you can easily make a basic podcast using the built-in microphone on your Mac and a set of Apple earbuds, but for best results you'll need something like an external USB microphone that you can move away from the computer to reduce the impact of fan noise being picked up. A decent pair of ear-enclosing headphones will also help to cut out spill and reduce any potential problems with feedback.

GarageBand is the weapon of choice for many podcasters, as it comes pre-installed on your Mac, and integrates neatly with iPhoto, iTunes and iWeb. The iLife Media Browser makes it a breeze to enhance your podcasts with photos from iPhoto or audio from iTunes. Before you embark on recording, it's a good idea to make a plan of what you'll be covering in your podcast, and exactly what you'll be saying in each segment. Prepare an intro that summarises the content, and think about what to say to round things off.

> "GarageBand is the weapon of choice for many podcasters"

GarageBand Delve into the podcasting world

01 Create new project
Launch GarageBand and select New Project from the intro screen's sidebar. Double-click the Podcast icon to create a new podcast project.

02 Choose a name
In the file dialog box, type a name for your podcast episode and choose a location on your hard disk to save it to. Click the Create button.

03 Select voice track
An Arrange window appears, containing several preloaded tracks. Choose one to record onto and click to select it.

04 Open track info
Click the 'i' button in the lower-right corner to reveal the track information pane for the track you have just selected.

05 Select recording source
Select the desired input source from the menu. If you have an external mic, select it here. Otherwise, just select your Mac's internal mic.

06 Monitor setting
If you have headphones connected, set Monitoring to On, so you can hear your voice as you record. Leave monitoring off for speakers.

Use GarageBand to podcast

Build a better podcast with GarageBand's help

Ducking

Podcast projects load with ducking enabled. This means you can set tracks to reduce in volume when other tracks are playing. Click the yellow triangles to 'promote' more important tracks

Export to iWeb, iTunes or hard drive

From the Share menu, your podcast can be exported to iWeb, or to your iTunes library. Alternatively, you can just write it as an audio file to disk

Podcast preview

Double-click the small Preview window in the podcast track's header to open a preview in a resizable floating window. This can be used to check visually how your podcast will play back

Speech enhancer

Use GarageBand's Speech Enhancer plug-in to help your voice sound clear and present. The noise reduction slider is a useful tool for eliminating background noise

07 Record voiceover

Click the Record button and speak clearly into the microphone, without shouting. Record your voiceover and hit the Spacebar when finished.

08 Open Loop browser

Click the Eye button to open the Loop browser, and click Podcast to reveal the jingles and sound effects. Audition effects by clicking on them.

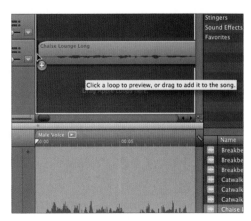

09 Add jingles/SFX

Drag the effects you like onto the jingles track and release the mouse button to import them. You can move them left or right by dragging.

Using iLife

Enhanced podcast
Enhance your podcast with images, chapter markers and weblinks

10 Prepare podcast track
Select the podcast track and click the button to open the Media browser. Click the Scissors button to open the Edit window if it's not already open.

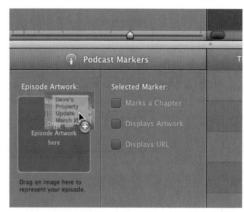

11 Add cover image
Add a cover shot for your podcast by dragging the required photo from the Media browser onto the Episode Artwork field.

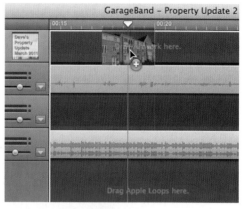

12 Picture this
Drag more images from the browser into the podcast track to mark specific points. Drag left and right to align each one.

13 Chapter markers
To add a marker manually, position the playhead at the required point, then click Add Marker. It appears in the track at the playhead position.

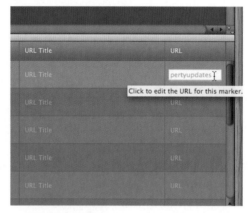

14 Add a URL
To add a URL to the marker region, close the Track Info pane and scroll right to reveal the URL column. Type in the URL.

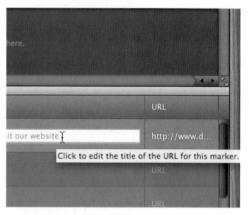

15 Add a URL title
Do the same in the URL Title field to give the URL its own title. This text will be displayed instead of the actual URL when viewing the podcast.

Edit out bloopers
Clean up your audio track

16 Isolate problem
To remove sounds, first position the playhead just before the mistake and choose 'Split' from the Edit menu. Then do the same just after it.

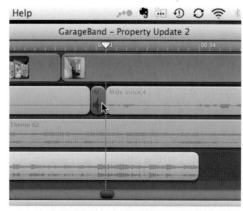

17 Delete
Click in the Arrange window to highlight the relevant region – the one containing the fluff – and remove it with the Backspace key.

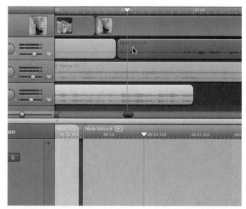

18 Join up
Drag the following region to the left so that it closes up the gap. You will know you're done when the timing sounds natural.

Prepare your podcast for iTunes

Make your podcast more appealing to download

Knowledge base

Toggle ducking

The ducking feature can be toggled on and off entirely with the Cmd+Shift+R shortcut, which is useful for enabling it without having to open the Track Info pane first. If you want a track to be neutral and not either a lead or a backing track, simply click the downward-facing arrow.

Check marker
Use these checkboxes to select whether or not a marker will function as a chapter marker or be able to display images and URLs

Episode information
The Episode Info pane appears in the Track Info pane when the podcast track is selected. Information entered here will be viewable in iTunes when the podcast is downloaded

Add marker region artwork
To add artwork to a marker region, drag an image from the Media browser to the artwork column of the marker's row in the Edit window

Start here
When you manually add a marker at the playhead position, its start time appears in the Time column on that marker's row in the editor

Knowledge base

Break it up

GarageBand's so easy to use that you ought to take advantage of its features and break up long elements of speech with musical interludes, jingles or even cool sketches you've written. You can create your own sounds for these or use the wealth of loops, stingers and jingles provided by GarageBand. It's up to you.

Top tips for podcasting

1: Regions
Once you've created a chapter or marker by dragging photos directly into the podcast track, the region boundaries can be dragged around to fit the required length of time.

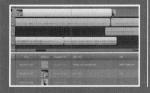

2: Stay in the loop
If the jingle you've selected to go underneath your voiceover is too short, position the mouse pointer over the top-right corner and drag it to the right. This will create a loop.

3: Use automation
When using multiple jingles and FX, use the volume curves to fade tracks in or out. These are revealed by clicking the small triangle found to the right of a track's Volume slider.

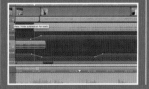

4: Slide it around
Try making title slides and transition panes in apps such as Photoshop before you begin recording. These can be dragged into the podcast track directly from the Finder.

5: Ducking
Open the Track Info pane and select the Master Track tab. At the bottom you'll find the Ducker plug-in slot. Click the icon; you can then adjust the effect's speed and severity.

Using the Master Track in GarageBand

GarageBand's Master Track controls the overall level of your project, but you can insert automation and effects on it too, just like a normal track

As a multitrack audio and MIDI workstation, GarageBand is capable of handling projects containing large numbers of tracks. In addition to all the regular tracks, however, each project also contains a Master Track through which the audio from the entire project passes before it reaches your audio outputs. This is normally hidden, but with the exception of pan, solo and mute controls, it behaves just like a regular track. Any effects you insert on the Master Track will be placed across the whole song, so you can use it to compress and EQ your mix and use automation to fade your track in and out. Which

brings us neatly to the subject of this tutorial. It's unusual for commercial tracks to have a structured, abrupt ending, the norm being to fade the track out over a repeated section at the end of the song. So if you want your song to have the classic 20-second fadeout, here is how you do it.

"Any effects you insert will be placed across the whole song"

Become a track master

Edit your entire track in one simple move

Track Info
Reveal the Master Track info pane by double-clicking the Master Track's header. Alternatively, you can also do it by clicking the 'i' button in the lower-right toolbar and clicking the Master Track tab

Fade away
You can place automation nodes anywhere you like along the volume curve to vary the overall volume of your song. Fadeouts are standard, but why not fade it in as well?

Automate effects
If you enable one of the Master Effects, all its parameters should become available in the automation menu in the Master Track's track header

Automation menu
As well as volume, you can choose to automate the master pitch or tempo settings by selecting the desired parameter from this menu and placing nodes on the curve in the same way

Knowledge base

Nodes job
Nodes are control points used to set particular parameter values at particular points in time. Clicking anywhere on an automation curve will create a node that can then be dragged up or down to set a level change. To delete an unwanted node, simply select it (currently selected nodes are displayed white and larger than normal) and press the Backspace key.

GarageBand Automate the Master Track

01 Show Master Track

Load your GarageBand project and choose the 'Show Master Track' option from the Track menu. The Master Track should appear at the bottom of the Arrangement window.

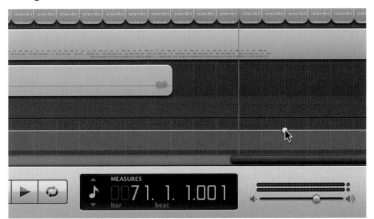

03 Set fadeout start point

If you want your song to fade out naturally at the end, you will need to start by clicking to place a control node on the curve at the point where you want the fade to begin.

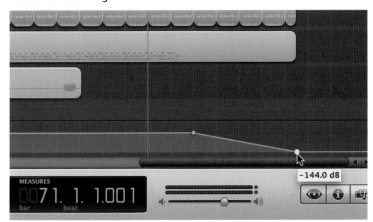

05 Fade down

Drag the second node down to the bottom of the lane until the value reads -144.0dB. This will create a straightforward linear fadeout between your start and end points

02 Enable automation

By default, the Master Volume automation lane is already showing when the Master Track appears. You will need to click on the purple button to turn the automation feature on.

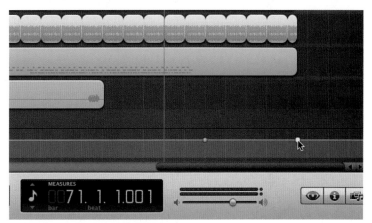

04 Set fadeout end point

Click to place another node on the curve at the point where you want the fadeout on your song to end. This will be the point at which the volume reaches zero.

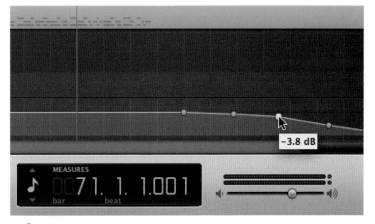

06 Add more nodes

Click as many times as you like between the original start and end points to create extra nodes with which to fine-tune the shape of your fadeout curve. This should give you the perfect fadeout to your song.

Export high-quality audio from GarageBand

The final stage of most GarageBand projects is exporting your finished track as an audio file. But how can you ensure that the quality is as high as it can be?

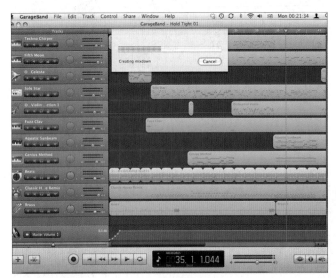

Due largely to it being a main component of the iLife suite, the audio export options in GarageBand tend to be geared towards sending finished tracks in .mp3 format to your iTunes library. In the majority of cases this makes complete sense, as it means that the audio files you export of your own GarageBand projects line up neatly quality-wise with all the other .mp3 files in your library, despite the trade-off degradation in sound quality that this involves.

The audio will still be of acceptable quality to most listeners, but every so often you will want to make sure that the audio file you are producing is of the highest possible quality, with no data compression whatsoever, for example if you are producing a mix for commercial mastering. It's a matter of just a few simple steps to make sure that your project is rendered at the highest possible resolution and bit depth to ensure a great-sounding result. So if you want to maximise the quality of your audio output, read on.

"You will want to make sure that the audio file you are producing is of the highest possible quality"

GarageBand Turn up the quality control

01 On the menu
Open the GarageBand project from which you want to export the audio. From the Share menu, select 'Export Song to Disk…'.

02 Empty the box
You will be presented with a window containing various export options. Ignore them all and just uncheck the 'Compress' checkbox.

Maximise your audio quality

The audio quality controls explained

Auto Normalize

Preserving the integrity of your exported audio means nothing if you don't exploit the full dynamic range available to begin with. Select the Auto Normalize checkbox to maximise loudness when exporting

Mix compression

Use mix compression to raise the overall level of your track. To do so, open the Track Info pane, click Master Track, click Edit, then click the LED button to turn on the compressor

Knowledge base
Data compression vs mix compression
MP3 is a form of data compression, meaning that an algorithm removes data from the file during the export process to reduce the amount of space it takes up on a hard drive, making it easier to send via email or fit onto an iPod. Mix compression, however, refers to reducing the difference between the loudest and quietest parts of a mix.

Audio Resolution

Set the Audio Resolution setting to Best, as this ensures that GarageBand will both record and export audio at 24-bit, the industry-standard bit-depth for professional audio recordings

Nice to meter

Watch the master level meters and adjust the master volume level slider as you play the track. When you export the project, the slider should be as far to the right as possible without the clipping indicators lighting

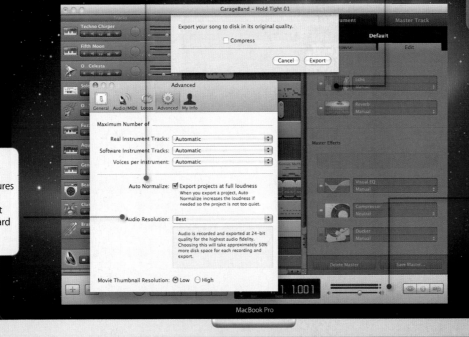

03 Push the button

The window will now ask if you want to export the file at its original quality setting. Click 'Export' to continue.

04 Select destination

Browse to the location on your hard drive that your want to export the file to and type a name for it in the box provided. Then click 'Save'.

Give your vocals some X-Factor treatment

GarageBand's new Groove Matching feature turns out not to just be an aid for sloppy musicians, but also a handy tool for remixers

At the heart of any remix lies the ability to synchronise a pre-recorded set of vocals with whatever new track you care to slot underneath it. With the powerful new tools in the latest version of GarageBand, it is hardly surprising to find users taking on the odd remix project or two.

The main reason for this is the addition of the new Groove Matching feature, which allows you to set one of the tracks in your project as the 'Groove' track and subsequently select which other tracks conform to its timing. Getting an existing vocal tightly in sync with a new beat is high on every potential remixer's

wish list, so here's a step-by-step guide to how the intriguing new feature can help with this tricky task.

> ## "Getting an existing vocal in sync with a new beat is high on every remixer's wish list"

GarageBand Groove Match your vocals

01 Launch project

We have a project containing a drum loop and a stack of four imported tracks, each containing a different take of the same backing vocal.

02 I am the Groove Master

Hold the cursor over the left edge of the drum track's header, click the star that appears in the rectangle to set that track as the Groove Master.

03 Analyse this

A dialog box will appear, asking if you want to continue with the analysis of the audio within the project. Click Continue to begin the process.

04 Follow tempo & pitch

A second dialog appears, asking if you want to enable the Follow Tempo & Pitch feature for the selected audio. This makes timing adjustments.

05 Match Groove

Click the Match Groove checkbox in the header of the first track whose timing you want to correct. You should see the waveform shift slightly.

06 Tick the boxes

Continue in this fashion for the remaining vocal tracks, ticking the boxes to ensure they are all in sync with the drums of your Groove Master track.

It's a groove thing

Make existing vocals sit with new drums

Star turn
To set a different track as the Groove track, drag the star from the header of the current Groove track to the header of another track

Unmatch of the day
To make a track not match the Groove track, simply deselect the Match Groove Track checkbox on the left-hand side of the track header

Bounce it down
As only one track in each project can be a Groove track, you can use the Export to Disk function to bounce the re-timed vocals down to a stereo file, and re-import it to free up the feature

Knowledge base

Import duty
If the Follow Tempo & Pitch dialog does not appear when you first click the Star button, you may have to enable it manually on any orange (imported) audio tracks in your project. To do this, double-click a region in the track to open the audio editor, then select the Follow Tempo & Pitch checkbox in the header of the editor.

No quantise
When a track is set to match the Groove track, conventional quantised timing becomes unavailable for the track, and is therefore greyed out

Knowledge base

Let's groove tonight
When you set the Groove track, all other tracks in the project are set to match the timing of the Groove track, except for tracks with quantised timing, and Real Instrument tracks with one or more (orange) imported audio files. You can select whether individual tracks match the Groove track or not with the checkboxes in the track headers.

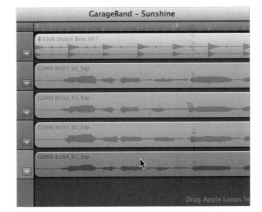

07 Open audio editor
Use Flex Time editing to correct anomalies. To begin, double-click the region where the error occurs to open the Audio Editor pane.

08 Flex time
Click with the pointer in the upper half of the waveform display, and drag the problem note or beat to its correct length or position.

09 Reset region
You can turn off Flex editing at any time for a specific region by clicking this button in the Audio Editor. This will restore its original timing.

Use Flex Time to remix to a new tempo

Until recently, digital audio limited what you could do with the speed of a piece of music. In GarageBand '11 however, those limitations are removed and the sky's the limit…

There have been a few milestones in the world of digital music regarding the level of control you have over the stuff you record. MIDI was one such milestone, and digital audio another. The problem that digital audio had for many years was that changing its speed would invariably also change its pitch and vice versa. To combat this issue developers eventually came up with file formats like REX, ACID and Apple Loops that would let pre-treated audio files stretch their tempo without changing the pitch. Now, in what could well turn out to be another milestone, GarageBand has inherited Flex Time from its older sibling Logic. Flex Time is a technology that lets you perform these kinds of changes on audio that you have recorded yourself, breaking down one of the final barriers in working with music digitally. This is particularly useful for remixing, so read on to find out how it works…

"Changing its speed would invariably also change its pitch"

Remix tempos with GarageBand

Let Flex Time do the hard work for you

Flex Markers
Hover the mouse above a Flex-enabled clip and you will find that you can drag parts of the waveform around to change the clip's timing but without altering the overall length of the clip

Knowledge base

Snap to it
GarageBand bases its time stretching calculations on beats or transients in the music and as such, works much better with material that is at least a little rhythmic. When you are dragging the Flex Time tool around an audio clip, it will obey the current Snap settings. Sometimes this is good but other times it stops you making precise adjustments. To turn snapping off, go to the Control menu.

Enable Flex Time
By clicking on the small icon next to the words 'Audio Region' you can enable or disable Flex Time for a particular audio clip. This means that changes you make are not permanent and can be undone

Follow Tempo & Pitch
This is a vital box to tick if you want to remix or manipulate digital audio. The clip will adjust itself to the project tempo, without changing its pitch

Project tempo
Click and drag up or down to change the project's tempo. All Flex-enabled audio, Apple Loops and MIDI parts will follow the changes

Knowledge base

Use a click
If you are recording audio, always record it either to a beat or to a click track. That way, if you give it to someone else to remix, it will at least be in time so their software will be able to analyse and stretch it accurately. To export a project track-by-track instead of as one big stereo file, just solo up each track one by one and choose Share>Export Song to Disk. Repeat for each track and the person doing the remixing has better control over the sound.

GarageBand Remix to a new tempo with Flex Time

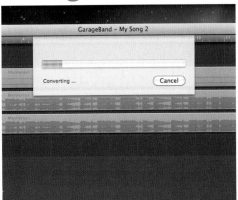

01 Open or create a project
If you are working with audio files from someone else, it helps to know their tempo. Open a GarageBand project and import the files.

02 Start with the beat
To change the tempo start with the beats. Double-click on the beats track. In the Audio Region tab, click Follow Tempo & Pitch.

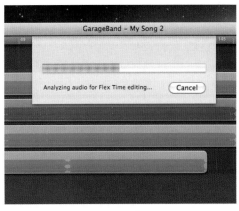

03 Analyse the audio
At this point GarageBand will analyse the file to make it available to the Flex Time tool. Repeat with the other tracks.

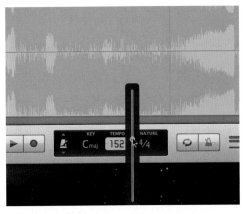

04 Try changing the tempo
To speed up or slow down without affecting pitch, change the project tempo. Line up the first beat of the track with a bar marker to sync.

05 Identify a beat
It's easier to time stretch and beat match shorter sections of audio. Isolate a section of the beat or a guitar riff then split the file to create a loop.

06 Edit the loop
Double-click on the loop to open in Edit view. Activate looping in the sequencer. Move to the larger view at the bottom of the screen.

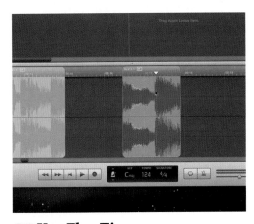

07 Use Flex Time
The pointer will become the Flex Time tool. Use it to pick up any transients or beats that need to be altered to change the feeling of the loop.

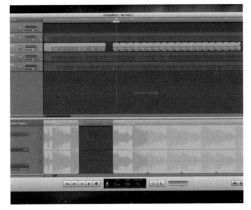

08 Duplicate the loop
Hover the mouse above the top right-hand corner of the loop in the timeline and drag to the right to repeat it. Repeat this with other loops.

09 Add loops
Open the Loop Browser section and drag in more loops to build up the remix. These can be MIDI or audio loops and will follow the project's tempo.

GarageBand Amp Guide

We look at the amps and stompboxes available to you for getting that guitar sound you're looking for

I n the past few years, GarageBand has shifted the focus of the software's target audience away from keyboard players, podcasters and DJs and aimed it at guitarists. GarageBand '09 took a big step forward with its 3D graphical representations of five new amp models and ten virtual stompboxes, which can be assembled in multiple combinations to create a vast array of guitar tones.

To provide consistency of control across the range, each amp has the same set of ten control knobs, even if some of those were not available on the original hardware versions. Although control of these parameters, and those of all the stompboxes, can be accessed by GarageBand's automation system, real-time changes while playing a guitar are hampered by the lack of MIDI control, so for most situations footswitches are out. You can now buy pedals that work with GarageBand, but most of the time they require additional drivers. Aside from that, both the amps and the pedals work and sound like the real thing, and are perfect for getting guitar ideas down quickly.

"Five amp models and ten stompboxes can be assembled to create an array of guitar tones"

GarageBand Role models

Each of the amps in GarageBand is based on a famous real-world model. Here's a breakdown of the classic gear that forms the inspiration behind your GarageBand guitar sounds.

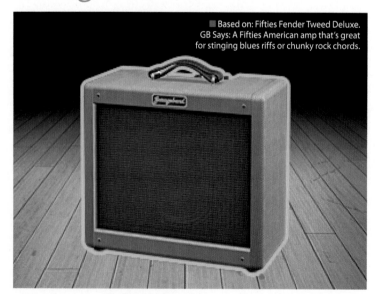

■ Based on: Fifties Fender Tweed Deluxe. GB Says: A Fifties American amp that's great for stinging blues riffs or chunky rock chords.

01 Small Tweed Combo

The Tweed Deluxe was a small 15W amp with a single 12-inch speaker. Later models introduced a warm distortion at high levels. Ironically, this made the Tweed one of Fender's most popular amps. This is probably your best bet if you're after a blues or jazz tone, but it'll also happily tackle rock chords.

■ Based on: Sixties Fender Blackface Super Reverb. GB Says: A Sixties American amp with a bright, balanced tone that really shines on clean rhythms or punchy leads.

02 Blackface Combo

Combining a 40W output and four ten-inch speakers, this amp was an attractive package, and became a favourite among the blues and rock fraternity. Although the GarageBand version doesn't include the bright switch, a tweak of the presence knob certainly compensates.

Take control

We take you through what all the knobs and buttons do

Gain controls

The Gain knob equates to the pre-amp gain stage of a hardware amp; turning it up results in a distorted sound. The Master and Output level knobs basically both do the same thing, controlling the overall output volume

Knowledge base

37 presets

If even setting up a virtual guitar rig seems like hard work, Apple has provided you with 37 preset rigs, covering a wide range of musical genres. Each rig consists of an amp with a set of stored control settings and stompbox setup. These are accessed by clicking on the selector above the amp graphic.

Grab that cab

Double-click the amp graphic and it will spin around and turn its back to you. The knobs will disappear and be replaced by the Input Source, Monitor and Record Level controls, along with the Track Effect parameters

EQ controls

The Bass, Mids, Treble and Presence controls work just the same as they would on any guitar amp, shaping the overall tone of the sound by increasing or decreasing the levels of the frequencies in the range they cover

■ Based on: Vox AC30. GB Says: A British Invasion amp known for sparkling highs and biting distortion.

■ Based on: Marshall JMP head with 4 x 12 Cabinet. GB Says: This powerful British amp helped define classic rock.

03 English Combo

Developed with the help of The Shadows, the AC30 featured two 12-inch speakers and a 30W power output. Vox's circuitry was not based around Fender designs, which led to a totally unique and punchy sound. This one is great for jangly, bright rhythm guitar with a cutting mid range.

04 Vintage Stack

The Marshall name became popular thanks to the likes of Eric Clapton and Jimi Hendrix. The 50W 1978 JMP Super Lead model had both low and high sensitivity inputs and simple controls. Mated with the legendary Marshall 4 x 12" speaker cabinet, its on-stage sound was devastating.

GarageBand Box clever

The ten virtual stompboxes found in GarageBand really expand the creative potential of the software for guitarists. Up to five boxes can be linked at one time. Here's a brief summary of what's included.

01 Vintage Drive (Overdrive)

The colourful Vintage Drive delivers that classic tube overdrive sound in spades. Featuring basic controls for amount of drive, overall tone and output level, it also has an additional 'Fat' switch for, er, extra 'fatness'.

02 Fuzz Machine (Fuzz)

No guitar rig would be complete without a fuzz pedal, and the GarageBand version doesn't disappoint. From a fat furry tone up to the thin comb-and-paper style sound, controls for amount of fuzz, tone and level will please all.

03 Grinder (Distortion)

The Grinder is far from your average distortion pedal. Aside from the level control, and the distortion amount (or 'Grind') control, this pedal also offers a filter. A flick of the Scoop switch switches the filter mode to band pass.

04 Phase Tripper (Phaser)

The Phase Tripper is a psychedelic stereo phaser that can have the effect of making you feel like your brain is being pulled out through your ears. The Depth control sets the amount of effect, and the Feedback sets how much it makes you wince.

05 Blue Echo (Delay)

Blue Echo is a decent stab at a vintage tape echo. The Time knob sets the speed of the repeats, and the Repeats control sets the number of repeats. The Tone Cut switch helps recreate that authentic dub reggae sound.

06 Retro Chorus (Chorus)

The Retro Chorus gives a lush swirling effect to add atmosphere to chords. It has only two main controls; Rate controls the speed of the chorus effect, and Depth governs how much effect is applied to your sound.

Which is right for you?

Get the stompboxes to suit your sound

That syncing feeling

All four modulation effects have a sync button, which ties the frequency of the effect into the project tempo, so that the effect will be in sync with your track

Choose your weapon

Double-click a stompbox on the stage and the full selection of ten pedals will appear below the stage. Simply drag and drop one into one of the yellow slots to add it to the current rig

Backstage pass

A single-click on each stompbox will bring up its control panel below the stage. As well as using the on/off button, you can turn each pedal on or off by single-clicking its name on the stage

07 AutoFunk (Envelope Filter)

A filter that responds to the dynamics of what you play, this works best on spiky funk riffs. The Cut-off parameter sets the frequency around which the filter operates, the Sensitivity control affects how it responds to your playing.

08 Robo Flanger (Flanger)

For the flanger effect, set the Rate, Depth and Feedback controls to the 11 o'clock position. The Manual knob appears to be an offset control to lengthen the time difference in milliseconds between the original and the effected signal.

09 The Vibe (Vibrato)

Controls for Rate and Depth govern the speed and the amount of vibrato applied, and there are six different types to choose from. Types V1, V2 and V3 offer standard vibrato options, while C1, C2 and C3 produce a more chorused effect.

10 Squash (Compressor/Sustain)

This pedal evens out the volume, raising the level of sustained notes as they die off. Attack controls the speed at which the effect kicks in, and Sustain alters the amount of compression. Use Level to compensate for any drop in level.

Add a greeting with your iSight Camera

The web's moving more and more towards video content. Thankfully, iWeb '09 and your Mac are well prepared for this shift. We'll show you how to create a video greeting for your site

Video is taking an increasingly important slice of our interaction with the web and if you're blogging, you should seriously consider adding video content as well. You could record what you have to say using your camcorder and edit the footage in iMovie, using fancy titles and special effects, but sadly, our lives are very busy and most of us don't have the time to do this. This doesn't mean that you have to ignore video and stick to text and images for your site, however.

Millions of people own either a laptop or an iMac and these machines are ideally suited to this task because they come with a built-in camera, the iSight.

Coupled with the media-friendly iWeb application, you have at your disposal everything you need to record a short welcome message for your site – or anything else, for that matter. This tutorial will show you how to achieve this.

"You have at your disposal everything you need to record a short welcome message"

Record a video for your website

Say 'hi' to your visitors using the iSight camera in your Mac

Hidden from view
If you're not too sure you want visitors to see your video just yet, make sure this box is unticked in the Page Inspector, so only people who know the exact address can access it

Knowledge base
Proper trimming
The trimming feature described in step 7 doesn't delete any footage, it merely hides it. If you'd rather edit your footage properly, you'll have to do your recording from iMovie. When no camcorder is connected to your Mac, you can use your iSight camera to record a message. Once edited, you can access your project from iWeb's Movies tab in the Media sidebar.

The final countdown
If you're not a fan of the countdown before the recording starts, hold down the Option key as you click on the red Record button to bypass it

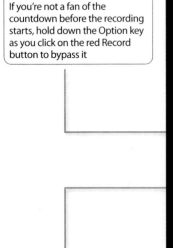

Video dimensions
You can control your video's dimensions just like you can a photo: by dragging one of its corners. You can also distort it by clicking on this tick box in the Metrics Inspector

The Media sidebar
If your Media sidebar isn't open, you can reveal it by clicking on this button (or by going to the Menu Bar and selecting View>Show Media)

iWeb Create a video greeting

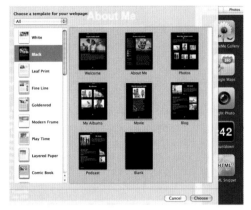

01 A Movie page

You can add a video to an existing page or create a new dedicated one. For this exercise, click on 'Add Page' and select a Movie page.

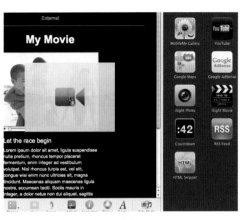

02 The Movie widget

Click on the Media sidebar's Widgets tab and drag the 'iSight Movie' widget onto the page's video placeholder.

03 Record your message

Click on the red 'Record Movie' button. You'll have three seconds to prepare and the recording will start. Click on the same button to stop.

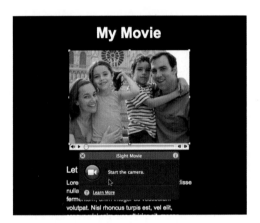

04 Re-recording option

If you're not happy, you can click on the blue 'Start the camera' button to re-record your message. Otherwise, click on the 'i' button.

05 Inspector parameters

This opens up the Inspector window's QuickTime tab. From there, you can choose options like displaying playback controls and looping the clip.

06 Poster Frame

The Poster Frame slider lets you choose a frame to display while the video is loading should you want one.

07 Rudimentary trimming

If you weren't quite ready at the start or end of your recording, you can use the 'Start and Stop' sliders to trim your clip.

08 Publishing

Once you've finished and you're happy with the look of your page, click on the Publish button (lower left of the interface) to upload your work.

09 Sharing

iWeb will offer you choices: you can visit the site or announce it to your friends. This last option will open an email message for you to fill.

Create a family tree website

iWeb is the perfect tool for creating and sharing a family tree. Here's a guide to making yours...

Designing family trees is often a very time-consuming process, and once you've collated all your research and gone as far back as you can, your biggest challenge is how to display your information and show it to the world – or at least to the family members concerned. The internet has made this latter process much easier to achieve, but designing a website has always been a little too tricky for most.

Thankfully, iWeb is there to help you create an attractive website in minutes using its bundled templates, or if you have a little time on your hands, you can create a completely original look with the help of an image-compositing program like Pixelmator (available through the Mac App Store if you're running Mac OS X 10.6.6) or Photoshop. But designing the tree is only a small part of your work; adding photos would make your site stand out and make it much more attractive for others to navigate. You can use a Photo template from iWeb's

themes and control the whole project yourself, or you could link to a MobileMe gallery page, for instance. This would offer you the option of letting others upload photos you may not have.

In this tutorial, we'll show you how to create a family tree from scratch, using many of iWeb's features to design the tree and link each person to their own individual page. So launch iWeb, and let's start linking your ancestry together.

> ## "iWeb is there to help you create an attractive site in minutes using its templates"

Family matters

Get your family tree website in order

Making active links
You don't have to publish your site to check if the links work as you expect them to. Tick this box and the next time you click on a link in iWeb, it'll take you to the desired page

Knowledge base
Link to a MobileMe gallery
Instead of creating a photo page, you could link to a gallery in MobileMe – so others can also contribute to it. When you do this, copy the gallery's web address then select An External Page from the Link Inspector's Link To pop-up menu. You'll find that whatever address you copied will already be pasted in the URL field.

Linking boxes
It's possible to link a text box rather than the text itself. This could confuse some visitors as linked text can look different than regular words, but it doesn't in this case

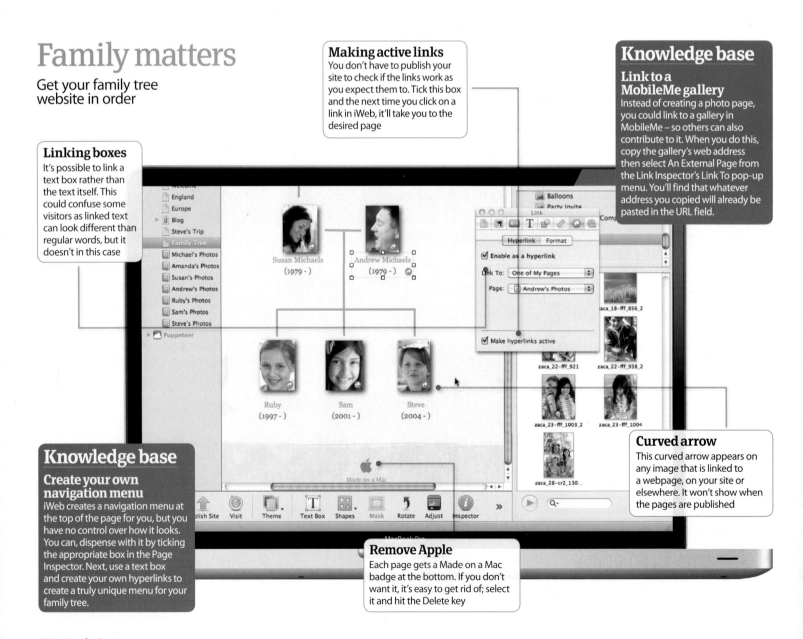

Knowledge base
Create your own navigation menu
iWeb creates a navigation menu at the top of the page for you, but you have no control over how it looks. You can, dispense with it by ticking the appropriate box in the Page Inspector. Next, use a text box and create your own hyperlinks to create a truly unique menu for your family tree.

Curved arrow
This curved arrow appears on any image that is linked to a webpage, on your site or elsewhere. It won't show when the pages are published

Remove Apple
Each page gets a Made on a Mac badge at the bottom. If you don't want it, it's easy to get rid of; select it and hit the Delete key

iWeb Create a family tree

01 New Site or New Page?

Start by creating a new site. Go to File>New Site. If you want to add your family tree to your existing website, go to File>New Page instead.

02 A blank page

You'll be asked to choose a theme and a template to build your page with. Whichever theme you select, make sure you click on its Blank page.

03 Renaming

A new page – Blank – will appear on your sidebar. To rename, double-click on it. You'll need the Inspector window, so go to View>Show Inspector.

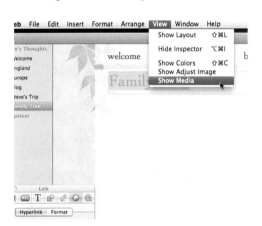

04 Show Media

Change the text to something like Family Tree, then ensure the Media sidebar is visible by going to View>Show Media. Click on its Photos tab.

05 Add a photo

You have access to your entire iPhoto or Aperture libraries from here. Select a photo of the first person on your tree, then drag it to your page.

06 Crop the image

You might want to crop the image to focus on their face. Go to Format>Mask and resize the mask and/or the image until the framing is right.

07 A text box

To add a title, click on Text Box in the bottom toolbar. Use the Inspector's Text tab to format your box. Resize and place it beneath the image.

08 Another photo

Add a photo of their spouse and place it next to the first one. To make the second image the same size as the first, go to the Metrics Inspector.

09 Resize the image

You can use the Metrics Inspector or the Alignment Guides to check an object's size, and resize it by typing in new values or dragging.

Using iLife

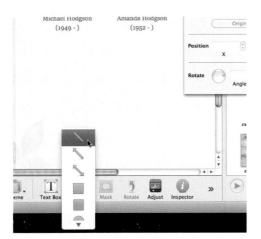

10 Add a shape

To join the two together, click on the toolbar's Shapes icon and select a straight line. Use the Graphic Inspector to alter its style, colour, etc.

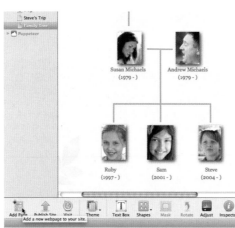

11 Build the tree

Build the rest of your tree. A small thumbnail of the person may not be enough. If you want to add more photos and info, create a new page.

12 A photos template

Select Photos from the available templates. You can then drag as many shots as you like from the Photos sidebar onto the page's Photo section.

13 Add more photos

You can use the Photo Grid pop-up menu to customise how the thumbnails are displayed and whether or not to include a caption.

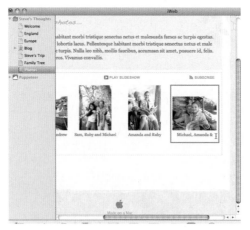

14 Caption customisation

To customise the caption, click on it (by default it bears the image's name). Use the text above to write about this particular family member.

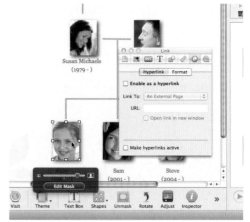

15 The Link Inspector

You need to link this photo page to the tree. Go back to the main page and select that person's thumbnail. Click on the Inspector's Link tab.

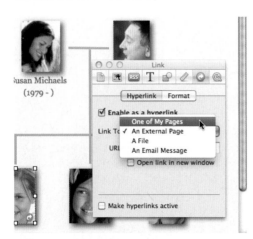

16 Create a hyperlink

Tick the Enable as hyperlink box and choose One of My Pages from the Link To pop-up menu. Select the relevant page from the Page menu.

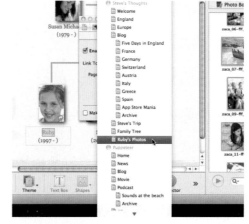

17 Link the words

Some people prefer to click on a text link, so make sure you select the words beneath your thumbnail and link them to the same page.

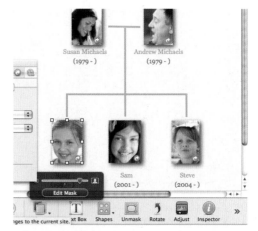

18 Repeat, check and publish

Repeat steps 12-17 for the other members of your family. Once you're done and everything looks as it should, click on Publish to upload to the web.

Family albums

Add media to your website

Flexible additions

Your media doesn't have to be in any of your iLife libraries for you to make use of them; you can also easily drag them from the Finder or even your web browser

Reorder

You can reorder the photos in your gallery as you would expect – drag them around until you've reached the perfect order in which to display them

Movie slideshows

You're not limited to photos in your gallery; you can add clips from your camera or movies made in iMovie, for instance. These could take an age to download, though

Knowledge base

Navigation limitation

Strangely, you can't add pages from other sites you've created in iWeb via the navigation menu, but the method described here solves this problem. You could find this a convenient way of managing your pages. In any case, to achieve this you'll have to open the site you wish to link to in your browser to grab the correct address from there.

Knowledge base

Useful widgets

Widgets are designed to easily add content to access other parts of the web and display it on your own pages. You can, for instance, add a YouTube video, paste in a Google Maps location or even use Google AdSense to pepper your site with ads. The RSS Feed widget allows you to display constantly updating data (like news) from other sites.

Searching

As long as your photos are properly labelled, you can find the exact one you need in seconds thanks to this Search field. You can also narrow down your search by clicking on the magnifying glass

Top tips for cool website functions/features

1: Change the page's dimensions

With our ever-increasing screen sizes, iWeb's default dimensions can feel a little too small – especially if your family tree is large. You can, however, alter the page's dimensions. Select the Page Inspector and click on its Layout tab to change everything about your page.

2: Hide pages from the navigation menu

iWeb adds all your pages in the navigation menu. This may not always be convenient as it can make your menu slightly cumbersome. To not display a particular page in the menu, select it, then go to the Page Inspector and untick 'Include page' in navigation menu.

3: Alignment guides

As you drag objects around your page, you'll notice blue lines appearing and disappearing. These are your alignment guides and are useful when placing objects next to others, so they are perfectly positioned. Go to Preferences and make sure the Alignment Guides boxes are ticked.

4: Link formatting

By default, text links take on a specific colour (which depends on the theme you've chosen). To alter this, select a hyperlinked text, then go to the Link Inspector. Click on its Format tab to gain access to all relevant parameters. You can also apply those changes to all new links on your page.

5: Image borders

When you add a photo to a blank page, it can look very bare with a lot of unwanted white space. You can, however, add a border around it by selecting the Graphic Inspector and focusing on the Stroke section. Click on the blue thumbnail to see all available options, which you can customise with the slider to its right.

Add a movie to your webpage

With more and more websites using video content, it's time to hop on the bandwagon and add movies to your own site

While not updated like some other programs in the iLife '11 suite, iWeb is still a powerful application that is capable of creating very nice-looking sites in next to no time. With the constant increase in video consumption on the internet, iWeb was there from the start with full support for either clips that have been posted on YouTube or those compatible with QuickTime.

In this tutorial we'll be showing you how to add your videos to your webpages. By adding video to a site, you engage your viewers on another level and give them something a little more interesting and appealing to look at. We will also take a look at how to customise the interface to display your work exactly how you want it to be seen. This means you're not constrained by the options iWeb provides and you can design it to fit in with your overall site. So launch iWeb, select a site you're currently working on (or create one from scratch) and let's begin.

> "By adding video to a site, you engage your viewers on another level"

iWeb Explore your options when adding a movie

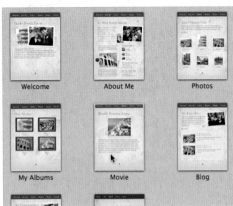

01 Page selection
You can create a new Movie page or add your video clip to an existing one. Choose the best option then go to View>Show Media.

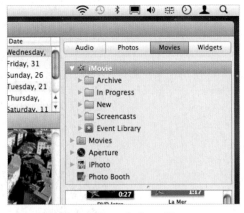

02 Finding the right clip
Select the Movies tab to access all the clips and projects created in iMovie, iPhoto, Aperture, Photo Booth, iTunes or your Movies folder.

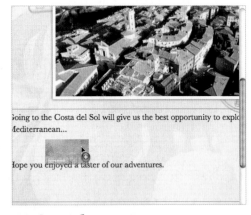

03 Onto the page
Find the movie you'd like to use then drag it onto your page. You can either drag it over the Movie page's placeholder clip, or anywhere else.

04 Resize options
You can resize your clip by selecting it and dragging one of the little white squares. You could also use the Metrics Inspector, if you prefer.

05 Inspector controls
Go to View>Show Inspector. The Metrics tab lets you revert to original size, or alter its dimensions by unticking the 'Constrain proportions' box.

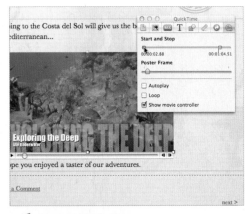

06 Start and Stop
The QuickTime tab offers many options. The 'Start and Stop' slider lets you cut the beginning and/or end of your video if you want to.

iWeb video options

How to alter the settings for movies

Resizing
Rather than dragging one of the movie clip's resize handles to alter its dimensions, you can type in the exact values you need here. You can also click the little arrows to the right of each parameter

Clips in Events
Not only can you access and use iMovie projects in your iWeb pages, you can also pick a single clip from one of your Events. They're all available within this menu

Knowledge base
Control without the controller
There's an option to hide the controls from your movie (see step 9). Although the controls may be absent, you're still able to start and stop playback: as the movie plays, click on it to pause. To resume playback, double-click on it. You can also use your mouse's scroll wheel to scrub through your clip.

QuickTime parameters
These three options can help turn a movie into a more immersive experience: you could for instance turn your clip into your page's backdrop, playing and looping automatically

Preview
If you're not sure which clip to use, select it in the list then click on this button. This will replace that list with a preview of the movie in question

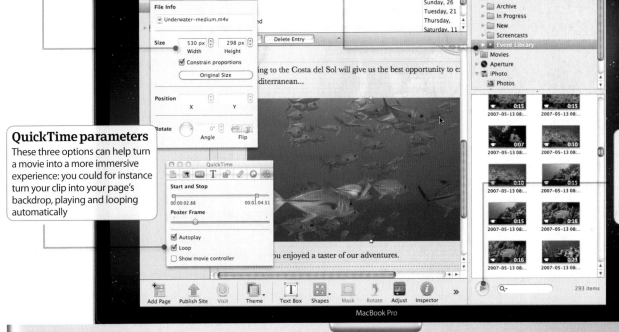

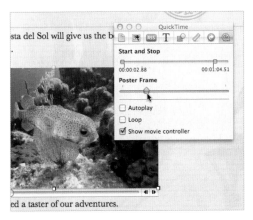

07 Poster Frame
The 'Poster Frame' slider lets you choose which frame to display before enough of the movie has been downloaded to be played back.

08 Autoplay
Ticking Autoplay makes the movie start playing automatically. The 'Show movie controller' option lets the viewer stop and start playback.

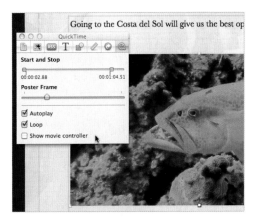

09 Loop and hide
The Loop checkbox will make the movie repeat itself. Unticking 'Show movie controller' will remove any means of controlling the video.

Use the Align and Distribute tools in iWeb

Use a few commands from the menu bar to quickly move multiple objects on your page in a way that is much faster than with the dynamic guides

By default, iWeb has alignment guides which are used to align objects with others on the page while dragging them: blue lines appear so that you will know if they are centred with each other or if their edges are aligned. This tool works extremely well when you're working with one, or a handful of items, but it can get tedious very fast if you have to move many items this way.

Thankfully, Apple's engineers have created other commands to help you speed up your workflow when dealing with many objects at a time (like, for instance, rearranging dozens of thumbnail images on a page). These are the Align and Distribute tools. They're tucked away in a submenu and they don't even have keyboard shortcuts assigned to them, but you'll be glad you have them when the time comes.

> "Apple has created other commands to help you speed up your workflow"

Tidy up design using Distribute and Align

Make sure all your images and text look nice and neat

Align and Distribute
All of the Align and Distribute tools are located inside the menu, broken down in horizontal and vertical alignments to make it easier for you to choose the correct one

Knowledge base
Create your own shortcuts
If you use the Align and Distribute commands often, you may want to create keyboard shortcuts for them. Go to System Preferences and select the Keyboard icon. Click on the Keyboard Shortcut tab, then on the '+' button. Choose iWeb from the Application pop-up menu, type in the command name exactly, followed by the shortcut you wish to use, and you're done.

Alignment guides
The default arrangement tool in iWeb, alignment guides appear as an object that you drag near another's edges. They can be most helpful if you need to drag single objects quickly

Corner handles
Grab one of those little white squares to resize the image. Hold down the Command key to rotate the object instead. You can also do both from the Inspector via its Metrics tab

Knowledge base
Disabling alignment guides
Though useful, alignment guides can get in the way of what you're trying to achieve. To disable them, select iWeb>Preferences from the menu bar. Untick 'Show guides at object centre' and 'Show guides at object edges' and they'll disappear. You can also change their colour by clicking on the blue rectangle above these commands.

Media
The media sidebar can be hidden and revealed using the menu bar command, as illustrated in this tutorial. You can also achieve the same result by clicking on this button

iWeb Align and distribute objects

01 Media sidebar

With the Media sidebar selected (if you can't see it, go to View>Show Media), click on its Photos tab, then choose four or more of your pictures.

02 Dragging pictures

Drag these images onto your page. They'll be overlapping each other, but all still selected. Go to the menu bar and click on Arrange.

03 Horizontal distribution

Start with Distribute Objects>Horizontally. The images will retain their vertical position but won't overlap any longer.

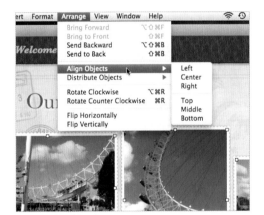

04 Alignment

If you'd like them to be aligned, as if on a grid, you need to use another command. Click on the Arrange menu and this time, select Align Objects.

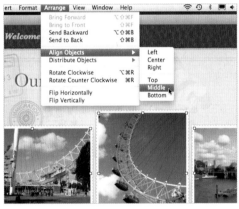

05 Three choices

Choose one of the last three options. Top or Bottom moves objects to match the highest or lowest one's position; Middle is an average.

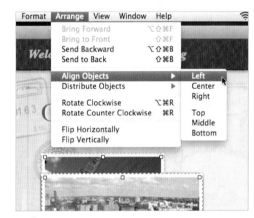

06 Vertical alignment

The top three options focus on the vertical axis. Select Left for all images to overlap each other, using the leftmost object as the alignment point.

07 Vertical distribution

To fix this quickly, go to Arrange>Distribute Objects>Vertically to evenly space out your images from top to bottom.

08 Inspector

Some may disappear off the page. Bring up the Inspector by going to View>Show Inspector (or using the Option+Command+I shortcut).

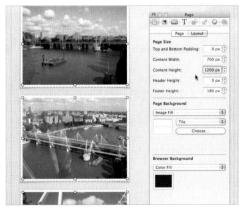

09 Layout alteration

Choose the Page Inspector. Click on the Layout tab and alter the Content Height parameter until you can see all your objects again.

Monetise your website

If you're spending a lot of time creating and promoting your site, you should get something in return

There are ways to attempt to earn some money from your website, even if you yourself have nothing to sell. Become an affiliate and advertise other people's goods and services. Should someone click on one of these banner ads and purchase a product, you'll get a cut of the profits. The more your readers do this, the more you stand to gain.

iWeb already has a built-in system for this, via Google's AdSense program. But just because Google has a prime position in iWeb's widgets doesn't mean you can't advertise other products, like Amazon, iTunes or any other company you'd care to represent on your website.

We'll show you how to can make the most of iWeb's AdSense widget to turn your webpages into potentially lucrative sources of income. We'll also touch on how to add other advertising options to your pages.

"The more readers that do this, the more you stand to gain"

Make money from your site

Use iWeb's AdSense widget to earn some extra cash

Dimensions
You can use various ad sizes on your page. The numbers to the left of each item refer to the width x height of the ad box in pixels

Can't resize
Despite the fact that the Google AdSense boxes have resize squares along their borders, you cannot alter their dimensions. You can, however, move them to a better location

HTML Snippet
Other companies with who you will register to become an affiliate will offer you some special HTML code to insert into your page. To make this work in iWeb, you have to use this widget

Knowledge base

Special links
Some companies let you advertise products within a page as opposed to a dedicated advert. These could appear as an image or a line of text your readers can click on. In order for these to work, you'll have to add a special URL in front of the actual link, which you can do from the Link Inspector.

Colour scheme
In order to make your ads blend in more with your page's overall design, you can select from several different colour schemes via this pop-up menu

Knowledge base

Become an affiliate
You can also advertise other goods and services from companies like Amazon, the Apple Store, the App Store or any other you'd like to promote. You'd have to register with them and they most likely will give you a few lines of code to use so that their ad shows up as expected. Drag an HTML Snippet onto your page and paste the code within it.

iWeb   Earn money through your website

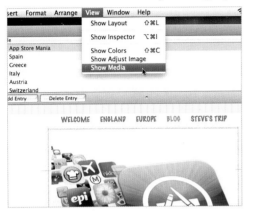

01 Show Media

Open one of your pages in iWeb. If the media sidebar isn't displayed on the right, reveal it by going to Window>Show Media.

02 Drag a widget

Drag the Google AdSense widget from the sidebar onto your page. It doesn't matter where you drop it in now, as you can reposition it later.

03 Account setup

A drop-down sheet appears. You can use it to create your AdSense account. If you already have one, click on 'I Already Have An Account'.

04 Email submission

Otherwise, enter your email address and click Submit. Check your inbox for a Google email. Complete registration by clicking the link within.

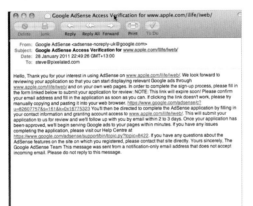

05 Confirmation

That link will take you to a page where you can add more information to your account (although this isn't necessary to carry on with the tutorial).

06 Pop-ups

You can now customise the design of your forthcoming ads to match your site, by using the two pop-up menus in the floating window.

07 Page layout

You can add as many AdSense widgets as you'd like. You could, for instance, add a banner ad at the top and a few others down the side.

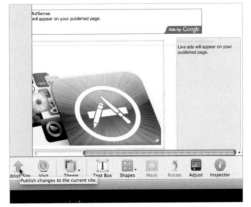

08 Publish to view

None of the ads will show up while in iWeb. The only way you can see the results is by publishing your pages online. Click Publish to do this.

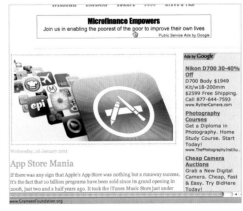

09 Visit site

Once your site is ready to be seen, a drop-down menu will appear. You can click on Visit Site Now to be taken straight to it.

Burn your movie to disc with Magic iDVD

Share your movies on a keepsake DVD complete with slideshows in a matter of minutes

There are many ways to share the movies you make in iMovie, such as emailing, adding them to an iWeb page or uploading them to YouTube. However, the original and best method is to burn them to a DVD using iDVD. If you're willing to get your hands dirty, you can add all sorts of incredible extras to your disc but, if you simply want a stylish disc containing the media you choose, the Magic iDVD option is your best bet.

In this tutorial we'll show you how to add your finished iMovie projects to iDVD, add slideshows and how to burn your disc. You can select from a number of themes in iDVD to enclose your movies and photos, and you can even pick the music to play behind your slideshows. When you're done it's simply a case of dropping in a blank DVD and letting your Mac do the rest of the work. Before you know it you'll have an amazing DVD to share with friends and family. It could even make a unique gift for someone!

"It's a case of dropping in a blank DVD and letting your Mac do the rest"

iDVD Burn with Magic iDVD

01 Add your media

Launch iDVD and select the Magic iDVD option to show the Magic iDVD screen. Start by naming your disc and then selecting a theme. Now use the Photos and Movies tabs to find the movies and iPhoto Events you want to drop into the vacant squares.

02 Background music

With your movies and photos added you can now pick some music to play behind the slideshows you have selected. Choose a song under the Audio tab and drag it on top of the relevant slideshow. Now click the Create Project button in the bottom-right of the screen.

Use Magic iDVD to burn a disc

Discover the options available to you in Magic iDVD

Media drop zones
You can add movies, photos and music to these drop zones to include them in your final DVD

Theme chooser
Pick from the numerous iDVD themes by using this slider and select theme collections by using the drop-down menu

Preview
Before committing to your chosen theme you can take a look at what your disc will look like by clicking this button

Create Project
Click this button when you are done adding media to set iDVD creating your DVD interface automatically

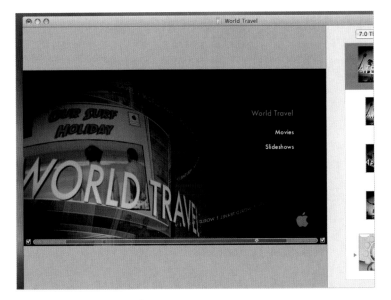

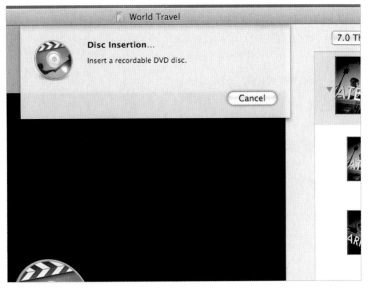

03 Finished product
Your disc will now be automatically built in iDVD with menus created for movies and slideshows. Check through the disc and preview it if you wish by clicking the Play button at the bottom of the screen. You can adjust any elements of the interface, including titles, by clicking on them.

04 Burn to disc
When you are happy with the way your project looks, click the circular button next to the Play button to launch the burning process. Now you will be prompted to insert a blank disc which, when done, will initiate the burning. You'll then have your finished work on your disc.

Back up your iPhone footage to iDVD

Saving content to a DVD may sound a
little old-school, but it's simpler and easier
than you might think

Most of us view iDVD as a way to create some kind of
physical copy of a creative project, but its remit goes
much further than that. Because it is fully integrated
into the iLife suite and Mac OS X, you can use it as a very simple and
effective way to back up your files.

iPhone clips are a perfect example of this. They are too lengthy and
take up too much room to keep on your hard drive and, over time, they
will probably be too much for a dedicated hard drive to handle. So, a
clean and simple way to save those files is to back them up onto a DVD,
and the best way to do this is using iDVD. Not only will this give you a
way to store the files, but you can also view them should you wish to
revisit clips from a particular holiday or party.

Getting clips into iDVD once you've got them stored in iPhoto is very
simple, and it will take us just four steps to show you how.

"Getting clips into iDVD from iPhoto is very simple"

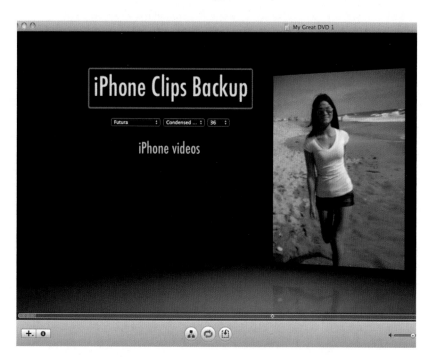

iDVD Back up iPhone files from iPhoto

01 Load, select, share

Load up iPhoto on your Mac, select all the clips that you wish to send to
iDVD (better yet, have them all in a dedicated album to save yourself some
time and effort) and then go to the top menu and click Share, then choose
'Send to iDVD'.

02 Spring to iLife

iDVD will now magically spring to life and will contain the videos you have
selected in the previous step in iPhoto. The title will already appear on the
main screen as well. Use the bar on the right to select a theme for your
backup DVD.

Back up using iDVD

Back up the photos and videos on your iPhone to DVD

Integration
iLife apps work in perfect unison, allowing you to easily share content and arrange projects between applications

Name it
Give your DVD a suitable name so that you can be sure it's got the clips on it you want to see when you are de-archiving later on

Themes
The themes in iDVD add some much-needed fun to an app that could quite easily be as dull as a Windows program!

Button it
The iLife apps are designed to be as simple as possible, which is why burning your DVD is as simple as clicking the Burn button

03 Customise
Drag and drop files (these can be photos or videos) into the dropboxes to complete the theme. These add a very polished look to the interface and act as a teaser for the DVD. Click into the Title to change that to something more appropriate.

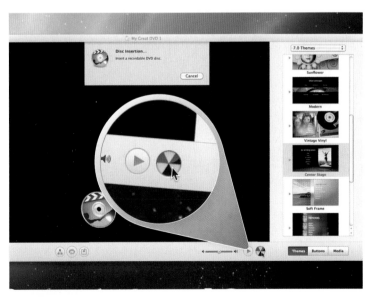

04 Burn it
Click the Burn button at the bottom of the interface and then insert your blank disc into your disc drive. The process will now be pretty much automatic. You can save your DVDs in a safe or bunker for future generations to discover…

Using iWork

From spreadsheets to word processors, iWork is a vital tool for any Mac user

Tip 1 Add style

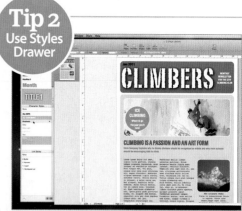

Tip 2 Use Styles Drawer

"You can use Pages to design impressive-looking leaflets and even small magazines"

Add your own unique style to your designs

Import your own assets into Pages to create a completely bespoke document…

If you don't like the pre-installed templates in Pages, or if you prefer to make your own mark, an alternative is to import your own design elements. It's really easy to do, and a great way to add your own personal touch to your designs. Following the recent revival for hand-rendered type and illustration, we've created our own elements by sketching them out with pen and paper, then scanning them into a computer and saving them. Don't panic if you can't even draw a stick-man though; there is a wealth of resources available online, such as clip art and textures – much of which is free. All you need to do is check the copyright if you intend to publish your project commercially. Here is everything you need to add your own creative flair to your projects.

"There's a wealth of resources available online, such as clip art and textures, much of which is free"

Online resources
Here are the most useful sites

01 www.sxc.hu
Stock.xchng is a free stock photo site. It takes seconds to set up an account and you have access to thousands of images.

02 www.istockphoto.com
iStock isn't free, but it is cheap. Anyone can set up an account, all you need to do is purchase credits to download images.

03 www.dafont.com
Add graphic elements to your projects using fonts or download a selection of free fonts from **dafont.com**.

04 www.pixelmator.com
Create assets in software such as Pixelmator. It's available to download on the Mac App Store for £34.99/$59.99.

Drop shadows
Use the Inspector pallette to add drop shadows to your design elements to give your project a more three-dimensional look

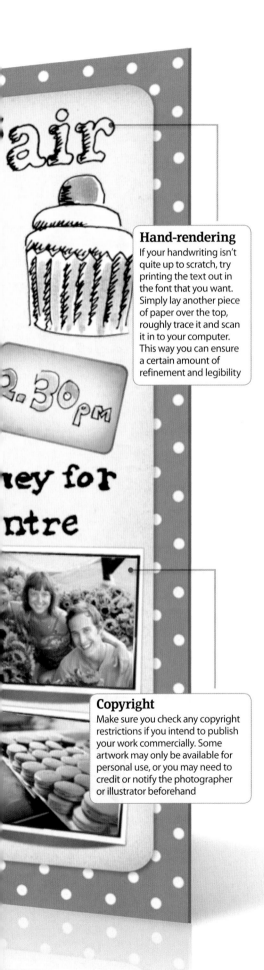

Pages Import your own assets

01 Collect assets

Collect the assets you think you may want to use and save them into a folder on your desktop. We downloaded this background from **www.sxc.hu**.

02 Blank template

Open Pages and select a blank template. Alternatively, select a template you like the look of and delete the elements you don't like.

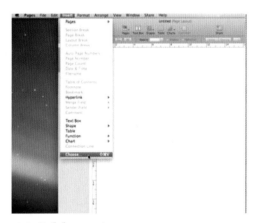

03 Add assets

There are two ways to import assets. The first is to go to the Insert drop-down menu at the top of the interface and select the option Choose.

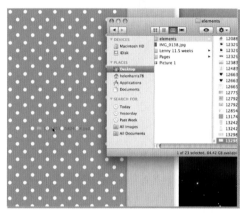

04 Alternatively

Another way to add your own elements is to select it on your desktop and drag it onto the Pages template.

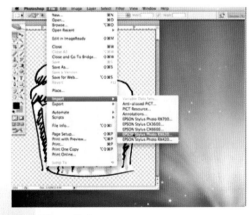

05 Sketching

If you have a scanner, try scanning in hand-drawn illustrations. If not, try creating them on your Mac using software such as Pixelmator.

06 Keep on adding

Keep adding your own elements until you're satisfied with your design. Experiment with how they sit on the page, so that you create a balance.

Hand-rendering

If your handwriting isn't quite up to scratch, try printing the text out in the font that you want. Simply lay another piece of paper over the top, roughly trace it and scan it in to your computer. This way you can ensure a certain amount of refinement and legibility

---

Copyright

Make sure you check any copyright restrictions if you intend to publish your work commercially. Some artwork may only be available for personal use, or you may need to credit or notify the photographer or illustrator beforehand

Use Styles Drawer to format work

Use the full range of style themes in every template by activating the Styles Drawer

Pages is a fantastic, easy-to-use application that can have you laying out cool pages in a matter of minutes with very little prior knowledge to how the application works. Each and every one of the templates that is available in the template chooser has its own unique style, and has been included because each one has a specific use. This style has its own fonts, which have been picked by the design team at Apple, to complement each other and make the page work as a whole unit.

The trouble is that you may not like all of the fonts used, or you may wish to use them in different places. Luckily the font styles of your template can be accessed using a tool called the Styles Drawer. Although this may sound rather complicated and something that's better left avoided, it's very straightforward to use. When activated, this is a virtual drawer that springs out of the left-hand side of your document allowing you to easily change the style of a text box you are working on. It's so simple it requires just a single click of your mouse, and before you know it you'll be tweaking the Pages styles to suit your own needs.

The Styles Drawer really is a fantastic way of making sure your pages have a consistently matching and complementary set of fonts, so your work always looks good and you have the typography style you desire. So if you want to personalise one of the styles in Pages, simply follow this four-step tutorial and in no time at all you'll have your very own styles to work from.

> "The Styles Drawer is a fantastic way of making sure your pages have a complementary set of fonts"

Pages   Activate and use the Styles Drawer

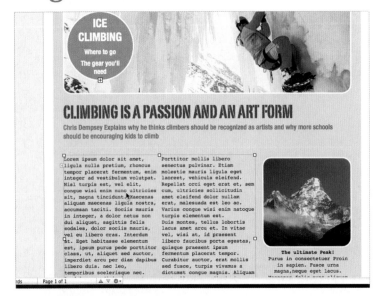

01 Load it, change it

Load a Pages document from the templates chooser and fill in all of the text with your new copy. If you want to mess around with styles first, you can do so with the dummy text that is pre-loaded in the template. By doing this, you don't have to worry if you accidentally delete any of your copy!

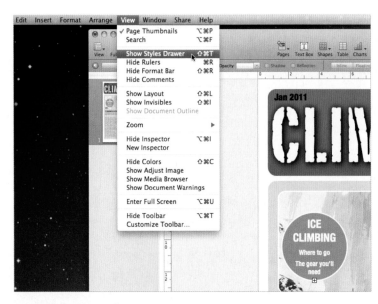

02 Menu, or shortcut

Go to the View section of the menu and select Show Styles Drawer. Alternatively, you can use the keyboard shortcut Shift+Apple+T. The drawer will now spring to life on the left of your document, bringing with it a whole new raft of options for you to explore.

What's in your drawer?

A closer look at this essential Pages tool

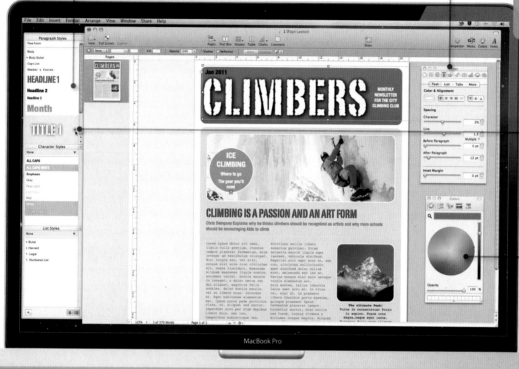

03 Click away
You will see all of the fonts and font styles that are currently used in your document. You can now select a text box and then select a font style on the left and click on it to activate it. The text in the text box will change instantly to what you selected.

04 Experimentation
The best way to find out what works best and which styles compliment each other is to experiment with different styles. A lot will depend on the content you are adding to the page and how you want it to work with other elements on your page.

Create a certificate in Pages

There's more to Pages than just a word processor. Learn how to use its arsenal of templates and tools to create your very own certificate to present to friends and family

The times when a word processor was essentially just a digital equivalent to the venerable typewriter are long gone. These days any respectable program of this type can handle photos and graphics with ease, allowing you to extend the functionality of the software and often leave little need to look elsewhere to create visually impressive documents. But some go even further than this, like Pages, which is actually a desktop publishing program masquerading as a consumer word processing application.

You can use Pages to design impressive-looking leaflets or even small magazines, and it comes with a vast array of templates that you can use to base your work on. One such template is the Certificate, which provides a great starting point for a brilliant, customisable award you can print for friends and family. It's also a great aid for teachers who want to reward their students. In a time when gold stars don't quite cut the mustard any more, giving a child a certificate to acknowledge good work or behaviour can be a great incentive for

> "It comes with a vast array of templates that you can use to base your work on"

the younger generation. This tutorial will familiarise you with the Page Layout section by helping you design a new certificate from scratch rather than copy Apple's default option.

Pages Use the Page Layout section to design a certificate

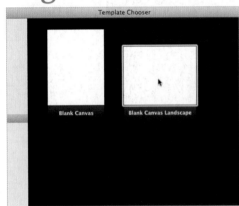

01 Get started

Create a new document. Go to File>New From Template Chooser. Click the Page Layout section's Blank option and select Blank Canvas Landscape.

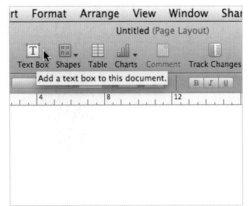

02 Add a Text Box

Unlike a word processor, you can't start typing right away – you need to add a text area first. Click on the toolbar's Text Box button.

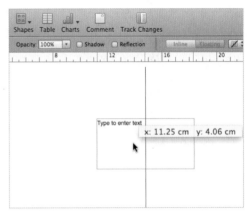

03 Moving and resizing

To move the box, click outside it to deselect it. Click on it again to reveal resize handles. You can now move it using alignment guides.

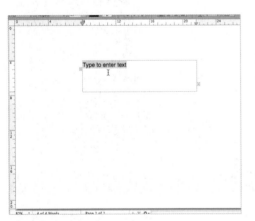

04 Edit text

To select the text itself, click on it again. If the text box isn't already selected, double-click on it to jump straight to the text editing mode.

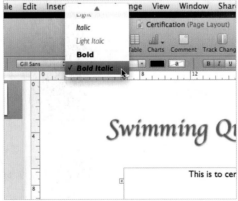

05 Customise its look

You can alter the font, size and colour just like you can in the word processing section; via the Format Bar (directly beneath the toolbar).

06 Add shapes

A certificate needs fancy graphics. Click the Shapes button and choose a curved rectangle. Move it near the top-left of your document.

Use Pages to design a certificate

Discover how Pages is more than a word processor

The Graphic inspector
The Inspector's Graphic tab is the perfect place to go when you wish to customise your shape. You can set a gradient, fill it with a photo, add a frame, a shadow, or even alter its opacity

Fill me in
If you wanted to, you could choose more than two colours to create a gradient. This is a new addition to iWork and we'll look at it in detail in a future tutorial

The colour palette
These little squares help you preserve a specific colour. To set one, drag the desired colour from the big rectangle at the top of this window onto it

Knowledge base
Customise a shape
When adding a shape you aren't bound by its default look. For instance, you can modify the star shape to have up to 20 points instead of the default five. Look closely on its inner circle and you'll find a small blue dot. Drag it to increase or decrease the spikes' size. Have a look at the other shapes to see how versatile some of them can be.

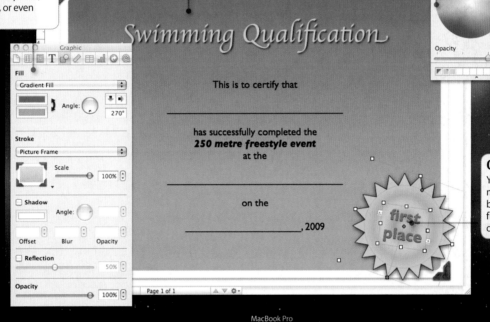

Group items
You can group items together to make changing their location a breeze: select them all (click on the first then Command-click on all the others) and go to Arrange>Group

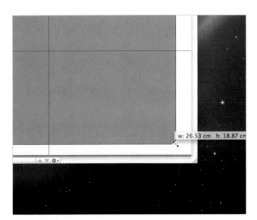

07 Shape customisation
Resize it towards the bottom-right. Notice an alignment guide appears once both sides are equal from the edge of the page.

08 Re-order objects
This square obstructs your text. To alter its position, go to Arrange>Send To Back (or use the keyboard shortcut Shift+Cmd+B).

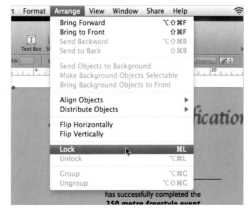

09 Lock into place
If you're happy with it, you can even lock it into position by going to Arrange>Lock (note that the Unlock option is just beneath it).

Use 3D charts to present your data professionally

Make your data more dynamic by mastering the art of using 3D charts in Numbers

Using 3D charts in Numbers is a great way to make your data look stylish, professional and more interesting. Although setting up a 3D chart is easy once you know how, there are so many options available that it can be mind-boggling. This guide not only includes a basic step-by-step, showing you how to create a 3D chart, but it also aims to give you an overall insight on how to utilise the many options available to you. From adding texture fills to using the Inspector palette and knowing the difference between a 3D-stacked bar and a 3D-stacked area, here's all you need to know and more.

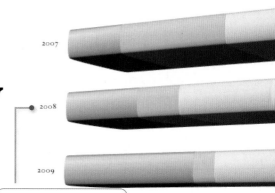

Axis
Choose the Axis option from within the Chart Inspector to determine how and what information is going to be displayed. From here you can also remove grid lines

Numbers Set up a 3D chart

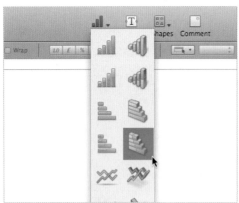

01 Select a graph
Go to the Chart drop-down menu at the top of the interface. From the right-side select the chart you want to use and click.

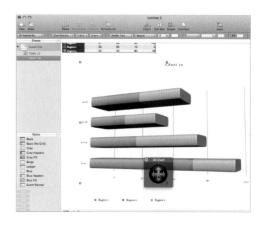

02 Input data
To input data, select the field and type. Use the Tab key to go across, Return to go down. To add rows or columns, hold down Control and click.

03 Resize
To change the size of the chart, select it, click on a corner point and drag. Use the 3D Chart box to change the angle (see right for more info).

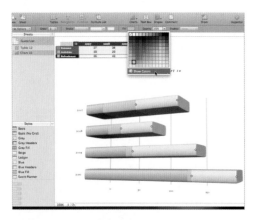

04 Change colour
Select the section of the graph you want to change, click on Fill and either select from the palette or click Show Colors for the colour wheel.

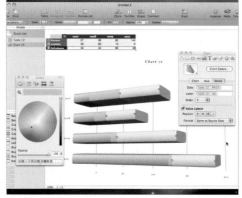

05 Series options
You can continue to edit the section individually. Go to Series Options (top-left) to display values or use the Chart Inspector to reorder.

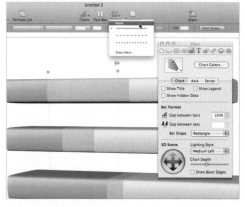

06 Inspector
Use the Inspector palette to continue editing your chart. To remove the lines, select them and at the top of the interface select None.

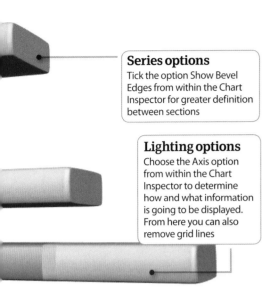

Series options
Tick the option Show Bevel Edges from within the Chart Inspector for greater definition between sections

Lighting options
Choose the Axis option from within the Chart Inspector to determine how and what information is going to be displayed. From here you can also remove grid lines

150   200

3D graphs explained

Using 3D graphs

Learn how to use these tools to achieve maximum impact

Angling
Use this box to change angles. The horizontal arrow (it will be highlighted pink when selected) will move it around, the vertical arrow will go up and down, or click in the middle to do both.

Texture Fills
Tap on the Chart Colors button within the Inspector palette and you have the option to add 3D texture fills to your chart. Choose from metal, marble or wood, among others.

Inspector
Not only can you change the style of the chart and the colour from within the Chart option of the Inspector palette, you can also edit the space between bars and sets, the lighting, angle and format. You also have the option to change the shape of the chart from a rectangle to a cylinder.

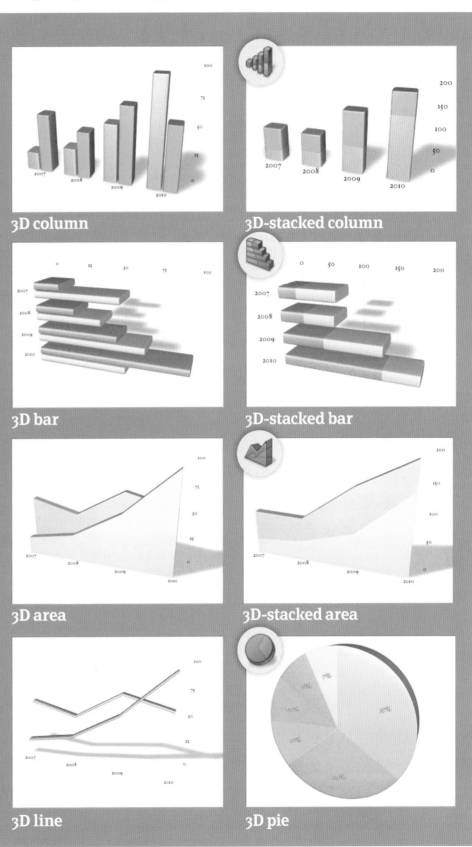

3D column

3D-stacked column

3D bar

3D-stacked bar

3D area

3D-stacked area

3D line

3D pie

Create an incentive chart for your children

Make tasks more fun for your kids by creating an incentive chart in Numbers

I f, like most parents, you find it difficult to get your children motivated, why not use your computer skills to give them a little inspiration? This fun and easy-to-make incentive chart simply comprises of a list of tasks to be done for each day of the week. Tick the box for each day that the child has completed the task, and if they complete that task for five days or more (everyone deserves a day off!) then reward them with a gold star at the end of the week. A set number of stars will be rewarded by a treat – the perfect way to get them to make their bed.

Of course, you don't have to make your chart exactly the same as the one shown here; you can make it as simple or as complicated as you like. All you need to do is create a basic table in Numbers, add a title and a name box, and then use the Inspector panel to add some professional-looking touches – such as a bright background, some bold text and lots of fun shapes to attract attention. It's as easy as ABC, so let's show you how it's done.

"You can make your chart as simple or as complicated as you like"

Numbers Make an incentive chart

01 Bright and bold

Launch Numbers from your Dock and choose a Blank template to work on. To capture your child's attention, use Inspector to add some bright shapes and colours – the more eye-catching the better. Don't forget to add a name box to make it more personal.

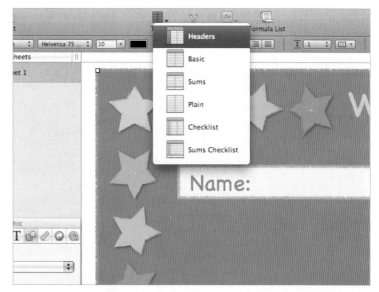

02 Add a table

When you're happy with the design you have worked up, head to the Tables icon (which you will find located in the top-left of the interface). Choose the table you want to add to your page and use the outside corners to resize it.

Design in Numbers

Create a reward chart to keep your kids in check

Tweak the text
Use these little icons to align the text in your table. Drag the cursor over the text and click the icon to align it left, right, top, bottom or centre. The same icons can be found in the Text Inspector

Shapes
To add shapes around the chart, use the Shapes icon at the top of the interface. Rotate them by heading to the Metrics Inspector and using the Rotate bubble at the bottom

Knowledge base

Distribute evenly
To make your columns even widths, select all of them and choose 'Distribute columns evenly' from the Table menu. To make one bigger, hover the cursor over the dividing line at the top, click and drag. Apply the same method to rows.

Graphic Inspector
Use the Graphic Inspector to add professional touches to your chart, like adding shadows to your shapes to make them more three-dimensional

Cell block
To change the background colour of a cell or the outline, select it and use the 'Cell background' option in the Table Inspector

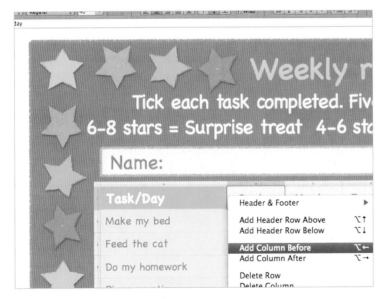

03 Add columns and rows
Add as many columns or rows as you like by Control-clicking on the table and selecting Add Column. Add your text by simply clicking inside each cell and use the Text Inspector to change the colour, size or font so it fits in with the rest of the incentive chart's design.

04 Print
When you're ready, save your creation and go to File>Print. You need to print bigger than standard A4 to use it effectively, so use the Print menu to make it A3 or bigger, tape it together and cover it with clear plastic so you can use it again and again.

Share spreadsheets with iWork.com

When collaborating with others on a document, not being in the same office can be a pain. iWork.com is here to help

iWork.com is Apple's answer to collaborating on a document remotely. The idea is simple: post your work online for others to see, comment on and even communicate during the process. This can be a great tool if you're working as part of a team, or simply if you're uncertain that the work you've done is the best it could be and you would like the input of others to provide feedback on where you're going wrong and what you can do to improve. This service is compatible with any program of the suite, be it Pages, Keynote or Numbers, but for the purpose of this tutorial we'll be illustrating how this works with the help of a Numbers spreadsheet.

Be aware though that this service is still in beta, which means it isn't perfected yet and is currently a work-in-progress. Some features may change over time and you may encounter the occasional strange glitch, but it won't damage your original file that's stored safely on your own Mac. After you have discovered just how simple it is to use this excellent feature, you'll find yourself using it all

> ## "This service is compatible with any program of the suite, be it Pages, Keynote or Numbers"

the time, and there's still the distinct possibility that Apple will add even more features over time to extend the abilities of iWork.com. So let's get cracking and share those files!

Numbers — Share, view and comment on a spreadsheet using iWork.com

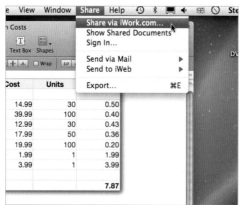

01 The Share menu
Open one of your spreadsheets and modify it if you need to. When you're ready to upload it, go to Share>Share via iWork.com.

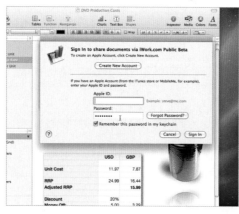

02 Signing in
You'll be requested to sign in. Your iTunes or MobileMe account will work for this, so there's no need to create a unique one for iWork.com.

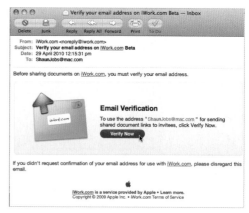

03 Email verification
You need to have your account verified if this is your first time. Click 'Send email' then follow the link in the email you receive.

04 Advanced options
Go back to Share>Share via iWork.com. A drop-down sheet will now appear offering you options. Click on Show Advanced to reveal more choices.

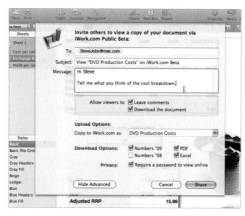

05 Send a message
In the 'To' field write the email address of the person(s) you wish to share your document with. You can also add a message. Now click Share.

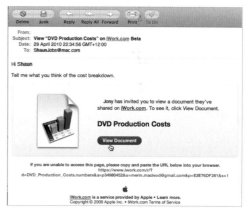

06 The colleague's view
The recipient will receive an email with a link directing them to iWork.com. Clicking on it will reveal the spreadsheet online.

Share your spreadsheets

Send your spreadsheets to iWork.com

The toolbar
The toolbar has very few buttons. From left to right they are; Add Comment, Show/Hide Comments, Print (turns the file into a PDF for printing) and Download

Exporting options
The Download button offers you three format options depending on your needs: Numbers, PDF and Excel. Only the Numbers format appears to preserve your iWork.com comments

Linked comments
When a comment is linked to a cell in your spreadsheet, a line connects the two. You can drag the comment anywhere and that line will keep it tethered to the correct cell

Floating comments
If nothing is selected when you add a comment, it'll remain as a floating window and not connected to anything. To delete a comment, click on its 'x' button

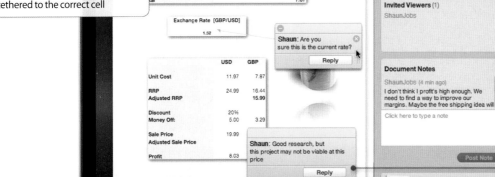

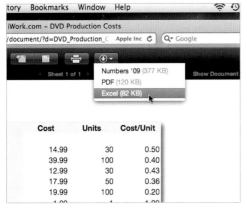

07 Download a copy
You can peruse the document but cannot modify it online. But you can download a copy by clicking on the fourth button in the toolbar.

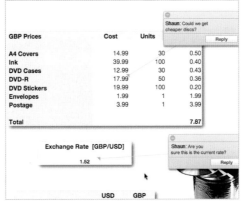

08 Post a comment
You can also post comments by selecting a cell and clicking on the yellow button in the toolbar. Click on Post in the yellow box to set it.

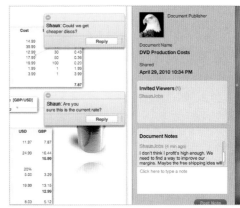

09 Document Notes
The Document Notes is for general information about the spreadsheet. The notes won't be saved when downloading the file, unlike the comments.

Create a vintage-style iMovie title in Keynote

Set the tone of your iMovie project by creating a beautiful vintage-style title sequence using Keynote themes and a little creative flair

Choosing the right theme, font and colours for your opening title sequence can really help to set the tone of your movie – just look to the big screen for inspiration. For example, you won't often see the opening credits of a horror film designed using a beautiful script font in a muted cream or pink, or a romantic love story using a distressed-looking typeface with a combination of black and blood red.

In this instance, we're going to create a title sequence to accompany a movie of an elegant birthday tea party. In keeping with the theme of the movie, we want to use a sequence that has something of a vintage feel to it. Although iMovie has some great themes, none are really suitable for this project, so we're turning to Keynote for some inspiration. This application is a great piece of kit that many will overlook, but we find an essential part of the iWork suite. The options on offer give you more choice than being confined to what iMovie

"None are really suitable for this project, so we're turning to Keynote for some inspiration"

brings to the table. Just a few simple steps will make all the difference to your iMovie project.

Movie title in Keynote

Use the iWork application to catch your viewer's eye

Master slides
The master slides will appear by dragging this icon in a downwards direction. To change the template of a slide, select it and then select the one you want to use from Masters

Sensitive colour use
Be sensitive when choosing colour for your text. Bright colours won't evoke the feeling of a bygone age. Muted colours, such as cream and gold, are much more appropriate

Hierarchy
Don't forget to make your headline bigger than your subtitle – this helps the audience navigate the page. Using two different fonts can also help differentiate between lines, as can using different weights such as Bold and Italic

Animating
If you're going to use animation between slides or for text, choose a build that is in keeping with your theme. Typewriter works well in this instance. To add animation to the text, make sure that it is highlighted first

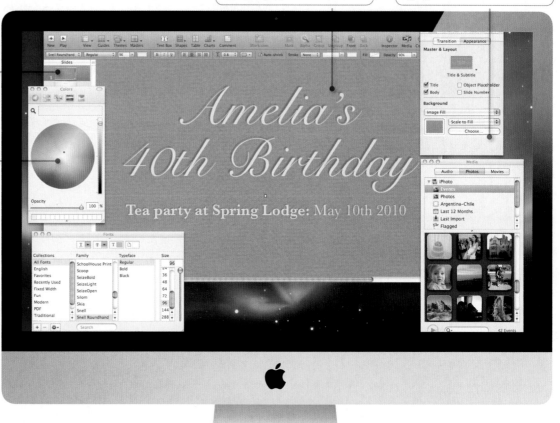

Knowledge base
Adding media
To add audio or graphics to your sequence, head to the Media panel (top right of the interface) and choose the Audio or Photo tab. If you do import audio, make sure that the 'Include audio' option is selected when exporting to iMovie.

Keynote
Create a vintage-style title sequence for iMovie

01 Choose a template
Open Keynote and select a template. Go to the Inspector, click the document tab and select 'Custom slide size' from the Slide Size menu.

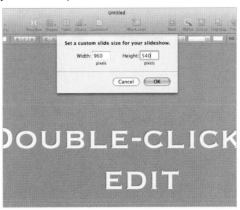

02 Check the size
Make sure your slide is set to a dimension that is consistent with your iMovie project's size. If it's a widescreen project, it should be 960 x 540 pixels.

03 Editing text
Click in the box to start typing and drag the cursor over the text to edit. In the Fonts panel, select a font that evokes the feel of your movie.

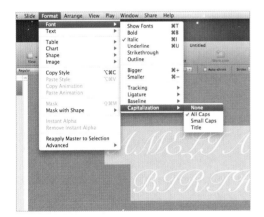

04 Lower case
You can change the text from upper to lower case by going to the Format menu and selecting Font>Capitalization>None.

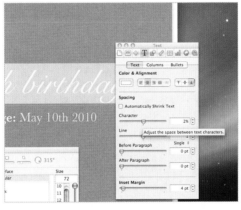

05 Tweaking
Go to the 'T' tab within the Inspector panel to make text adjustments. You can change the alignment and colour, or change the spacing.

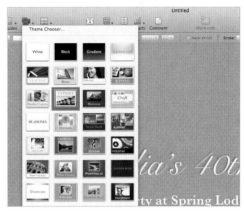

06 Change of heart
If you decide that you don't like the selected theme, it's not too late to change. Simply go to Theme Chooser and choose another.

07 Builds
Click Shift+Cmd+N simultaneously to add a new slide and select a new design from Masters. Add animations by going to the Build Inspector.

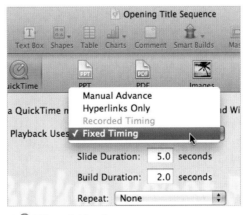

08 Fixed timing
When you're finished, go to Share>Export and choose the QuickTime option. Under the Playback Uses pop-up menu, select Fixed Timing.

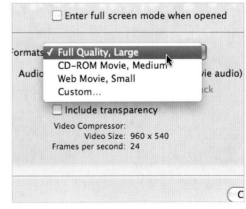

09 Exporting
Using the Formats pop-up menu, select 'Full Quality, Large'. When you're done, click Next to name and save. Now you're ready for iMovie.

A grand finalé for your presentation

Use animation in Keynote to give your presentation a climatic ending

Some people might say that a climatic ending is what makes a good movie. Whether that's true or not, it's definitely the part that everybody remembers. Be it a movie, book, piece of music, videogame or – as in our case – a presentation, suspense, pace and drama are crucial to keeping the audience captivated and hanging off your every word. You also want the viewer or reader to feel that everything that went before it was worth it, and you want to leave them satisfied with the ending.

This common technique of slowly building suspense to culminate in a grand finalé is especially useful when creating presentations, particularly if you are building up to a big announcement that's going to really appeal to your captivated audience. The example that we are using here is the annual financial report for a small business. The big announcement at the end is the net profit

– which for many people is what the presentation is all going to be about – so we are going to use a combination of animation techniques in order to give it

> ## "Suspense, pace and drama are crucial to keeping the audience captivated"

extra importance and to emphasise that this is the highlight of the presentation. Follow these easy steps to learn how and discover ways in which you can blow your audience away with an explosive finalé.

Go out with a bang!

Make sure you finish your presentations on a high

Suspense
Keep your audience captivated by teasing them. Create suspense by adding a cliff-hanger at the end of the penultimate slide

Magic Move
Make an image move from slide to slide using Magic Move. It only works with identical images and works best if the image is resized

Knowledge base

How it works
From the first to the second slide, the cupcake will decrease in size and move bottom-left. At the same time, the images will align themselves to the right. The big figure will appear one number at a time with a sparkly effect over the duration of eight seconds. Once this has finished, the figure will spin around.

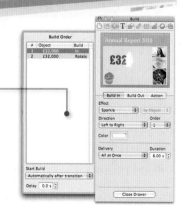

Duration
Edit the duration of your animation by using the arrows in the Duration box. From the Start Transition menu, you can opt whether to start the animation yourself with a click or start automatically

Play
Tap in the image to view each animation. From within this palette you can also choose your Builds and Actions, from the duration and order to colour and direction

Keynote Use animation to emphasise your presentation

01 Duplicate slide

Try using Magic Move to create impact. Begin by duplicating what will be the penultimate slide. Control-click and select Duplicate.

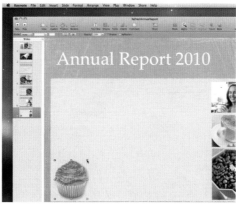

02 Resize

Magic Move works best if you resize and rearrange your images. On the duplicated slide, click the image and drag the corner points.

03 Magic Move

Go back to the previous slide. Open the Slide Inspector and select Transition. From the Effect drop-down menu, select Magic Move.

04 Format text

Type the data onto the last slide and open the Font palette. Make the text as big and bold as you can for maximum impact.

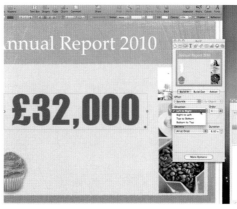

05 Build

With the box selected, go to the Build Inspector and choose an effect. We've chosen Sparkle. Edit the effect by direction, order and duration.

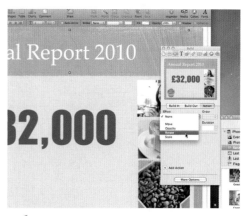

06 Rotation

The data will appear onto the slide with the effect. Once completed, add a rotation for extra emphasis. Click on Action and choose an effect.

07 Full circle

Edit the rotation by the direction and degrees. The Order refers to its position within the sequence. For more on this, tap on More Options.

08 Build Order

This menu shows a list of your animations. Drag them around to change the order. You can determine how they start and the delay.

09 Play

Play each animation from within the Inspector palette by clicking on the image, or to view the entire presentation full-screen click Play.

Rehearse your slideshow and customise the display

If you want a slick presentation you're halfway there using Keynote, but you'll have to practise what you want to say. Luckily Keynote has a great tool to help you do just that

If you want to give presentations the way Steve Jobs does in his keynotes, you will need to rehearse. A lot. First of all you'll need to build a slick, interesting and engaging presentation, which is easy to accomplish using Keynote's broad range of tools and easy-to-access functions.

Once you've done this you'll need to practise what you want to say as each slide appears. You'll also want to check that all the animations, effects and other elements are working as strongly as they should be. Keynote has a great full-screen tool to help you do this. The full-screen nature is incredibly important as it gives you the 'Keynote Feel'. There are timers on the bottom of the screen as you practise so you can make sure that you are adhering to any time limits, whether they are imposed by yourself or others. Not only that, but you can customise the display so it is working as hard as possible to help you hone and perfect your speech.

"You'll need to practise what you want to say as each slide appears"

Keynote   Use the Rehearse Slideshow tool in Keynote

01 Make it, rehearse it

Once you have built your scintillating presentation, go to the Play section of the top menu and then click on the Rehearse Slideshow option. Everything will then fade into full-screen mode and you can begin your presentation once ready.

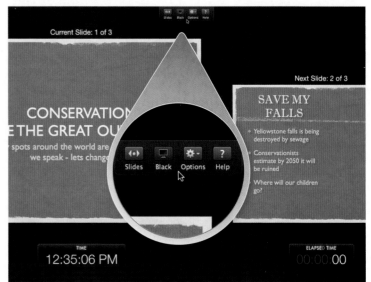

02 Mouse to the top

Flick through the slides to rehearse your presentation and the timers will then begin. If you wish to make any changes to the display at this point, direct your mouse to the top of the display and a hidden menu will magically appear.

Rehearsal is key

Give presentations Steve Jobs would be proud of

Tick them
Use the tick boxes to select elements you want to see on screen. Experimentation will help you find the right combination. When you are finished click the Done button

Slides
Position these wherever you like. We have ours arranged so slides move from right to left but you can go the other way or even up and down too

Make it big
You can drag and resize any of the windows you like. Here we've made the time remaining window as big as possible, so it's easy to see as we practise the presentation

Slide indicator
At the bottom of your current slide is an indicator to show you how far through the presentation you are

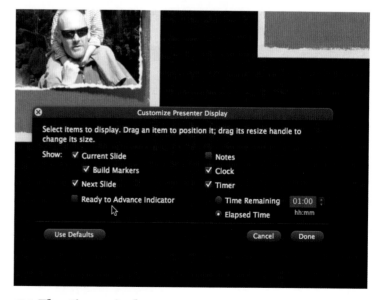

03 Options
Click on Options in the menu and then select Customize Presenter Display. This will freeze the presentation at the current point and allow you to rearrange the elements that are present on screen. You will just need to click and drag them around.

04 Floating window
A floating options window will also appear that will let you pick the elements that appear on screen. Tick boxes are used so you can simply click to add or remove elements from your display. Once you're happy you can then continue to practise your presentation.

Apple Essentials

"Mail on the Mac is a smart way to manage your emails"

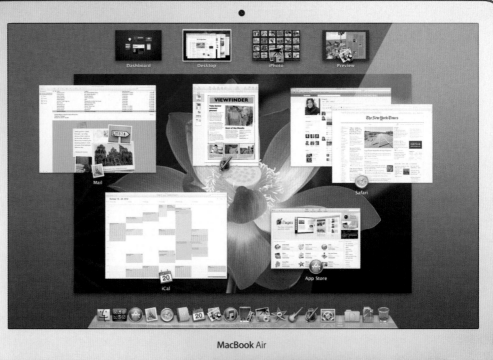

From Mail and iCal to Safari and Photo Booth, discover how to use these essential applications

Tip 4
Set up FaceTime

Tip 5
Discover ClickToFlash

Tip 6
Share your snaps

"Extensions are fun and can be useful in a number of situations"

Set up Mail on your Mac

Mail on the Mac is truly as painless as an application can get. Follow these nine quick-and-simple steps to get started and confidently send and receive your emails with ease

It's easy to overlook Mail on the Mac when we're accustomed to browsing emails on the web. And with social networking becoming ever-more popular, many people will communicate solely through the likes of Facebook and Twitter. But if we're lucky enough to own an iMac or MacBook, we really should make good use of our sophisticated machines and allow them to do what they do best: make life a whole lot easier! Mail on the Mac is a smart way to manage your emails as you work and play in Apple's safe hands.

Now, the beauty of your Mac is of course its simplicity. But when that simplicity is a new application staring at you expectantly, it can feel a little intimidating. Pushing buttons at random in the hope you will eventually work it out is never going to be the best approach, so with this helpful little guide to

setting up Mail on the Mac, we'll have you sending and receiving emails to and from your favourite people in no time. We'll also show you how to customise

"Mail on the Mac is a smart way to manage your emails as you work and play"

your messages to give them that personal feel, and explain how to attach documents and keep the Mail interface clean and tidy so you know where all your messages are.

Mail Get your mail up and running

01 Run Mail

Click on the Mail icon in your dock to kick it into motion. After a quick bounce you should be prompted by a Welcome to Mail pop up window.

01 Mail's Setup Assistant

This wizard can configure accounts that use the most popular email services, including Gmail and Yahoo. Choose your favourite.

03 Enter your details

Enter the full name, email address and password for your existing email account the same as you would in the browser of your service provider.

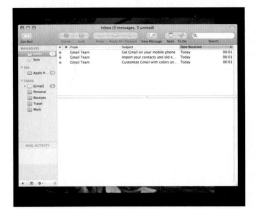

04 Create and enjoy

Click on Create in the Mail Setup Assistant and be taken to your new Mail Inbox. You'll have the same mailboxes as in your web-browsing version.

05 Compose a message

Hit New Message to summon an email draft. Enter the address of your recipient in the To field and fill in your Subject and message accordingly.

06 Attach a file

To send your recipient a file, click on Attach and choose the file from its location. Be mindful of what you're sending to avoid large email sizes.

Master Mail on your Mac

Everything you need to send and receive emails

Happiness is shortcuts

As Mac users, we love our shortcuts. Ctrl and click on the emails in your Inbox to bring up various time-saving options: Reply, Forward, Mark As Unread, Delete, Move To folders of your choice etc

The Mail toolbar

You'll find handy buttons for all the most-used functions right at the top of your Mail interface. Delete, send mail to the Junk folder, Reply, Forward and create New Messages till your heart is content

Knowledge base

Notes and To Do lists

We all need reminders now and again. Mail's handy To Do function creates a list of important email tasks – simply set the Date, Priority and set an alarm for anything you don't want to forget. Notes are helpful post-it style reminders that can also be added to your To Do list and get sent to your Inbox for added importance.

Keep it tidy

Creating folders to store your emails for quick reference is a great way to prevent oversized Inboxes. Go to Mailbox>New Mailbox and set the Location and enter a Name for your new folder

Sort and search

It's there but it's hiding. Sort by From, Subject or Date Received, and use the Search field in the top right to track messages with specific words in the Entire Message, From, To or Subject

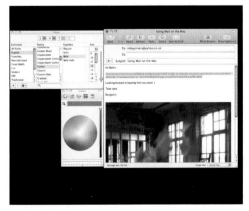

07 Add some style

If you're feeling adventurous, you can change your fonts and add colour by clicking on the appropriate Fonts and Colors buttons.

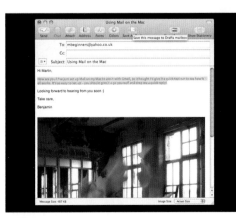

08 Save or send

If you're not yet ready to send, click Save As Draft and it'll wait in your Drafts folder. When happy, hit Send to start your message on its journey.

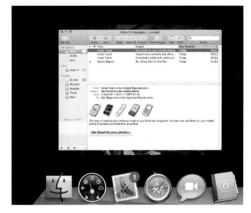

09 You've got mail

Click Get Mail in the top left to download emails. Unread messages are highlighted by blue dots – the icon in your dock also shows new messages.

Set up the Junk Mail filter in Mail

Nobody likes getting spam emails, so get organised and filter them out for good

S pam is seen by many people as the bane of the emailing world. It seems that no matter how careful you are not to give your details away when you don't have to, you still end up getting unsolicited messages dropped into your inbox at a rate that is hard to fathom.

Spam can quickly turn a mail account into a cesspit of scams, unlicensed drugs and terrible products. At that point it takes all the fun out of getting emails – who wants to have to delete a ream of rubbish before you can settle in and read a message from a friend? Luckily, as Mac users we have Mail – and it's possible to customise it to help filter out all the rubbish and keep your inbox full of the emails you want. The

"The amount of spam that you receive will then reduce dramatically"

process is simple and will mean that as emails pour into your inbox, spam will be immediately filtered out. You may have to tell Mail where to put a few rogue spam messages, but it will then learn from that and the amount of spam you receive will reduce dramatically. You will then be able to enjoy the feeling of receiving a new message, safe in the knowledge that it will be something worth reading and not asking you to enter your bank details because you've won the Nigerian lottery…

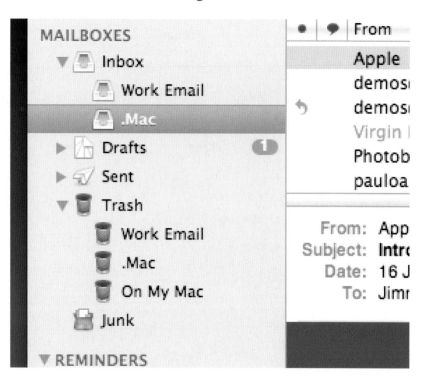

OS X Mail   Filter out your junk emails

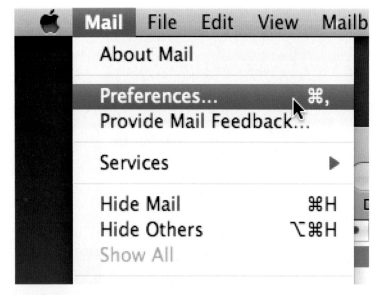

01 Go to Preferences

Once you have opened up Mail go to the top menu, click Mail and then click Preferences. This will bring up the Preferences window. From here you can customise a number of elements in Mail, personalising it and making it work how you want it to.

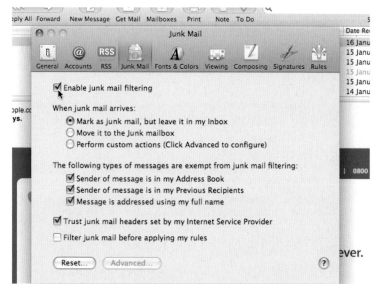

02 Junk tab

In the window that appears, simply click on the Junk Mail tab at the top of the window as shown above and click the 'Enable junk mail' filtering tick box. There are a number of other options presented here, but we'll walk you through them in the next step.

Employ the Junk Mail filter in Mail

One-button vetting
You can also mark or unmark your emails by using the button at the top of the interface

It gets smart
Mail will, over time, come to recognise junk mail and will get more proficient at filtering it out

Knowledge base
Junk in the cloud
If you use MobileMe from other computers a lot you can also enable Junk Mail filtering there too. When logged in to MobileMe select Preferences from the Action menu and then click Enable Junk Mail filter. Now, all potential junk emails will be flagged the same way as in Mail.

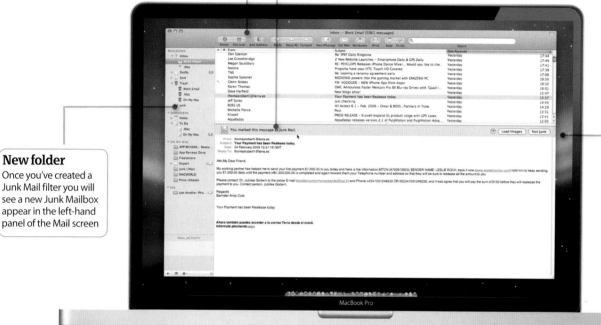

New folder
Once you've created a Junk Mail filter you will see a new Junk Mailbox appear in the left-hand panel of the Mail screen

Marked messages
You can mark mail as junk from within the email itself. You will be prompted at the top of an email as to whether you wish to mark or unmark it as junk

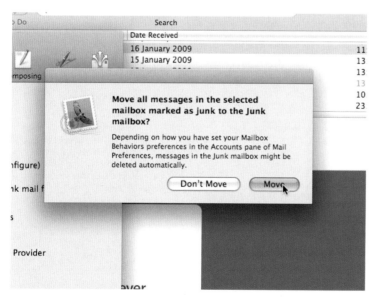

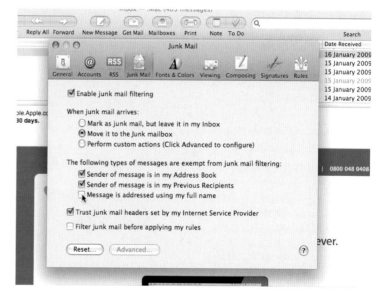

03 When it arrives
In the 'When junk mail arrives' section, tick the 'Move it to the Junk mailbox' box. You will now be prompted about moving mail, so hit the Move button. By selecting this option, when Mail determines something is junk, it will move it to a separate folder instead of cluttering your inbox.

04 Further customise
You can now alter the behaviour of the Junk Mail filter by ticking the boxes you want to apply to your Mail. Your changes will be saved automatically and you can return to this window and alter the settings as and when you wish if you find they're not working for you.

Change the fonts of the Mail interface

Using Mail's Fonts & Colors preference pane, it is possible to change the default typeface of the various text elements and adjust the colour scheme of quoted text in message replies…

Whether you have a preferred font type or a compulsion to customise every single item you possibly can, Mail offers a comprehensive set of options to add a personal touch to its interface. Maybe you want to use a smaller font size in order to see more items or, conversely, you have an aversion to a cramped-looking application interface and prefer to give a lighter feel to its various elements. The Fonts & Colors preference pane is the place to go. The options presented there also give you the opportunity to alter the colour scheme of quoted text in your replies to messages.

In some cases, the choice of a specific typeface can lead to confusion. Fixed-width or mono-spaced fonts, like Courier, or varying width fonts, like Helvetica, can lead to uncertainty with characters like upper-case 'i', '1' or lower-case 'L'. This tutorial guides you through the font settings for the Mail viewer window.

Customising Mail fonts

Choose a typeface that will improve the look of your messages

Message list font
Most of the lists displayed in the Mail interface are affected by typeface adjustments made in this text box; this applies to Messages, RSS news, To Do and all types of lists available in Mail

Mailbox font
The font type and size adjustment selected here will be applied to all mailboxes, reminder items, folders, RSS feeds listed in the sidebar and section headers. This also applies to the item counters

Notes fonts
Unlike the settings for messages, Notes' font setting is the same for the list and content. However, the font size of items in the Notes list is identical to the Message list size setting

Knowledge base

Plain text messages

The plain text message format is the simplest and oldest format used to send emails. Its ease of use, simplicity and light weight are only a few of its unique qualities. It can be read by all email applications; supports attachments; can be scanned easily by antivirus software; and does not allow something dangerous to be concealed within the message.

Message font
In the Fonts & Colors preference pane, the selected font and size settings for the Message font also apply to the content of the RSS items; thus, it is not possible to change the text colour for any of these items

Mail New fonts for the Mail interface

01 Locate Fonts & Colors pane

Open Mail's Apple menu and select Preferences; the Fonts & Colors section you are after is fifth on the toolbar.

02 Preference pane layout

Fonts & Colors preferences are in two sections. The first lets you change the font displayed; the second caters for quoted text options.

03 Change the font settings

To change the font type for all the Mail interface panes, click on the Select button next to each of the five text boxes in the first (upper) section.

04 The Fonts panel – part one

This shows all the collections, families, typefaces and font sizes available; a single click on one immediately applies it to the selected element.

05 The Fonts panel – part two

In the present context, most options in the toolbar are not applicable. You can only modify Mail's typeface and size through the Fonts panel.

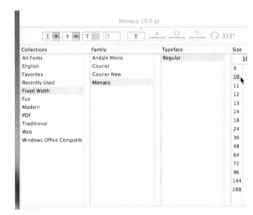

06 Fixed-width fonts

For these, choose from the fixed-width category. This allows the use of an alternate font when receiving a message in an unknown typeface.

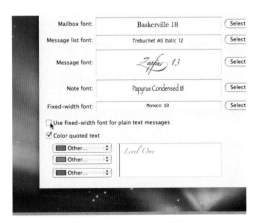

07 The fixed-width fallback

Tick the 'Use fixed-width font' checkbox to apply it to plain text messages. Then Mail has a fallback solution for messages in an unknown font.

08 The quoted text options

It is possible to modify the colours of the quote-level markers up to the third level. Click the drop-down list and select one to change the setting.

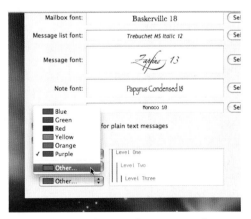

09 Other colours for quoted text

For a more appropriate standard colour or to help distinguish quoted text, select Other in the drop-down list and pick a colour in the Colors window.

Get to know iCal and MobileMe calendars

An incredibly important app that can help organise your life

iCal is one of the unsung heroes of OS X and iOS. It is the Mac-based predecessor to Calendar on your iPhone, iPad or iPod touch. This powerful application has the ability to help you organise your life and, when paired with MobileMe, it can be with you everywhere you go by offering synced calendars across all of your Apple devices. As you would expect, Apple has made the application very simple and yet very effective. It has even made it possible for you to access it over the internet, should there ever be a time when you are without a Mac, iPhone or iPad (unlikely, we know).

In this introduction to the application we'll show you how to add a new calendar, add an event and how to sync calendars with MobileMe, as well as how best to view your busy schedule. Armed with this information, you can then get your appointments, meetings and reminders all added to the application and synced across your devices.

> "It can be with you everywhere you go by offering synced calendars across all of your devices"

iCal view options

Track your life daily, weekly or monthly

iCal Get started with iCal

01 Add a calendar

The very first step will be to open up iCal on your Mac. Use the + button at the bottom of the iCal interface to add a calendar. These can be added to your Mac or to the MobileMe calendars you have set up. You can add as many as you like.

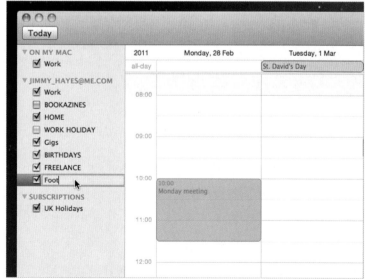

02 Name it

Naming your calendar is important, as it will specify the kind of events you add and help you divide the kinds of tasks you complete in your everyday life. You can, once your calendar is made, tick and untick it to reveal and hide those events.

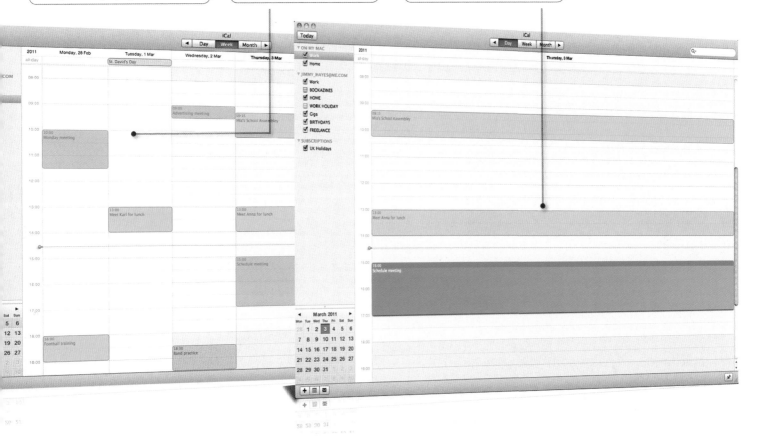

Month view
This is the best way to view the year and to get a feel for how busy you are. You can easily skim through months at a time, which makes it the best place to plan holidays and larger projects

Week view
This is our favourite view as it offers enough detail to see entire days well-planned-out, but it also offers an overview of the entire week. We live in this view

Day view
If you're a really busy bee, this is where you'll need to be to organise every moment of your life. A great way to keep yourself abreast of each minute of the day

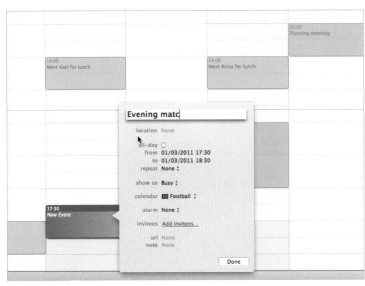

03 Double-click
Double-click on a day and time to add a new event. A pop-up window will appear, allowing you to add all the pertinent information you want to the new event. Be as detailed as you can, as this will help you recall the event when the time comes.

04 Done
Once finished, click Done. If this event has been added to a MobileMe calendar, the information will be synced with the Cloud and then shared with all your other MobileMe devices. You can then manually refresh whenever you need to.

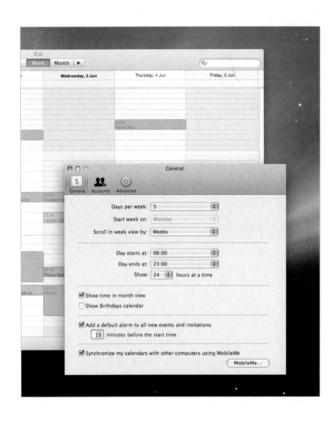

Change the days per week in iCal

iCal has the flexibility to keep things relevant to the way you live your life. If you only want to see weekdays, it's just a couple of clicks away......

Having iCal on your Mac can be an absolute godsend. Not only can it sync with your iPhone or iPod touch, but it works seamlessly with Mail and your Address Book so you need only do the bare minimum in order to organise your life. This is all pretty common knowledge and often touted on the Apple website, but what a lot of people don't know is that iCal can be easily customised to suit your life. If you use it primarily for work, for instance, you can shorten the number of days shown in the week view to five. You can also, if you work irregular hours, increase the amount of time you can see and edit in the week view. These tweaks may seem like cosmetic fiddling to some, but for those who want to use iCal as a serious organisational tool it can make an impressive difference. In this tutorial we'll take you through the basics of making those changes.

"You only do the bare minimum in order to organise your life"

Change the week view in iCal
Customise the amount of days and hours shown

Knowledge base

Sync the iPhone and iPod touch
The iPhone and iPod touch don't have a week view, so when you make the changes to iCal from this tutorial you won't see an immediate difference. But if you go into the day view on the iPhone and iPod touch, however, you will see that the new number of hours viewable in a day has been synced to your device.

Hit it
Click this button to see the week view. This is where all your changes will have taken shape

Hard work
You will now just see the days of the working week on the week view. This is a much more efficient way to view your life if you use iCal for work only

All the hours
The number of hours you set as being viewable in the Preference window will now be available to edit and add events to

Full month
You can still see the weekends in the month view box here, or by clicking the Month View button at the top of the interface

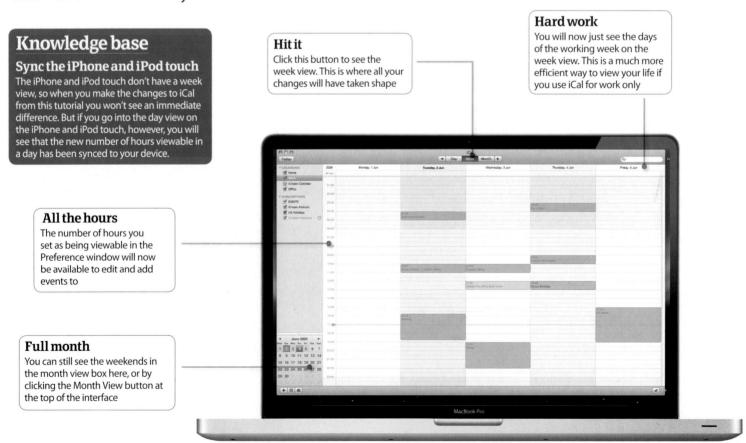

iCal Customise the week view

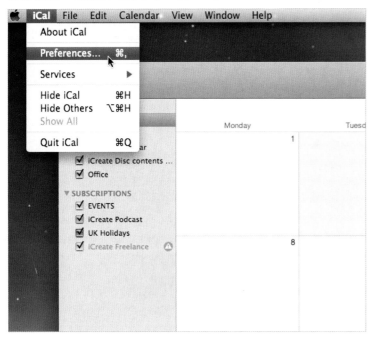

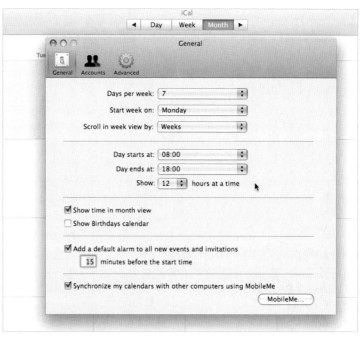

01 Go to the top

Open iCal from your Dock or from your Applications folder, wherever is easier for you. Now go to the top menu and click iCal>Preferences, as shown in the screenshot above. The Preferences pane will now pop up in the middle of your screen.

02 All happening here

The General section will now appear with lots of options on offer. Here you can make changes to the way you view and use iCal. If you make a change here and then you decide it's not working for you, you can return to this screen and change it back.

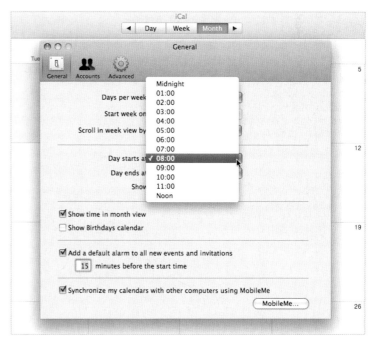

03 Let there be five

You can change the number of days in the week shown in iCal by using the drop-down menu and clicking '5'. A tick will then appear next to it and it will return to the default view with five days in the field instead of the usual seven days.

04 Time it right

You can also change the number of hours of the day viewed in the same way. Just use the drop-down menus and click on the value you want to be shown in iCal. This can be handy if you do shift work, or don't want to show the hours you'll be tucked up in bed!

Apple Essentials

Add iCal events using Automator

Tired of opening iCal and manually adding Events?
Use Automator to simplify and speed up the process…

i Cal is a fantastic app for managing your events, birthdays and to-do lists, and in general keeping track of where you are and where you should be. With only a few clicks of your mouse you can add a custom event to any date, with location details, from-and-to dates, repeats, attendees, attachments and alarms.

But what if you're busy working in an application and quickly want to add an event to iCal without actually having to close the current window and switching programs? Don't worry, all is not lost. There's an easy solution using Automator – Apple's clever scripting program that takes time-consuming processes and simplifies them into one click. Follow us over the next two pages as we explain how to create an Automator script that enables you to add an event to iCal with a minimal amount of fuss.

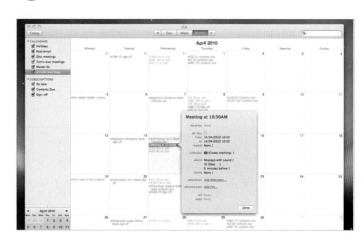

Automator Quickly update iCal with new events via Automator

01 Launch Automator
Open Automator from your applications folder and choose Application from the drop-down list that greets you upon startup.

02 New iCal Events
Click on the Calendar listing in the left-hand column, and double-click New iCal Events. The details will appear in the main window.

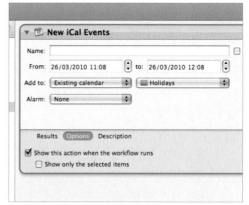

03 Detailed options
Click the Options button at the bottom of the action window, and enable the button that says 'Show this action when the workflow runs'.

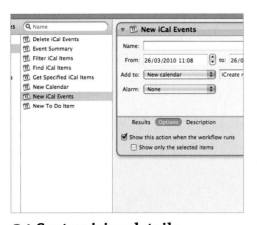

04 Customising details
By clicking this button you're telling Automator to make this action interactive, enabling you to customise the details of each new iCal Event.

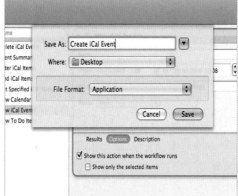

05 No need to name
Don't worry about adding a name right now, as it's likely each new iCal Event will be unique. This is how our new iCal Events box looks.

06 Saving…
Click the File button in the Finder and choose Save. Give your new action a name. Under File Format, choose Application.

The Automator
iCal Events action

Discover how easy it is to use Automator

The results field

After you've created and run your new iCal Events action, click the Results button to see a visual log of it

All day event

If an Event is to last all day, simply tick this button in the upper-right corner to tell iCal to create a 24-hour long Event

Other iCal actions

The column to the left enables you to create other Automator actions that simplify using iCal. If you ever need to quickly delete an iCal Event, you can easily create an Automator application to do this

Add to options

If you wish to add Events to new Calendars, click the 'Add to' drop-down menu and select 'New calendar'. Calendars that already exist in iCal can be chosen from this same menu

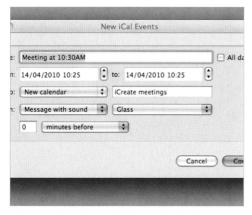

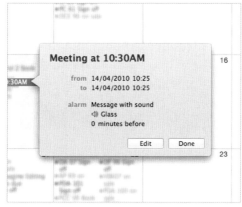

07 Testing

You've now created your own custom application that adds new Events to iCal. Test it by closing both iCal and Automator, and running the app.

08 Event added!

Once you've entered the details into the application window, click the Continue button and the Event will be added to iCal.

09 Finer details

It's not possible to add attendees, URLs or attachments via this method, but it's still a great way to add simple Events without opening iCal.

Set up and use AutoFill

Save yourself an extraordinary amount of time online by using AutoFill. It's easy to set up and edit so you always have the right information at your fingertips…

We've all been in that situation: you need a product or service from the internet and yet cannot face the repetitive nature of filling out form after form in order to get the best deal. Thankfully Safari has a thing called AutoFill to keep you from this monotony.

AutoFill works very cleverly with Address Book; it takes the information you feed it and can summon it at will when you need to fill in a form. For the sake of a couple of minutes' work it can save you an untold amount of annoyance when you find yourself repeatedly tapping details into the web. It's important in the first instance to add as many details as you think you will need to your Address Book card so that Safari can do as much of the form as possible, therefore lessening your need to go in and fill in any blanks. This is such a cool feature that once you've set it up you'll be wondering how you ever lived without it.

"Once you've set it up you'll be wondering how you ever lived without it"

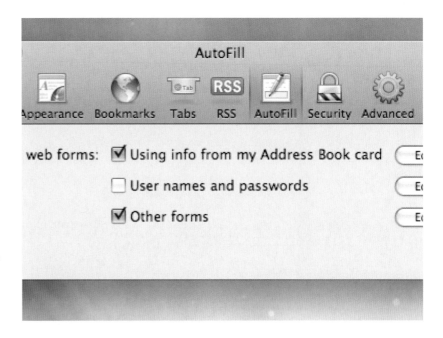

Use AutoFill in Safari

This tiny little feature can be a great time saver

Menu
You can use the menu to access AutoFill. It's in the Edit section but will cost you a couple of mouse clicks

A breeze
With AutoFill set up you can very quickly negotiate online forms and get exactly what you're after in no time

In action
When you activate AutoFill, Safari will populate the fields it thinks are right. Occasionally it will repeat data, so be warned and be vigilant

Knowledge base

Users
Remember that AutoFill will only work for each individual user on their account so you have to log in to your user account or change which Address Book card represents you should you not be using your own user account.

Safari   Set up AutoFill from your Address Book

01 From A to B

To kick things off you will need to open up the Address Book and find your details. If you don't have any, click the plus button to add a new contact and fill out as many of the details as possible. This will come in handy later on and save you time filling in extra fields.

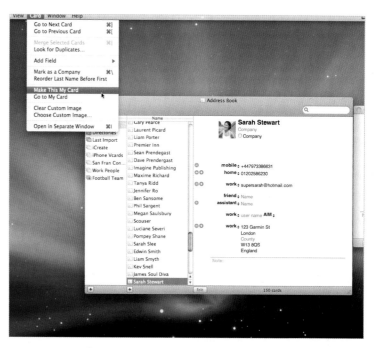

02 My card

Double-click on the finished contact card so it opens in a brand-new window. With this window actively selected, go to Card from the top toolbar and select Make This My Card from the drop-down menu. A new icon should appear next to the name.

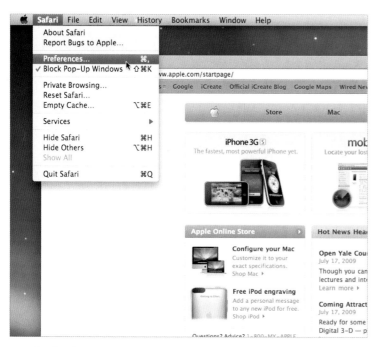

03 Safari

Now open Safari and head to the top menu. Click on the Safari menu and select the Preferences option (the keyboard shortcut for this is Cmd+,). The Preference window will now pop up allowing you to continue with the next step of the tutorial.

04 AutoFill

Click on the AutoFill tab and then tick the 'Using info from my Address Book card' box. This will then allow you to populate forms using the information you added earlier, saving you an endless amount of time when the next form you need to fill out appears.

Block unwanted adverts on websites

Discover how Cascading Style Sheets (CSS) can be used in your favourite browser and learn how to configure advanced Safari preferences to block adverts on your favourite websites

Modern websites have elaborate marketing policies that throw all sorts of nonsensical advertising at you. This is the way a lot of sites make money, and no matter how annoying and intrusive you may find them, they won't be going anywhere for some time to come… or will they? Fortunately, many of these are implemented by using CSS (Cascading Style Sheet) techniques that can be easily blocked by Safari. Even if ready-made, advert-blocker CSS files are widely available on the internet, finding the right one is a question of trial and error.

A simple Google search for CSS and adverts returns numerous hits, from the infamous userContent.css (from **floppymoose.com**) to AdSubtract.css (from **code. google.com/p/adsubtract**), or even fanboy-adblocklist-elements.css (from **fanboy. co.nz**). Once the chosen file is safely downloaded onto your Mac, Safari is then

able to use it to hide the advertisements from view. Other types of advertisement that are encountered on many websites consist in the opening of a new browser

"Many are implemented by using CSS techniques that can be easily blocked by Safari"

window. These 'pop-up windows' can also be easily blocked by Safari. Following these simple steps will free you from all those flashing banners and having to close endless window after window.

Safari adverts

Enhance your browsing experience and banish any distractions

Safari Advanced Preferences
In Safari's Preferences, the Style Sheet area of the Advanced section allows for the selection of a CSS advert-blocker file. The effect of the CSS advert-blocker is immediate upon selection in the drop-down menu

A blocked advertisement
Once the CSS advert-blocker, downloaded from **www.fanboy.co.nz**, is selected, notice how the Google results page is devoid of all the sponsored links at the top and the advertisement banner to the right

Block Pop-Up Windows
In the Safari menu, the activation of this option is indicated by a tick-mark to the left of the menu item. When activated, it will prevent window-based advertisements from opening automatically when navigating to a new website

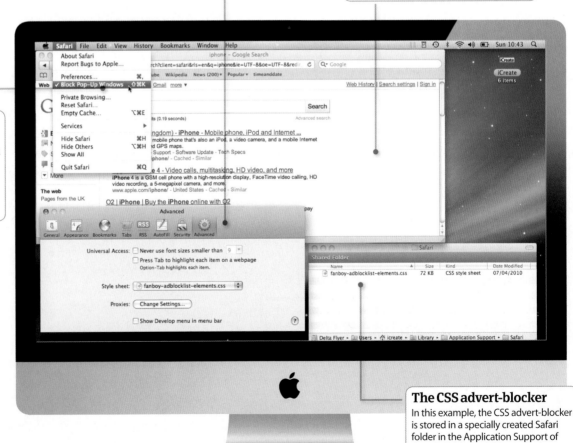

Knowledge base

What are Cascading Style Sheets?

A CSS file, or Cascading Style Sheet, is a text file that contains instructions to enable your browser or newsreader to apply styles and formatting (fonts, colours, spacing, etc) to any web documents. It is an essential part of any website design and allows the implementation of extensive styling policies. For more information, check out **www. w3.org/Style/CSS**.

The CSS advert-blocker
In this example, the CSS advert-blocker is stored in a specially created Safari folder in the Application Support of the User's Library folder. Any other convenient location is acceptable

Safari Block adverts on webpages

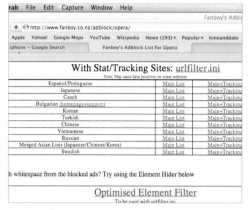

01 Select an advert blocker

Open Safari and choose one of the online resources mentioned before. Navigate to the website and locate the link for the CSS document.

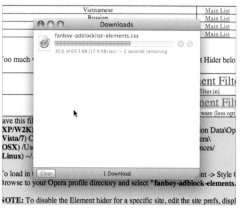

02 Download the CSS file

Locate the link for the CSS advert-blocker file, right-click on it and select the relevant download option. The Downloads window will appear.

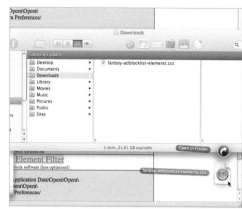

03 Locate the CSS advert-blocker

Once the operation is complete, either open a Finder window to access your Downloads folder or click on the Dock's download stack. Locate the file.

04 Create a folder

With a Finder window showing your Downloads folder and another showing your location to store the file, create a new folder for the CSS file.

05 Advanced preferences

Activate Safari and select Preferences from the Safari menu. Select the Advanced section and locate the 'Style sheet' drop-down menu.

06 Select the CSS advert-blocker

Select Other from the menu. In the resulting Finder window, navigate to the newly created folder storing the CSS file. Select the file and click Choose.

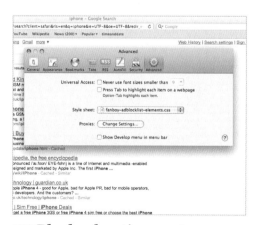

07 Block advertisements

Check that the webpage now displays only the relevant information. Otherwise, restart from Step 1 with a different online resource.

08 Block Pop-Up Windows

With Safari active, click on the Safari menu and locate the Block Pop-Up Windows option. If the option has a tick to its left, it is already activated.

09 Activate the blocking

In order to turn on the Block Pop-Up Windows option, simply click once on the text of the option. A tick-mark will now appear to its left.

Add extensions to Safari

Extend the capabilities and features of Safari and customise your web browser

One of the reasons people have chosen other web browsers such as Mozilla Firefox in the past is because of the large number of clever plug-ins and extensions that are available for it. Well, finally there's no need to look elsewhere for third-party browsers because with the introduction of Safari 5 there is a very easy way to find and install extensions for Apple's very own web browser.

Safari extensions are a fantastic way of extending the capabilities of the web browser and adding new and cool features that were previously not available to you the user. Now you can block irritating adverts on the web, translate foreign pages with a single mouse click, tweet and access Facebook from any webpage, and a whole lot more. Extensions are fantastic, fun, and can be really useful in

a number of different situations. They are also very easy to find and install. Like Widgets before them, as popularity grows and functionality increases the range of extensions will grow. For the moment, there are more than enough options to keep you very busy, so let's explore how you can customise Safari and add your own extensions.

> "Extensions are fantastic, fun, and can be really useful in a number of different situations"

Safari Add and use handy extensions

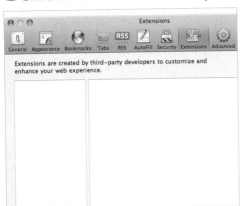

01 Enable extensions

Make sure that extensions are enabled in Safari. Go to the Safari menu and click Preferences>Extensions. Turn on the feature.

02 Go to the gallery

There are several ways to open the Extensions Gallery and with Preferences open click Get Extensions. You'll also find it on the Safari menu.

03 Browse the extensions

All the extensions are on one page, so scroll down and read the info. As the number grows the gallery may be redesigned.

04 Install an extension

When you've found an extension you like, click the Install Now button. We are going to add the official Twitter for Safari extension to our browser.

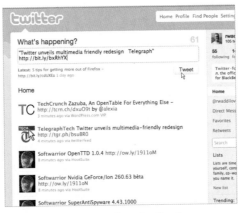

05 Use Twitter for Safari

Extensions can add anything to Safari and each is different. With Twitter there's a toolbar at the top of the page. Click Tweet to post a message.

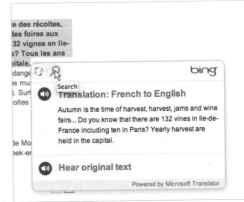

06 Bing search and translate

With Bing you select some text on a page and a magnifying glass appears next to it. Mouse over it and you'll see translations and more.

Time for extensions

Increase Safari's usuability by adding extensions

Enable and disable extensions
Enable tick box so you can choose whether it is operational or not. There's also a global extensions On/Off button at the top, and also buttons to uninstall extensions

Toolbars and buttons
Some extensions are invisible and work in the background, so you see nothing on the screen, but others add extra items to the right-click menu. Some add toolbars and buttons to the browser window

Check for updates
If updates are available for any of the extensions you'll see a number just to the right. Here there's one update. If you click Updates you can choose to have Safari automatically install them

Configure your extensions
Some extensions are just plug and play, but others have an extensive array of configuration options that you can use to customise the way that they work. Check each extension carefully

07 Update your extensions
Extensions are sometimes updated. Go to Safari> Preferences>Extensions and click Updates. Click the ones you want or Install All Updates.

08 Disable an extension
You may not want every extension running all the time. In Preferences choose the ones you need. Select extensions and tick or clear the Enable box.

09 Remove an extension
After trying an extension you may find it's not for you. Go to Safari>Preferences>Extensions, select the extension and click the Uninstall button.

Learn about ClickToFlash

Discover ClickToFlash, a clever Safari extension that gives you control over embedded Adobe Flash elements. Your browsing experience will become faster and free of those pesky Flash-based adverts…

Like all modern browsers, Apple's Safari allows for the development of third-party software in order to extend its abilities. Among these so-called plug-ins, ClickToFlash is an interesting addition that relates to both the browsing experience and the blocking of adverts, and allows you to improve the efficiency and productivity of your browser.

Indeed, with the release of Safari and the official support for third-party extensions, surfing the web with this excellent browser has reached a whole new level. Although the modern media that is the web is cool, it has also brought about the nasty trend of websites becoming cluttered with adverts and irrelevant content that simple gets in the way of you accessing the information you're after. Back on page 208 we had a simple tutorial showing you how to block some of these adverts, but one of the main vectors for this nonsense is the ubiquitous

Adobe Flash component. For the regular web surfer, it can become vital to regain control over the irritating and omnipresent features of many websites. Enter

"The nasty trend of websites becoming cluttered with adverts and irrelevant content"

ClickToFlash; a Safari extension that improves productivity and browser stability, reduces processor temperature, and extends laptop battery life, and is so simple anyone can use it.

Improve Safari browsing

Stop Flash ruining your browsing experience

Uninstall the ClickToFlash extension
Should the need to uninstall ClickToFlash arise, the launch of the uninstallation process can be initiated at the click of a button in ClickToFlash preferences. One further click in a confirmation dialogue and it's done

Preferences
The ClickToFlash preferences are extensive, from 'Video Settings' through 'Contextual Menu Items' to a 'Whitelist' facility. The extension is powerful and simple to configure. It even caters for 'Scalable Inman Flash Replacement' (sIFR) text

Knowledge base

What are extensions?
Extensions, plug-ins, add-ons… all different names for the same utility software that can expand or enhance your use of a given application. They can help you turn Safari into a personalised browser. Extensions can become a toolbar item, a contextual menu item or a behind-the-scenes addition to Safari functionalities that interact with a webpage.

Safari's Extensions Preference pane
From 'Safari Preferences', the 'Extensions' pane is easy to access and offers a handy management facility for your installed Safari extensions. It lets you turn off 'Extensions' – either completely or individually – and control how these are kept up

A blocked advert
When the ClickToFlash extension detects any Flash advert or content from a source or on a location not in the 'Whitelist', it fills the Flash content embedded in the webpage with a grey backdrop and label

Safari Download and install ClickToFlash

01 Locate the extension

In the Safari menu, select Safari Extensions Gallery. From Apple's selection of plug-ins, scroll down to Productivity to find ClickToFlash.

02 Download ClickToFlash

In the ClickToFlash section, click 'Install Now'. Once completed, a green tick box with 'Installed' will appear at the bottom of the section.

03 Enable-Disable ClickToFlash

Select the Safari menu and choose 'Preferences'. Click the Extensions tab, find ClickToFlash, tick/ untick the Enable ClickToFlash checkbox.

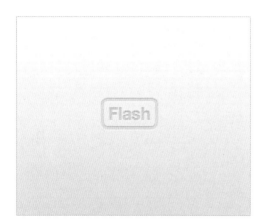

04 How does it work?

Once ClickToFlash is activated, no Flash advert or content is displayed. It's replaced by a grey area in the page on which the word Flash is embossed.

05 Unblock Flash content

To unblock Flash content, click anywhere in the grey backdrop replacing the ad or video. The page element will load, allowing you to watch it.

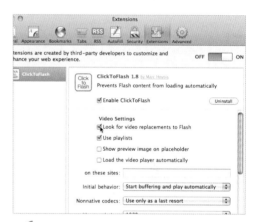

06 Get HD video

From Preferences choose to enable HD-quality videos. Tick 'Look for video replacements to Flash' in 'Video Setting' to load only these.

07 Create Whitelists

From the Whitelist section of Preferences, add entries to a list of sources and locations you wish to allow/disallow Flash content to play.

08 Use the contextual menu

In Preferences, the Contextual Menu Items section allows you to access shortcuts to the extensions via a right-click on the Flash content.

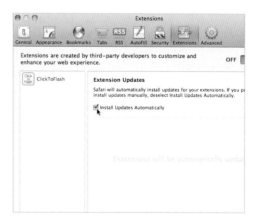

09 Get Auto-update

Keep extensions up-to-date by selecting 'Updates' in the Safari Preferences Extensions pane. Tick 'Install Updates Automatically'.

Importing from your iPhone/iPad/iPod touch

Preview can make it easy to import photos from your iDevice directly onto your Mac

From the early days of Mac OS 9 to the present Snow Leopard, Preview has constantly evolved. In fact, with the advent of portable devices, such as smartphones, digital cameras and tablets, Preview is doing more than just keeping up with these modern tools; it allows you to simplify and improve their use in ways you may not be aware of.

Indeed, Preview now offers the unique ability to retrieve photos and pictures from iPhone, iPad or iPod touch and, through a set of smart features, ensures that your time spent downloading photos from your portable device is not wasted. The extended information – displayed for each of the documents – and handy editing tools allow Preview to go further than just matching your adoption of new technology with a few appropriate functionalities. Since some of the more relevant features of Mac OS X's built-in photo download utilities have been integrated to Preview, there are now new ways to retrieve and edit the pictures coming from your iPhone/iPad.

"There are now new ways to retrieve and edit the pictures in Preview"

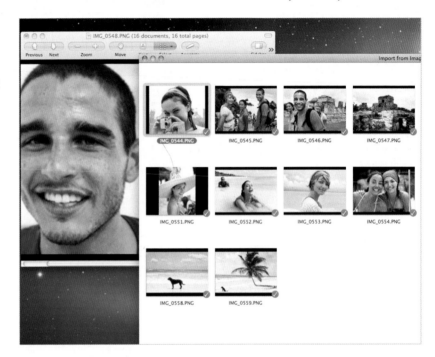

Preview Import photos with Preview

01 Get set

Ensure that your iPhone, iPad or iPod touch is plugged in correctly and that it is turned on. Launch Preview from your Applications folder. In the File menu, select 'Import from' and the name of your portable device which should be visible in the menu.

02 View your pictures

A window showing you a list of all the pictures on your iPhone/iPad will now open. Information, such as thumbnail view, name, size, creation date and extensive photographic parameters, will be displayed for you to peruse in the main area.

Navigate the import window

Get to grips with the import procedure

The list of pictures
Once imported, the pictures listed in the 'Import from' window will display a green tick mark, indicating their status. Double-click on any imported photo to switch to the Preview window to see the results of your import

Imported photos
When the import procedure begins, Preview will open a single window in the background to show the imported files. You can then navigate through these using Preview's sidebar and further edit them once the import is complete

The toolbar
All the tools displayed in the toolbar help make this utility flexible and easy to use. Below the Import buttons, a sliding cursor even enables to you to change the size of the thumbnails

Import location
The 'Import to' drop-down menu offers three default options: the Pictures, Desktop and Documents folders of your current User's Home folder. To choose to import the files to a different folder, use the fourth option: Others

03 Get organised
Below the picture list, a set of buttons in the toolbar allows you to toggle between list and icon view, rotate and delete pictures, change the location to which the documents are to be imported and also change the thumbnail size if you wish.

04 Import
To the right-hand side of the toolbar, the Import and Import All buttons enable you to choose a single retrieval or a complete download of all the photos available. Click the relevant button to start the Import. If you're importing a lot of images, this make take a little while.

Master Preview preferences

The Preview preferences are useful, and understanding how to utilise them can streamline your usage of this handy application. This tutorial shows you how to make the most of them…

In its introduction to Mac OS X Applications and Utilities, Apple describes Preview as a smart, straightforward, image and PDF viewing application with limited searching and editing functionalities. This is not entirely true as there is far more to Preview than first meets the eye – and all the more so when it has been properly configured to suit your individual needs and perform to its full potential. Although Preview is indeed simple to use, a closer inspection of its Preferences cannot fail to expose its resourcefulness. Preview has four groups of settings: general operations, PDF editing and viewing, image editing and viewing, and PDF bookmarks.

Undeniably, Preview's claimed simplicity of use and niftiness are completely genuine, but with just one or two judiciously set Preferences, your usage of

this application can be greatly changed for the better. Let us take a look at how configuring its Preferences can leverage these functionalities, and discover how

"A closer inspection of its Preferences cannot fail to expose its resourcefulness"

your image and PDF viewing can be improved no end by simply tweaking just one or two settings.

Preview Learn about Preview settings

01 Preview Preferences

You can launch Preview from your Applications folder or Dock. Access to the Preferences is via the Preview drop-down menu.

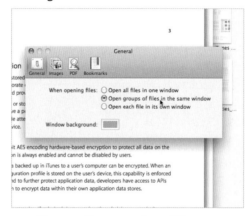

02 General – opening files

The 'When opening files' option configures whether groups of files are opened in a single window or each one in its own window.

03 General – background colour

'Window background' lets you to alter the colour of the empty space which surrounds documents. Click the colour selector and choose a shade.

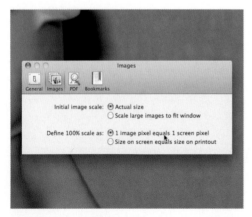

04 Image size

'Initial image scale' lets you fit large images in the window. 'Define 100% scale as' sets the relationship between image size and screen size.

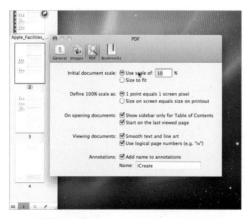

05 PDF – size

'Initial document size' is similar to the 'Initial image scale' option; it shrinks PDFs to fit. It also allows you to choose the zoom level.

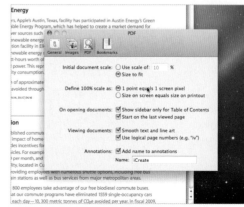

06 PDF-to-screen ratio

'Define 100% scale as' sets the relationship between document size and screen size, avoiding the impact of screen res on displayed size.

Master Preview

Familiarise yourself with Preview preferences

Bookmark editing
The Bookmarks menu presents you with a list of bookmarks and the ability to edit and remove them. Selecting one bookmark at a time, click the Remove button to delete it

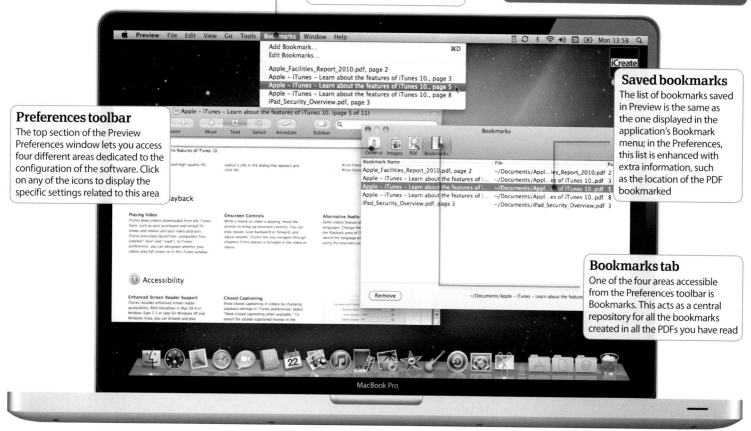

Preferences toolbar
The top section of the Preview Preferences window lets you access four different areas dedicated to the configuration of the software. Click on any of the icons to display the specific settings related to this area

Saved bookmarks
The list of bookmarks saved in Preview is the same as the one displayed in the application's Bookmark menu; in the Preferences, this list is enhanced with extra information, such as the location of the PDF bookmarked

Bookmarks tab
One of the four areas accessible from the Preferences toolbar is Bookmarks. This acts as a central repository for all the bookmarks created in all the PDFs you have read

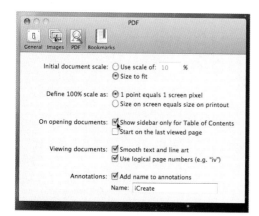

07 PDF – opening PDF files
'On opening…' allows auto-opening of the TOC, if available, and permits the automatic return to the last page being read prior to closing.

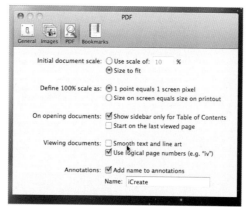

08 PDF – rendering quality
'Viewing documents' options enable anti-aliasing for graphics and text, and aid searching of Roman and Arabic numbers.

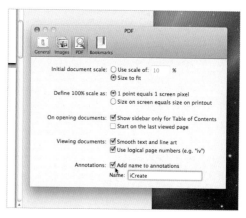

09 PDF – annotations
The last option in the PDF Preferences pane permits you to enter the name of your choice, to be added to any annotations made to a PDF.

Share your Photo Booth snaps

Photo Booth is a very practical tool, able to make videos or take snapshots with your Mac and share them in a few simple steps

Have you ever wanted to possess your own photo booth or simply make a fun auto portrait? No need to go looking for an expensive solution, as you can do all of this and more with an ingenious little application called Photo Booth and the help of the built-in iSight camera on your Mac. Although the pictures created here may not be ones to fill up a family photo album, they're good fun and a little bit more entertaining and interesting than having the same straight-laced pictures all the time. They can also be great if you want to make a humorous birthday card for a friend or family member, or just experiment to see what you would look like if you suddenly put on a lot of weight!

Whether you need a single photo, a 4-up snapshot or a video recording, Apple's Photo Booth is here to provide all your needs. It allows you to take a picture or make a video and apply various effects – some arty and inspiring, some funny and slightly ridiculous. Then, from a number of integrated options, it lets you choose how to publish and share the result of your work. This fun application is gifted with

"They can be great if you want to make a humorous birthday card for friends or family"

all the capabilities offered by digital age technology, and you can then compare your photos with your friends.

Get the most out of Photo Booth

Instant account photos and fun effects

1, 2, 3 and action!
The red camera button is your digital shutter button. It is used to start/stop your video recording or to take pictures and 4-up snapshots. Pressing this digital shutter button will always trigger the three-second countdown

Apply an effect
Choose to apply an effect to your work by clicking on the effects button. Browse through the effects library with the right and left arrows. To cancel your choice, select the centre effect

Photo or video
Click on any of the three pictograms located in the left-hand corner below the live feed window to choose between the different types of picture taking: single shot, 4-up snapshot or movie clip

Knowledge base
File types and names
In the Photo Booth folder of your Pictures folder, single photos are saved as a single JPEG image while 4-up snapshots are saved as four distinct files. Video recordings are saved as one Apple QuickTime MOV file. All file names reflect the date and time of creation; 4-up snapshots are further numbered from one to four.

Thumbnail view
The result of your work is displayed below the live feed window. Each thumbnail can be deleted by clicking the cross to the bottom left of it. Browse through the collection with the left and right arrows

Photo Booth Understand how Photo Booth works

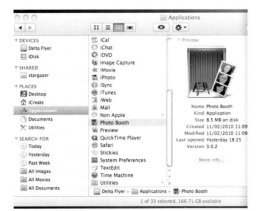

01 Get ready

From the Applications folder, locate and launch Photo Booth. When using an external camera, make sure it is properly connected.

02 Choose photos or video

At the bottom-left corner, three icons allow you to choose single photo, 4-up snapshots or video recording. The red camera button is your shutter.

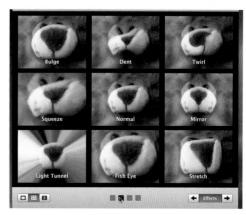

03 Apply an effect

You can choose an effect for your photo or movie with the Effects button. If they aren't suitable, return to the Normal display.

04 Strike a pose

When ready, click the shutter. After a countdown, Photo Booth will take its shots or begin the video. Click the stop button to terminate the recording.

05 Check the results

Your photo or video recording will appear as a thumbnail in the window. Click the camera button to initiate a new picture acquisition.

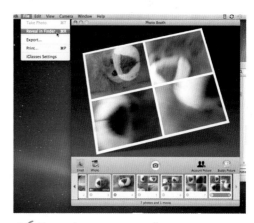

06 Locate your work

Your work is saved in a Photo Booth folder in your Pictures folder. Select a thumbnail and use 'Reveal in Finder' from File to navigate there.

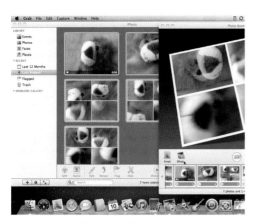

07 Transfer to iPhoto

To share your work on Facebook, Flickr or MobileMe, export it to iPhoto. Select a thumbnail, click on the iPhoto icon, and iPhoto will open.

08 Custom account picture

Select a photo thumbnail and then either click on the iChat or Account Picture icon to use it as your application custom account picture.

09 Send it away

To attach your work to an email, select the thumbnail and click on the Mail icon. Mail will open and insert your work into a new message.

Create a buddy pic in Photo Booth

The integration in OS X means creating a new buddy picture for iChat in Photo Booth is simple

When it comes to software integration, Apple pretty much thinks of everything. The lengths it goes to in order to make our lives easier is obvious throughout its hardware and software, and there are very few times when you're left wondering "Why doesn't this work like this, it would be much easier".

The point is that Apple constantly improves its software so that actions can be completed with the minimum amount of fuss. It's the reason why people who make the move to Apple fall in love with the OS and can't fathom why other people aren't following suit. It makes all those years struggling with your Windows PC seem like a huge waste of time. Adding an iChat buddy picture directly from Photo Booth is a great example; it requires just a couple of clicks.

"People who make the move to Apple fall in love with the OS"

Take a new buddy picture in Photo Booth

Use OS X's integration to create a new iChat buddy picture

Easy booth
Having iSight and Photo Booth on your Mac makes creating profile pictures incredibly simple. Add to that the number of cool effects you can use and it's also a great deal of fun

Updates
The updated picture will populate all the necessary windows, replacing the previous or default picture

Get it spot on
iChat is also very easy to use and the Buddy Picture window is the perfect example: resize it with a slider and just grab the image to move it around

One-button fun
Photo Booth has a number of integrated buttons that allow you to easily use pictures in other apps. Just select a picture and then click the button

Knowledge base

Mac mini users
Obviously Mac mini users don't have a built-in webcam so they will need to buy their own in order to use Photo Booth. Most third-party webcams will work with OS X. Photo Booth still comes loaded on Mac minis, so once the webcam is up and running Photo Booth will detect and use it.

Photo Booth Change your buddy picture for iChat in Photo Booth

01 Load and snap

Load Photo Booth from the Dock or from your Applications folder and click the camera button to take a new picture. Use whatever effect you like the look of. The new picture will drop into the reel at the bottom of the window.

02 One-click wonder

With the newest picture selected on the bottom panel simply click the Buddy Picture button that's found on the right-hand side of the interface. This will launch iChat and the preference, which allows you to change pictures.

03 Slide and grab

Use the slider in the newly opened Buddy Picture window in iChat to resize your image. You can play around with this until you decide that the dimensions are just right. You can also click on the image and drag it into the correct position.

04 All set

When you are happy that the image has been moved and scaled to perfection, click the Set button. The new buddy picture will then populate your open iChat windows. If you change your mind at any point though and want to select a different picture to use, click Cancel.

Discover FaceTime for Mac

With FaceTime for Mac, video calls are now only a few clicks away. Learn how to install and configure this great tool

One of the most acclaimed features of the iPhone 4 and iPod touch is now available on your Mac. Indeed, if your Apple computer runs Mac OS X Snow Leopard version 10.6.4 or later with FaceTime for Mac, video calls are now only a few clicks away. From the comfort of your laptop or desktop Mac, FaceTime for Mac now makes it possible for you to have a chat or share a smile with your friends and family who also possess an iPhone 4, iPod touch or Mac. It is even possible to engage in video calls over your local network.

With the simple, further requirements of an email address and an Apple ID, a world of enhanced communication is now easily accessible. The sleek, simple and powerful interface of the FaceTime for Mac application is fully integrated in your Mac OS X environment. This two-page tutorial takes you through the few simple steps needed to install and configure it. Let's see how this is done.

"Engage in video calls over your local network"

FaceTime   Set up and use FaceTime

01 Download

In your web browser head on over to **www.apple.com/uk/mac/facetime/** to install the necessary software. Click Download. Safari's download window will open and show the installer's package being transferred to your Downloads folder.

02 Install

Once the download is complete, the installer will open automatically. If it does not, go to the download location and you will need to double-click on the installer's disk image file. Then double-click on the installer and follow the on-screen instructions.

Find your way around FaceTime

Make video calls to your friends and family with ease

Your Favorites list
It is possible to create a list of preferred contacts in the Favourite list. Click the Favorites button, then select the '+' sign and select the relevant name from the contact list

The video call window
During a call, the video call window shows a picture-in-picture display of your contact which you can drag to any corner of the video call window. Use the Video menu to enter full-screen display

The Recents call list
In the Recents call list, all the incoming or outgoing calls are listed. It is possible to filter the list to show only missed calls. Click Clear to empty the list of all calls

The Contacts list
Upon installation, FaceTime will automatically add all your Address Book contacts to its contact list. Changes to any Address Book entry will be immediately reflected in the FaceTime contacts list

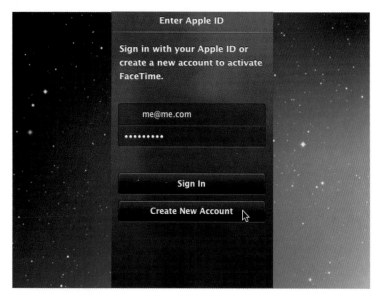

03 Configure
From your Applications folder, double-click the FaceTime icon. Enter your Apple ID or if you haven't already got one, click Create New Account. You will then receive a confirmation email where you will be required to click the link to complete the procedure.

04 Make a Call
Select Contacts and click on the name of your chosen contact. You can only make video calls to contacts with an iPhone by clicking a phone number and with an iPod touch or Mac by selecting an email address. All that's left now is for you to have a nice long chat!

Use the built-in OS X Dictionary

Find out how the built-in Dictionary application can become an essential part of your working day

Ever read an email or a webpage and hit a word whose meaning you didn't know? Or maybe you keep using the same word over and over and wish you could expand your vocabulary? We have all been there. However, this could all be a thing of the past, because when reading a webpage or eBook on your Mac, the invaluable Dictionary application comes rushing to your aid. With its integration inside the Apple OS, Dictionary's contribution knows no bounds.

Indeed, Dictionary is accessible through a contextual menu item in the Apple suite of utilities and applications – like TextEdit, Safari, and Mail – making checking definitions simple. The addition of a Dashboard widget Dictionary, which also operates as a thesaurus, makes for a highly accessible reference tool. Furthermore, it is not only based on the New Oxford American Dictionary and Oxford American Writer's Thesaurus, but also uses such online resources as Wikipedia and can be extended with the addition of other dictionaries.

"The Dashboard widget makes for an accessible reference tool"

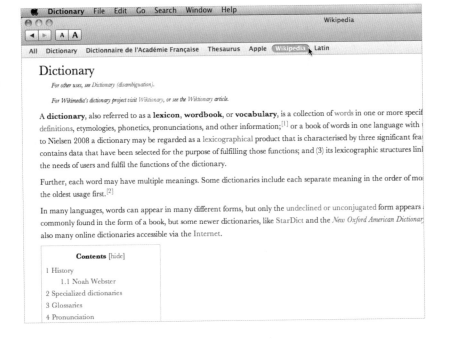

Using the Dictionary

Discover the options at your fingertips

Dictionary application toolbar
From left to right, the toolbar contains two arrows to browse through the history of search terms; two buttons, which control the font size of the entries found; and the search field where you can type the word being searched

Select your reference source
Below the Dictionary toolbar, a banner shows the names of all the enabled inline and online reference sources. The first item on the banner allows the results from all sources to be displayed

The Dictionary panel
Once the Dictionary panel option is activated, the panel appears whenever you select the 'Look up in Dictionary' item on the contextual menu. It permits changing from word definition to thesaurus and launches the Dictionary application

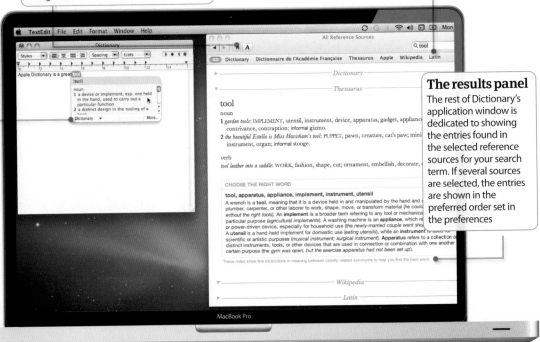

The results panel
The rest of Dictionary's application window is dedicated to showing the entries found in the selected reference sources for your search term. If several sources are selected, the entries are shown in the preferred order set in the preferences

Knowledge base

Need more dictionaries?

If your mother tongue is not English, or if you are looking to enlarge your vocabulary, it is possible to expand Dictionary reference sources to include jargon and professional terms, or even some foreign-language dictionaries. Check your favourite search engine for free Dictionary plug-ins and the Apple Home & Learning Download section at: **http://www.apple.com/downloads/macosx/home_learning** for a few more.

Dictionary   Learn about the built-in Dictionary

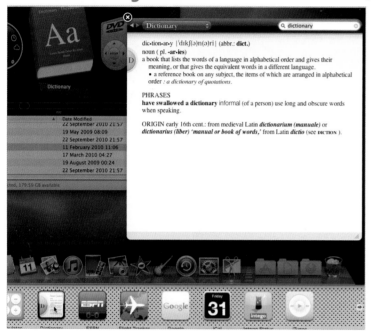

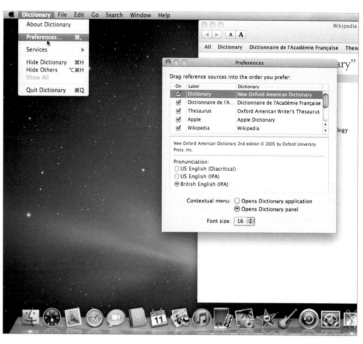

01 Where is Dictionary located?

Dictionary is located in the Applications folder but can also be accessed via the contextual menu item 'Look up in Dictionary'. Adding the widget to the Dashboard is part of the default set of widgets that are installed with Mac OS X.

02 Dictionary Preferences

Preferences are accessed through the Dictionary menu. The pane consists of two sections: the top one shows the list of available reference sources, the other configures how Dictionary reacts to your actions. Set the Preferences to suit your needs and how you work.

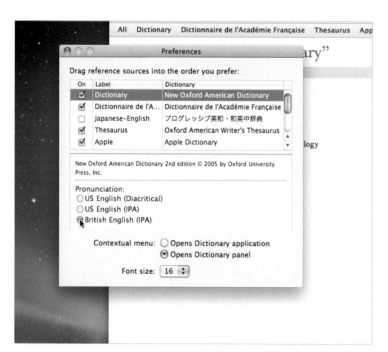

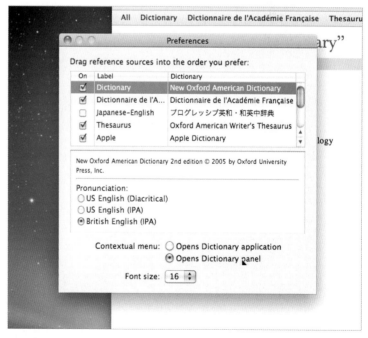

03 Configure additional reference sources

Each reference source on your system can be enabled/disabled. Rearrange the list by dragging items in the order preferred. Further configuration parameters are displayed for each source, if applicable. Here you can also change the font size and pronunciation.

04 Decide how Dictionary behaves

Dictionary's reaction when invoked with the contextual menu can be configured in the second section. You can open Dictionary or superimpose a panel on top of the word, with the relevant definition or synonyms for the word you have looked up.

Quickly check MobileMe syncing

Learn how to stay up-to-date with all your MobileMe syncs

MobileMe syncing is a great feature in Apple's online service that works seamlessly with Mac OS X. Once set up, it works quietly in the background making sure all of your contacts are in sync between multiple computers and your iPhone. Sometimes, however, it's handy to know a little bit more about what's going on with your information – especially if you suspect things aren't running as smoothly as they should. You could, of course, head to the MobileMe System Preferences pane to check things out, but in order to save time this handy tip allows you to find out some basic information, as well as open up System Preferences or diagnose a fault, right from the desktop Menu bar.

It's a quick tip, but one that's easily overlooked and could help you fix errors, or at least give you some peace of mind that your information is as up-to-date as possible. With the power of a Mac at your fingertips it's worth getting to know how to use features like these when they are available to you.

> "It works quietly in the background ensuring all of your contacts are in sync"

MobileMe Stay updated with MobileMe

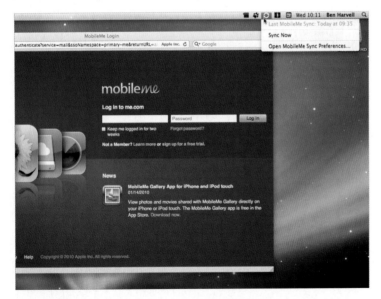

01 Standard view

This Menu bar symbol lets you know how syncing of your MobileMe contacts and calendars is going. When clicked it shows you the last sync, and provides a quick way to initiate a sync of all your info. It's worth remembering that it is there…

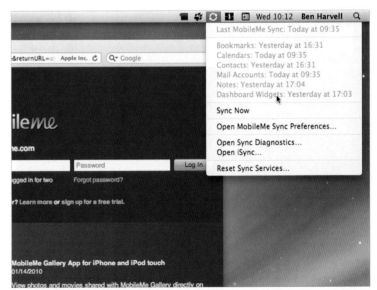

02 Take a closer look

The small amount of info provided in the last step may be enough for you, however if you hold down the Alt key and click the symbol again, you get a much more detailed view that will show you when each MobileMe element was last synced.

Stay on top of your syncs

Keep an eye on MobileMe and its synchronisation

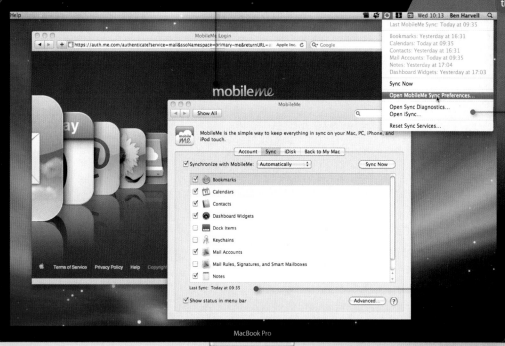

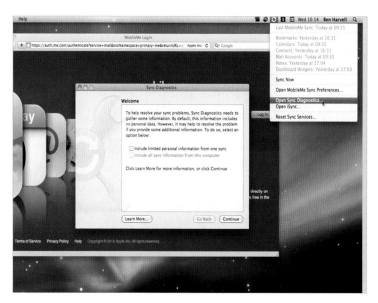

03 Quick preferences

This menu provides a quick way to make changes to your MobileMe syncs – by clicking on the Open MobileMe Sync Preferences option you will immediately be taken to the correct preference pane as shown above, giving you a few more options to investigate.

04 Got a problem?

If your adjustments to the sync preferences don't help, you can troubleshoot your syncs by launching Sync Diagnostics from the same menu to help highlight any issues. This will then inform you of any problems MobileMe may be experiencing.

Mac Apps

The top apps to extend your Mac's functionality

"For casual users looking to build a personal website, this is a fantastic solution"

Thoughts
Page 245

Twitter
Page 248

Opera
Page 251

Daylight for Mac
Page 253

"It's cheap, addictive and very entertaining; a great game to have"

Price: Free   Developer: Evernote Corporation

Evernote

Take notes and jot down ideas wherever you are

Evernote is a sort of organiser and though it is not quite a project planner, it does enable you to gather items for a project you may be working on. It is suitable for anyone that has business or home projects, students doing schoolwork or even someone with a hobby or interest that includes collecting and storing information.

The first thing to realise about Evernote is that it is not simply an app for your Mac; that is just one component of a far-reaching web service, and there are Evernote apps for other devices including the iPad, iPhone and iPod touch. No matter which device you use, however, you can create one or more notebooks and in them you can store text, images, audio, PDF files and more. Every time you add something it is uploaded to Evernote's online storage and then synced with every device you use so you don't have to worry about transferring data.

A panel on the left shows a list of notebooks that have been created, and when one is selected, the notes can be displayed in another panel as a text list, thumbnails or a mixed mode. A third panel shows the content of a note. There are various ways to create notes and anything that appears on the screen can be grabbed; text can be copied from the clipboard, there's a free Safari plug-in to lift content from webpages, you can take snapshots with the Mac's iSight camera, you can drag and drop files from Finder windows and you can type in text.

Evernote is free, but there is a 60MB limit per month to the amount you can upload. If you think you'll create more than this, you can upgrade to a Premium account costing $5 a month (approximately £3.10). A Premium account also enables you to store a wider range of file types in notebooks and you'll soon see the limitations of the free version when you try to drop various files on it. However, there is still a lot of useful things you can do with a free account.

Evernote is a very useful organiser to have on both your Mac and iPhone, and the interface is flexible so you can view your notes, files, images and other documents in a range of different ways. Notes can also be re-arranged and emailed, and getting the items out of Evernote and into your project is very easy and won't take up too much of your time.

Rating ★★★★★

■ Evernote is used to create notebooks and then images, text, web clippings and audio files are stored in these for quick and easy access.

■ Notes can be viewed as lists, thumbnails or a mixed mode, and they are useful when organising projects and work.

■ Photos can be taken with the Mac's iSight camera and then stored in a note along with text and other information.

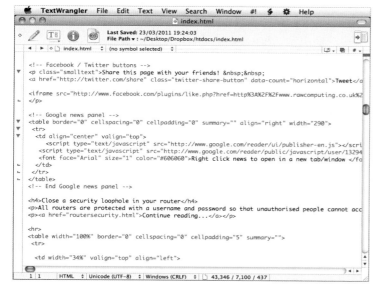

■ TextWrangler is ideal for projects like creating webpages and the colour coding helps to make it clearer.

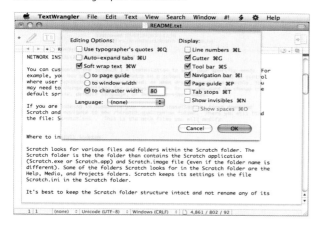

Price: Free   **Developer:** Bare Bones Software

TextWrangler

A great text editor with extra features that's ideal for programmers

TextWrangler is a text editor, and you might wonder why you need one as OS X includes TextEdit, but this is different. TextEdit is more of a word processor and TextWrangler is a pure editor that works with plain text files. It is a favourite of programmers and website designers, but don't let that put you off because it can be used by anyone who needs to create or edit plain text files.

When used as a simple text editor it works much as you would expect, enabling you to type in text, optionally wrap it at the window edge, check the spelling and so on. However, there are some advanced features such as the ability to find and replace across multiple files, compare two documents and find differences. Multiple files can also be opened and worked together or in separate windows. The really useful feature is that it recognises lots of different types of content such as HTML and JavaScript code, C++ and other programming languages. A great utility not just for programmers.

Rating

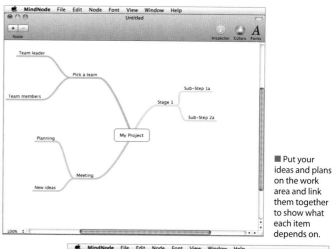

■ Put your ideas and plans on the work area and link them together to show what each item depends on.

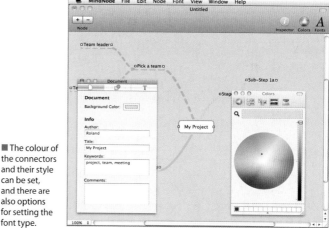

■ The colour of the connectors and their style can be set, and there are also options for setting the font type.

Price: Free   **Developer:** Markus Müller

MindNode

Plan your projects and store your thoughts and ideas with this great free app

MindNode is a mind-mapping application and it enables you to plan projects and put ideas and thoughts into a sort of web. It's not like traditional planning software and you are free to place items almost anywhere on the page. You start off with an idea or a task and then one thing leads to another, literally. You join ideas or tasks together, so step A leads to step B, which leads to C and so on, in something akin to a flowchart.

Mind mapping is one of those things that is easy to use once you try it, and it can be invaluable in some circumstances, but it is hard to describe. It's a bit like jotting down ideas on a sheet of paper, but in mind maps they are all linked, so you can see what tasks depend on other things.

The functions are straightforward, you can set the colours and fonts and change the look of the connecting lines. There is a good selection of export formats including PDF, FreeMind documents, HTML and more, and though there's a Pro version, this free one may be all you need.

Rating

Mac Apps

Price: £1.79/$2.99 Developer: Vito Technology

Solar Walk for Mac – 3D Solar System model

Explore the solar system and discover the wonders of the universe

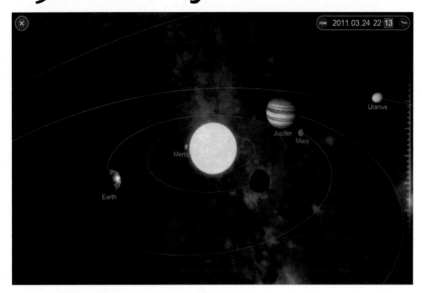

If you want to learn about the solar system and our nearest planetary neighbours, then Solar Walk is well worth considering. As the title says, this is a 3D solar system model and the emphasis is on the graphical display of the planets. The app starts off full-screen as if you are travelling in space, and the Sun and planets spin around as you move. You zoom in to a position some way off the Earth and view the spinning globe with the numerous satellites orbiting it. An interesting feature of the program is that it can be switched into 3D mode and all you need to view it are a pair of cardboard specs with red and blue cellophane in them, the kind you get with some 3D films. It really brings the display to life. You can also zoom out to view the solar system and then choose any of the individual planets to look at up close. A time bar on the right enables you to see where the planets are in relation to each other at any time and an information panel can be displayed with some basic facts about each planet. It's a delight to watch, but could be improved with more information.

■ You can fly around the solar system, viewing it at your leisure from different angles and at different points in time.

Rating ★★★★☆

Price: Free Developer: AudioGuidia

World Explorer

You'll never be bored or stuck for things to do again with this travelling app

■ You can view street maps, lists of places nearby and explore the fascinating links to articles in Wikipedia.

Online services like Wikipedia and Google Maps enable you to explore the world and discover facts, sights and information about this planet we live on, and they are both excellent. World Explorer is a sort of mashup of these two services, and the app window is even split down the middle with Wikipedia on the right and Google Maps on the left.

The app aims to work out your current location so that it can show a map of your immediate area and a Wikipedia entry for something relevant nearby. This is fine on recent Macs, but it doesn't work with older ones which don't have the right hardware or software to determine their location. This is not important, though, because you can type any city or place into the search box at the top to go straight there. The Google Map is split horizontally and the lower half shows the map while the upper half displays a list of places of interest along with the distance and star rating. Any of these places can be selected to see the Wikipedia entry on the right, making World Explorer a great way to research places you are planning on visiting, or are already at if you have taken your MacBook with you.

"World Explorer is a great way to research places"

■ Combining Google Maps and Wikipedia enables you to explore any city, town or place that interests you.

Rating ★★★★★

Price: Free **Developer:** Zongyao Qu

MPlayerX

Optimise your viewing experience with this handy utility

The Mac isn't short of ways to play media files like movies you may have downloaded or shot yourself on a camcorder or iPhone, but there is always room for another app, particularly if it adds some useful features. MPlayerX is an open source program, which means it is free of charge and it's a nice media player.

You can open almost any type of movie file on your Mac or even a stream from the web, and play it. That's not unique of course, but you do get a very useful video tuner panel that enables you to adjust the brightness, contrast, saturation, gamma and hue. You can also sharpen the image and apply noise reduction. There is an equaliser for adjusting the quality of the audio and there are ten sliders ranging from 30 to 16kHz. All this means that MPlayerX is able to enhance the quality of the playback, and the ability to watch movies full screen and use an Apple remote is great. Multimonitor support also enables you to play a movie on one monitor while working on another. MPlayerX is free and so it costs nothing to try. You might just like it, we did.

Rating ★★★★☆

■ You can play all your iPhone videos and other movies using this handy media player with a good range of features.

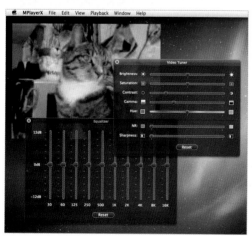

■ Here you can see some of the extras, such as the audio equaliser and the video tuner panels for enhancing the playback.

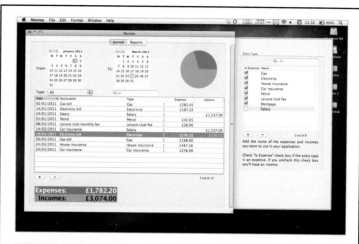

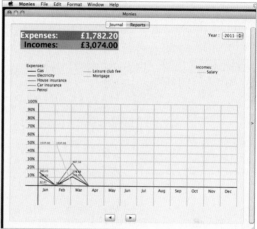

■ Your bills, expenses and income are stored in a journal and you can filter the entries by date or by category.

■ See where your money is going with a useful display that charts each month's spendings and outgoings too.

Price: Free **Developer:** Silviu Turuga

Monies

Keep track of your finances and chart income and bills

Online banking is commonplace now and we can see how much is left in our current and savings accounts with a few clicks of the mouse, but this doesn't actually tell you where your money is going. When there is little left at the end of the month you might end up wondering where it has all gone, and this is where the free app Monies comes into the equation.

Monies does not import statements downloaded from your bank, which is its only flaw, because that means you have to manually enter incomings and outgoings. It stores everything in a journal in date order and you can see at a glance all your bills, expenses, salary and other income. Two calendars at the top enable you to filter by date and you can filter by category of transaction too.

A nice feature of the app is the pie chart and text display of expenses verses income, and on the Reports tab you can see a chart for the whole year that shows what you have spent and what on. It is a simple app, but one that is very useful for tracking those pesky finances.

Rating ★★★★☆

Price: £2.99/$4.99 **Developer:** Rovio Mobile Ltd.

Angry Birds Rio

More mayhem, puzzles and antics from those avian protagonists

Angry Birds has been a phenomenally successful app on the iPhone and iPod touch with millions sold, has become something of an obsession for many, and no sooner was the Mac App Store opened for business than a Mac version was launched. *Angry Birds Rio* is a new release based on the original title and the gameplay is very similar, but whether you're an old hand at saving your feathered friends or a newcomer to the series, you'll find lots to enjoy and engage here.

In 20th Century Fox's animated movie *Rio*, two birds Blu and Jewel are kidnapped by bungling animal smugglers and must escape. The game follows this story and the original angry birds are kidnapped and taken to Rio. They escape and must then rescue their friends. This is where you come in. There are several levels and each is in a different location, such as the smuggler's den or the jungle. Each level has many sublevels to solve and to release the captives you fling angry birds at them using a catapult. The graphics are excellent and the scene is displayed side-on. You click and drag with the mouse to pull the catapult to fling your birds through the air, hit the cages and break them open.

It sounds very simple and it is, but it becomes increasingly challenging because the cages may be precariously balanced on top of or underneath other objects, such as blocks, crates, stones and so on. All the objects act realistically and you can use them, for example, to knock one into another to topple them over. Some objects can be broken and some fall on others and break. The design of each screen presents a puzzle that must be solved as at first it seems that there aren't enough angry birds to rescue everyone, but if you can work out the right places to fling those feathered fiends, you can always succeed.

There are a large number of levels to work through and it is fun for all ages. It can become quite addictive, however, as you try to work out how to solve the next level. The game can be played at full-screen, or in a window on the desktop, and if you don't like the sound effects or music you can easily mute it out. It runs on quite limited hardware, so you don't need the latest Mac with Nvidia or ATI graphics, and it runs fine on an Intel Mac with GMA 950 graphics. It's cheap, addictive and very entertaining; a great game to have.

Rating ★★★★★

■ The levels become more complicated as you progress, and objects must be toppled and broken.

> "It's cheap, addictive and very entertaining"

■ Not all the birds are the same and some have special capabilities, such as splitting into three for extra points.

■ Fire the angry birds using the catapult and try to break the cage holding your friends captive.

■ Watch out, there are aliens about! Keep your finger on the trigger and blast those aliens back where they came from.

■ There isn't much of a story, but with this type of game it isn't really necessary. Some nice graphics also add to the atmosphere.

Price: £3.99/$6.99 **Developer:** Awem studio

Star Defender 3

Blast your way through level after level of alien invaders

Star Defender 3 is an old-style shoot-'em-up game that is fast paced, gets the adrenaline pumping and sharpens your reflexes. A one-sentence description of the gameplay could be: if it moves, shoot it, if it doesn't, shoot it anyway. What, you want a story? It's not really necessary, but the year is 2743 AD and it is set a couple of years after a war in space with the Insectus. Humans are weak from their previous battle and it is up to you to save the universe from being overrun by the alien scum.

The story doesn't matter and this is basically a space-based shooter in which you have control of a spaceship that sits at the bottom of the screen. Alien craft stream on-screen from the top and the sides, and some just fly around while others shoot at you. There are extra weapons to be picked up, power-ups, big boss aliens at the end of each level and all the usual features you'd expect from this type of game. It's fairly cheap, but the graphics are good and it runs on quite limited hardware well. If you like fast action shoot-'em-ups, you'll like this one.

Rating ★★★★★

■ Knock the monsters off of your books in this fun physics game.

■ You must complete each level before you can move on to the next.

Price: Free **Developer:** Geek Beach

A Monster Ate My Homework

A physics game with a puzzle on every level

Physics games have really taken off in the app stores recently, and here is another entertaining puzzler that is simple, but surprisingly addictive. There is a cardboard box in a pond and on top of it are piles of books making up your homework. In addition to these are boxes that have animated monster faces on their sides – naturally. You basically have to throw balls at the monster boxes to knock them off the cardboard platform so that they fall into the pond, but without losing any of your piles of books.

You can spin the box around in 3D so you can view it from all angles and then position a target using the mouse to show where you want to throw each ball. Everything behaves like real-world objects, so you can expect the ball to dip as it travels and the boxes to tumble and bounce. You have to clear each level to move on in this combination of luck, skill and accurate throwing. If you like this game genre, it's sure to be a winner.

Rating ★★★★☆

Price: £34.99/$59.99 **Developer:** Pixelmator Team

Pixelmator

Enhance your photos and produce original artwork

There is no doubt that Adobe Photoshop is a fantastic application for photo editing and generating artwork, but unless you are rich or can persuade the people you work for to stump up the cash, it is out of reach for many because of its high price. Pixelmator aims to offer most of what Photoshop has, but at a more affordable £35, give or take a penny. While it might not have every feature of Adobe's flagship product, Pixelmator is a powerful app in its own right and is useful for touching up digital photos, creating new artwork and any graphics related tasks.

The interface consists of a collection of separate palettes and windows, and this can look untidy and confusing if you run it on top of several other apps, so it is best run on its own. It then looks really good with its dark interface and nicely designed tools and palettes. Among the features are the Lasso and Magic Wand for selections, Crop and Slice, Pencil and Brush for drawing and painting on the image, Gradient and Paint Bucket for filling areas, Blur, Sharpen and even Clone for repairing or erasing items from images. Quite an impressive list.

On the Filter menu is a large collection of special effects you can apply to photos and images. There are ten categories, such as Distortion, Blur, Sharpen and Stylize, and some have subcategories beyond that. Pixelmator enables you to build images using multiple layers one on top of the other. They can be blended in a variety of ways including Difference, Subtract, Divide, Color,

■ The interface looks good and there's a palette for everything. However, it is best displayed on a plain background.

Multiply and more. The opacity can be set too and you can even import a layer from the Mac's iSight camera into an image. There are lots of tools for enhancing photos and they can be imported directly from iPhoto albums using the built-in browser. If you need to tweak a photo there are some useful tools in Pixelmator such as Levels, Curves, Exposure, Brightness and Contrast, Hue and Saturation and many more. There is a multi-level undo facility, so you can always step back to a previous version.

Pixelmator is one of the best-selling apps in the Mac App Store and it's little wonder. It is straightforward to use and has a wide range of image editing and enhancement tools. Adobe hasn't got much to worry about, but Pixelmator is the best at this price point.

Rating ★★★★☆

■ The range of filters is excellent and you can do some clever things with images and layers in the app.

Price: Free **Developer:** Autodesk

SketchBook Express

Let your artistic side loose with this intuitive drawing app

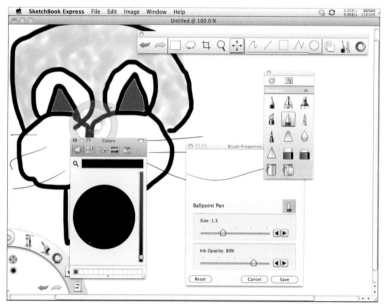

Autodesk is well known for its high quality and powerful drawing applications, and SketchBook Express is a feature-limited version of its SketchBook Pro illustration software. Although it is a cut-down version, it is still a powerful program with a good range of drawing tools. The interface is unusual and is like nothing you have seen before. The toolbar is an arc in the bottom-left corner of the window, and clicking a button displays a palette of options arranged in a circle. You draw a line to the one you want. It's weird, but it's fun.

There are lots of drawing tools such as Pencil, Airbrush, Marker, Ballpoint Pen and Paintbrush. Select one and you can adjust its properties such as the size and opacity. Your own images or photos can be imported onto the canvas and there are five popular image formats for saving artwork.

SketchBook Express supports multiple layers so you can build up an image from several different components, but a limitation is that only six layers are allowed. However, that will be plenty for most people. Slightly more limiting, though, is that images are flattened to one layer when they are saved. Despite a few restrictions, this is a cracking app for creating artwork.

■ No matter how good the tools are, it won't make you a brilliant artist. Some talent is required!

Rating ★★★★★

Price: £0.59/$0.99 **Developer:** Daniel Miller

Daily Cardio Workout

Keep in shape with these simple but effective exercises

■ The app isn't much to look at and it could be graphically better, but it does the job of getting you fit.

There are four apps in the health and fitness category by Daniel Miller, and these are Daily Cardio Workout, Daily Ab Workout, Daily Arm Workout and Daily Butt Workout. They are only 59p each, so you could get all of them for about the price of a Starbucks latte and you would have a complete fitness regime at your disposal.

Each app on its own is quite simple, and Daily Cardio Workout is a series of exercises that are designed to get your heart pumping. There are two workouts and there are ten exercises in each one giving a total of 20. You can start from the beginning and perform a complete workout or you can choose whatever exercises you want and do them in any order you like. In each case, most of the screen displays a video clip of a woman demonstrating the exercise and you just have to copy her. A timer counts down from 60, but only advanced people should do the full 60 seconds. Beginners and intermediate people are told to stop and rest earlier.

Bearing in mind that this is a very cheap app, it is easy to use and encourages you to get fit, so it's worth the money.

"It is easy to use and encourages you to get fit, so it's worth the money"

■ The exercises are straightforward and easy to copy. Just watch the demonstration and away you go.

Rating ★★★★★

Price: £11.99/$19.99 **Developer:** plasq LLC

Comic Life 2

Turn your life into an action-packed comic book with this brilliant piece of software

■ The vivid interface makes it fun to create comics.

With so many adaptations hitting the big screen recently, comic books appear to be more popular than ever before. If you want in on the action but aren't exactly a whizz with a pencil, then Comic Life 2 might be just what you need. Instead of tasking users to draw comics from scratch, Comic Life 2 enables you to import photos from iPhoto or any other folder on your Mac, then turn them into comic book storyboards. It's also incredibly easy to use. When first opened, the program gives you a choice of a variety of templates, including a science fiction comic, ancient history comic or road trip-themed comic. Once you've chosen a folder of photos, you can simply drag them onto the individual panels of your story, then resize them in real-time, add captions and speech boxes. As well as being straightforward, it's incredibly fun to use. The entire interface is skinned like a comic and as you manipulate objects you'll hear sound effects such as dragging, lasers and oohs and aahs.

Once a comic has been completed it can be uploaded directly to a single friend via email, or shared with all of your friends via Facebook. The entire process of choosing a template, adding photos and exporting as a comic takes mere minutes and as a result this is one fascinating and enjoyable way to create original and engaging comic-themed photo albums.

Rating ★★★★☆

Price: £11.99/$19.99 **Developer:** The Iconfactory

Flare

Give your photos a retro look with this fun app

Have you ever used Instagram on your iPhone to add retro effects to your photos? Well, Flare is similar, with dozens of built-in presets that can be instantly applied to an image, but it's far more powerful than anything you're likely to have used on your iDevice before.

Flare is easy enough to operate, simply open the app, drop a photo onto its window and then apply a preset to achieve the desired result. You can save the photo to your Mac, export it to Flickr or email it to a friend. Where the strengths of Flare really lie is its Effects window. Three groups are included; colour effects, lens effects and creative effects. These can be accessed by clicking the Edit button at the top of the screen, with each presenting a range of sliders that can be manipulated to tweak a multitude of settings. Exposure, tint, saturation, blurs, textures, borders and more can all be tweaked and applied to an image, and when combined with the built-in presets, Flare can be an incredibly powerful image editor.

This app won't be replacing the professional tools used by image editors and photographers any time soon. It doesn't have the smart fill found in Photoshop or the brushes effects found in Painter. But for casual image editing, tweaking Facebook shots or applying a retro effect to a holiday snap, this is an intuitive and affordable app.

"This is an intuitive and affordable app"

■ Instantly apply a number of preset filters.

■ You can tweak images using slider bars in the Effects pane.

Rating ★★★★☆

Price: £14.99/$24.99 **Developer:** Byoni Ltd.

Perfect Diet Tracker

Track exactly how many calories you're consuming each day

With so many diet plans, tips on losing weight and warnings about particular foods, it's hard to work out what's the best way to stay in shape. Perfect Diet Tracker can help. It's a tool that enables you to create a personal diet plan, keep a food diary and add exercises to see how your daily calorie count is really adding up.

When setting up the app for the first time, Perfect Diet Tracker asks you to enter your name, age, height and weight, then displays an estimate of your BMI. You can use a slider to tell the program how physically active you are, how much weight you wish to lose or gain and what food types you wish to monitor in your food diary within its slick and accessible interface.

Adding items to your diary is a simple process. Once you've clicked the plus icon you can enter a search term and find the exact foodstuff. Perfect Diet Tracker references the international food database, which has more than 80,000 food items for countries including the UK, USA, Canada, Europe and Australia. As a result, you'll find the exact food almost every time you search.

Adding an exercise is also an easy process. It's possible to search through dozens of preset entries, enter the duration and add it to your diary. Perfect Diet Tracker will automatically work out how many calories you've burned and add them to a daily chart at the bottom of the screen. This chart also displays the amount of calories consumed, calories remaining and can break down your daily intake into its nutritional values – which is a really helpful way to see if you're consuming too much fat, carbohydrate or even alcohol.

Perhaps the most useful indicator in the program is the Remaining counter. Seeing exactly how many calories can be consumed before the day's end is helpful, but also strangely addictive. It won't be long before you're working out what simple exercises can be done to add more to the counter.

"A genuinely helpful app. It might well change your life"

As you might imagine, this is the kind of app that gets more useful each time you open it. It tracks your calories and exercise over time, so it's possible to generate a chart that displays your progress and current BMI. Just seeing the numbers go down is an encouraging feature, and the quick access to additional information makes planning the next stage of your personal programme a cinch. For anyone who is serious about losing weight, staying in shape or keeping an eye on their diet, Perfect Diet Tracker is a genuinely helpful app.

Rating ★★★★☆

■ Keep a daily diary of your food intake and exercise.

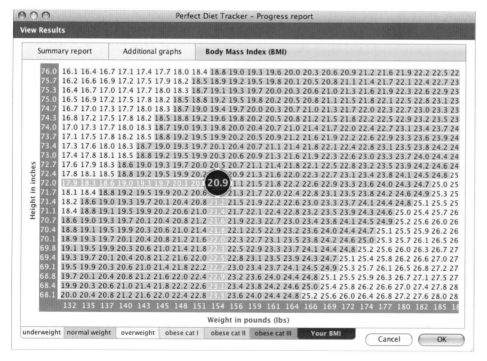

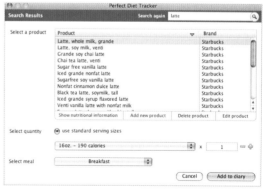

■ Quickly find an item of food using the built-in search engine.

■ At any point you can pull up a graph displaying your current BMI.

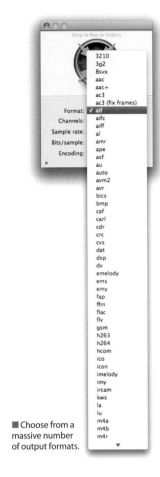

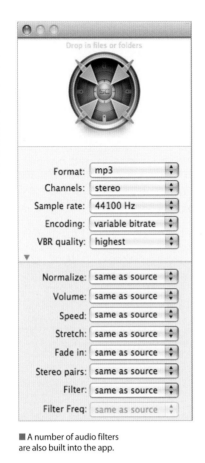

■ Choose from a massive number of output formats.

■ A number of audio filters are also built into the app.

■ Drag your music onto the plates to start.

■ You can add samples to the music in real-time.

Price: £5.99/$9.99 **Developer:** Steve Dekorte

SoundConverter

Convert any audio format from one to another with this easy-to-use app

We're sure you've experienced the problem of not being able to play an audio file in iTunes or on your iDevice. With support for only MP3, AIFF, WAV, MPEG-4, AAC (.m4a) and Apple Lossless, sadly a large number of audio files on the web won't playback on your Mac without the specific software. Thankfully, SoundConverter is here to help. It can import audio files in 83 different formats, and output them in 78. As a result, you can pretty much guarantee that any audio files you wish to convert and play will be supported.

Using the program is a breeze. Once opened, you only need to choose an output format from the drop-down menu, then drag any audio files that need to be converted to the black and green icon above. SoundConverter will automatically begin to convert the audio file, and will save the new file alongside the original. As you might imagine, it's possible to choose whether the output file will be in stereo or mono as well as other options such as its sample rate, bit rate and encoding method. SoundConverter also includes a number of audio effects such as Speed, Stretch, Normalize and Fade in, and these are accessed by a small arrow icon at the bottom of the interface. For anyone looking for a quick and simple audio converter, you won't find a better option in the Mac App Store than this.

Price: Free **Developer:** Atomix Productions

VirtualDJ Home

Mix music tracks and videos in real-time with this intuitive free DJ app

This really is a fun app to use – even if you're not a full time DJ. Load it up and a vivid black interface awaits. To import music, you need to select a track or album using the left-hand pane of the Browser panel, then drag a track to either of the plates above. The program automatically scans each track to determine its beat, so when two tracks are playing simultaneously, all you need to do is press the sync button to play them together in harmony. It really does work, and by using a slider in the centre of the screen you can fade between tracks. As you might imagine, it's possible to 'scratch' a music track by clicking and holding on a plate and moving it with the mouse cursor. There's a wealth of other clever features included too, such as the ability to create a loop in real-time, change the pitch, add sound effects, play with a mixer or jump to any part of a track. There's even a small video mixer in the centre of the screen that enables you to fade between two videos.

Mixing music and video in real-time gives both mediums a new lease of life. The best aspect of all is that VirtualDJ Home is free, so there's no excuse not to download it to your Mac and give it a spin.

Rating ★★★★☆

Rating ★★★★★

Price: Free **Developer:** Running with Crayons Ltd.

Alfred

Open applications, find files and search the web with incredible ease

Ask many productive Mac users what their favourite app is and, chances are, they'll name a quick-launcher app. Alfred is one such program, enabling you to launch applications, search the web and more with just a few keyboard taps.

Available for free, Alfred is launched by pressing Alt+Space. Up pops a quick panel, enabling you to type a search query to see instant results. One of its most useful features is the ability to open programs from your Applications folder. For example, if we wanted to open Photoshop, we need to type "ph" then click on Photoshop – which is the top search result. This great method of launching apps not only saves us from opening the Applications folder, but also enables us to keep the Dock tidy by not filling it with dozens of icons.

Of course, launching apps isn't the only great feature built into Alfred – powerful search abilities are also a massive draw. By typing a search query into the pop-up window you can instantly access the relevant web service to find what you're looking for. So a search for 'Bob Dylan music' will enable you to search Google, Amazon and Wikipedia. You can limit search results to individual websites by entering the domain before a search query. So by entering 'youtube music videos', for example, you can instantly view search results limited to that specific field and that specific website. Other websites

supported in that way are all of those you would expect, including eBay, Twitter, Flickr and Facebook. It's also possible to search your Mac for files and folders by starting search queries with the word 'find'. Results appear instantly thanks to Alfred's ability to use the Spotlight feature included with Mac OS X.

A Powerpack is available to buy for £12 (approximately $20), that adds even more features to Alfred. These include file actions such as email, copy, move and delete, the ability to control iTunes, open websites within applications and further tweak the Preferences pane. Those who find themselves using Alfred consistently throughout the day will certainly like these extra abilities.

Using Alfred to search for apps, web results and files isn't exactly second nature. Even after the program was installed, for a day we were still tempted to double-click the Applications folder or use the search field in Safari after forgetting to press Alt+Space. But with enough time it did become more natural, and as a result Alfred has made our busy lives far easier. For speeding up search queries and app launches, Alfred is worth getting used to, hard to beat and highly recommended.

Rating ★★★★★

"Alfred has made our busy lives far easier... hard to beat and highly recommended"

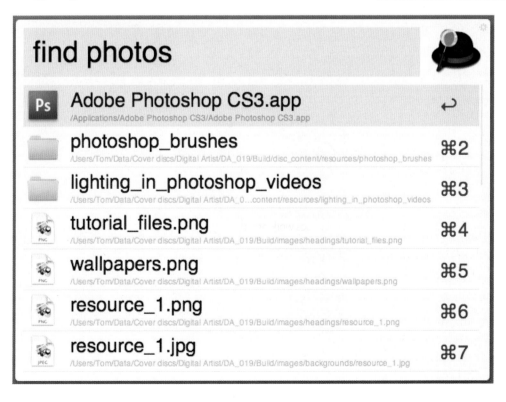

■ Open apps by entering just one letter.

■ Access files and folders by starting a query with 'find'.

Price: £5.99/$9.99 **Developer:** LittleFin LLC

Compartments

Create an inventory of your entire household in next to no time

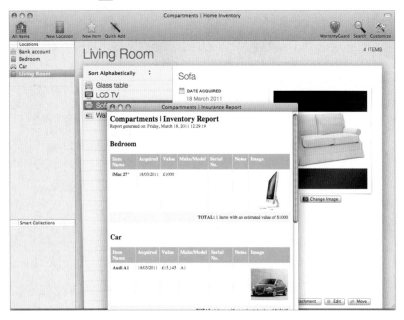

Your home probably contains the most precious items and valuables that you own. Chances are, however, that you don't have an extensive inventory of every item of worth, which can be very useful. Compartments is here to help you, with an easy-to-use interface that makes adding and cataloguing items an incredibly easy feat to accomplish.

When first opened, the app gives you the option to create locations in and around your home. Once a location has been created it takes only a few mouse clicks to add an item. It's possible to enter details such as value, warranty details, model name, serial number, notes and tags. You can also upload a photo, or capture a new image using the Mac's iSight camera. Compartments doesn't only just cover home contents, but also items in your office, car and bank account – each with its own icon. Once you've finished entering items you can generate a PDF report with just a single click, which is particularly useful when estimating the total value for insurance purposes.

There are a few improvements that could be made to the program. The ability to add more than one image would be useful, as would an online backup. Nevertheless, Compartments is a great solution.

■ Generate a report with just one mouse click.

Rating ★★★★★

Price: £17.99/$29.99 **Developer:** Realmac Software

LittleSnapper

Capture your screen, a window and more with this clever grabber

■ Organise and catalogue your images from the Library.

With so many distractions on the web, it's often a good idea to take snapshots for later reference. LittleSnapper enables you to do just that, with the ability to capture the entire screen, a user-determined portion of it, a window, entire webpage or a timed, countdown shot. It sounds clever, and it is – with shortcuts that enable you to capture a moment at any time. Snaps are saved to the program's Library, but can also be sorted into collections and types which is particularly handy for those that capture a large amount of images.

LittleSnapper doesn't only grab snapshots, however, but enables you some fun edits like adding text and shapes, cropping to a particular size, highlighting areas and blurring specific sections. It's a really intuitive system that anyone will pick up in an instant. Once images have been captured and edited they can also be uploaded to Ember, Flicker or an FTP account, or exported as a PDF, PNG or JPG.

We have a couple of niggling issues. Nearly all of the capture tools can already be used for free on your Mac. Take capturing a window for example – simply press Command+Shift+4+Space and your Mac saves whatever window is open as a PNG. Also, the program was prone to crashing while we were testing it. Look past these small issues however, and you'll find a great image annotation app with some handy sharing features.

■ Easily add graphics, effects and text to captures.

Rating ★★★★★

Price: £29.99/$49.99   **Developer:** Realmac Software

RapidWeaver 5

Create your very own website with this intuitive software

Creating a new website can be an incredibly daunting challenge. Not only does it have to be designed and coded, but the site must be tested on a range of browsers, analytics code added and uploaded to a domain. Helpfully, there are a number of WYSIWYG (what you see is what you get) programs that automate much of the hard work by enabling users to simply drag and drop content onto a blank window to build a website. Apple has created its own, iWeb, which is included with every copy of iLife, but the program hasn't been updated for quite some time leaving competitors to step in and provide alternatives. RapidWeaver is perhaps the best-known WYSIWYG software for the Mac. It includes 48 built-in themes that enable users to quickly create an attractive looking website. Getting started is fairly easy, RapidWeaver asks for the website's FTP details (so you'll need a registered domain and web hosting details) and the basic information about

the site. Once those are entered, you're free to choose a site template and get started. When adding a new page, RapidWeaver presents a series of page templates including a blog, contact form and photo album. Adding content to these pages is incredibly easy, with the ability to drag media from the desktop to RapidWeaver's window, add text fields and quickly link items. Content can be resized in real-time, or tweaked further via the small Preferences window. To help aid the content creation process, a slider at the bottom of the screen enables you to swap to a preview mode that shows how the website will look in a browser so you can get an idea of how it will come across.

Perhaps RapidWeaver's strongest asset is the large community that can be accessed via the program's website **www.realmacsoftware.com**. Hundreds of user-made themes can be purchased and installed, with further plug-ins that add additional features you might want included on your site such as checkouts, search engines and more. A large forum can also be found that's filled with helpful members, always on-hand to answer your site-building questions.

There are a handful of limitations when using RapidWeaver to create a website. Editing the built-in themes is rather tricky, with only a few settings for tweaking button layouts and background images. Advanced features such as div tags and CSS can't be used without editing back-end code and there can often be rendering bugs when swapping between editing and preview mode. That said, for casual users looking to build a personal website, this is a fantastic solution. RapidWeaver is easy to use, builds attractive websites and has an enthusiastic community that's constantly building new content.

■ RapidWeaver enables you to quickly create your own video gallery.

Rating ★★★★☆

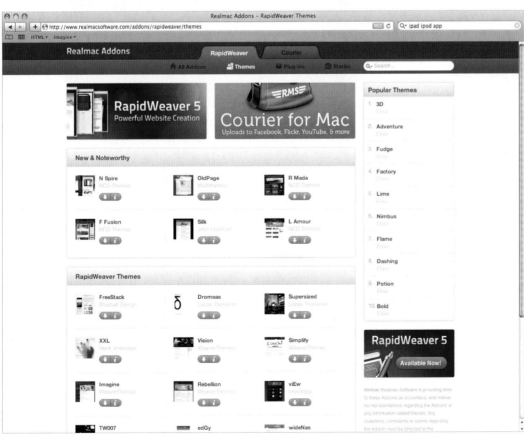

■ Setting up a blog takes mere seconds.

■ Plenty of third-party themes can be downloaded from the web.

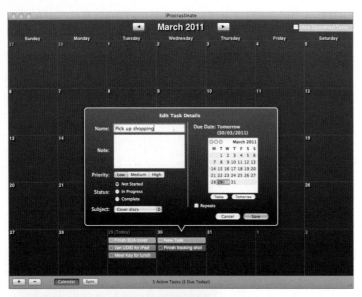

■ Manage your busy life with ease.

■ Enter tasks via the built-in calendar.

Price: Free **Developer:** Craig Otis

iProcrastinate

Manage classes and schedules with this free task manager

This free to-do app is one of the easiest ways to manage a busy life. It works by grouping tasks into subjects, then displays them in a field in the centre of the screen. It sounds simple, and it is – requiring no knowledge of task managing software before the application can be used to its fullest. Subjects can take any form, so students may wish to list tasks by class, socialites could use friend groups – the list goes on. The easiest way to add a task is via the calendar, accessed by clicking the Calendar button at the bottom of the screen. Anyone who has already used iCal will be familiar with how iProcrastinate works; simply double-click a date, enter a name, choose a subject and click Save. It's possible to repeat tasks daily, weekly, monthly or yearly, give them a priority and even update their status in real-time. It isn't possible to assign times to each task however, so if you have a meeting or class at a particular hour, you'll need to enter it in the task's title. Those with iPhones will be pleased to hear that iProcrastinate has the ability to sync with its iPhone cousin, either via DropBox or direct to the iPhone if it's plugged into your Mac. With so many abilities packed into one free app, this is an essential download for those juggling busy lives.

Rating ★★★★☆

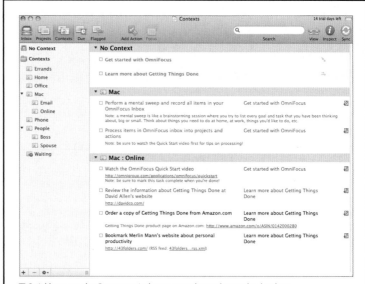

■ Quickly access the Contexts window to see what tasks need to be done.

Price: £44.99/$79.99 **Developer:** The Omni Group

OmniFocus for Mac

Record events, organise ideas and much more with this clever app

Another in the range of apps out there to help keep your desk from becoming a forest of post-it notes, OmniFocus is our second task managing program and includes some powerful tools such as a Quick Entry panel, Contexts and the ability to sync the software with the iPhone and iPad apps.

Getting started with the program is easy thanks to a selection of video tutorials linked to via the home screen. We would certainly recommend watching them, as OmniFocus isn't entirely intuitive to those new to task managing software. The Inbox, for example, isn't an inbox in the same sense as your email client, but rather a place to dump ideas, tasks and other information.

OmniFocus has a clever solution to capturing ideas and tasks that suddenly pop-up; the Quick Entry panel. At any point while using your Mac, simply hit Control+Alt+Space on your keyboard and the Quick Entry panel will appear. Once you've noted down your idea, simply click the Save button to store it within the program. One of our favourite features of OmniFocus is its ability to sync with an iPhone and iPad via a MobileMe account, Bonjour or WebDAV server. It's a little tricky to set up, but once you are up and running it means you can enter and edit tasks and see them synced instantly across all of your various devices. You'll need to buy the iOS app separately to this Mac app however.

OmniFocus isn't exactly cheap, but if you're struggling to stay on top of tasks then it might just be worth the asking price.

Rating ★★★★☆

Price: £23.99/$39.99   **Developer:** Andreas Monitzer

Thoughts

Create and manage virtual notebooks on your Mac

It seems a little odd that the Mac doesn't come with a built-in notes app. After-all, both the iPhone and iPad have one. Thoughts goes a long way to fixing this small problem, however, by enabling you to create notebooks and store them on a virtual shelf.

It's incredibly easy to use. When the program is opened for the first time, an empty shelf appears with a New Book button beneath. Simply click the button and your very first book springs into view, and double-clicking opens it. When adding and editing text, Thoughts works just like a basic word processor. It includes a multitude of text editing options, with the ability to set fonts, text size, formatting and colour. You can add as many pages as you like to a notebook, each easily accessible via a panel on the left side of the interface, useful for brainstorming and multiple projects. Controls at the bottom enable you to view your book in full-screen, flick through its pages (with a great page-turning animation), view a calendar that displays when pages were added as well as importing and exporting pages in RTF, PDF, Word and ODT format.

The beauty of Thoughts is how simple it is to use. A welcome tour video is available for those that like to discover every feature before embarking on usage, but it really isn't necessary with this intuitive and accessible program. After only minutes of installing the program, we had created a series of books and added the notes we had stored on our iPhone to them, and it wasn't long before we had a shopping list added, some script notes and the opening chapter of a book all outlined and neatly saved. The ability to store all of these text notes within one application certainly beats saving them across several folders.

■ Your books are stored on a virtual bookshelf.

There are a few improvements we'd like to see, though. The book icons on the virtual shelf are rather large, so if you have more than three you have to scroll. The title text of each is also too large, which results in long words being split over several lines. All these issues are cosmetic touches that could easily be fixed – we didn't have any problems with the functionality of the program itself. As a result, we can easily recommend Thoughts to anyone who wishes to store notes, ideas and lists on their Mac; it really is the kind of program that should be included with the Mac OS by default. If only the asking price wasn't quite so high.

"We can easily recommend Thoughts to anyone who wishes to store notes, ideas and lists"

Rating ★★★★☆

■ Add and edit notes with ease.

■ Type your notes
in full-screen mode.

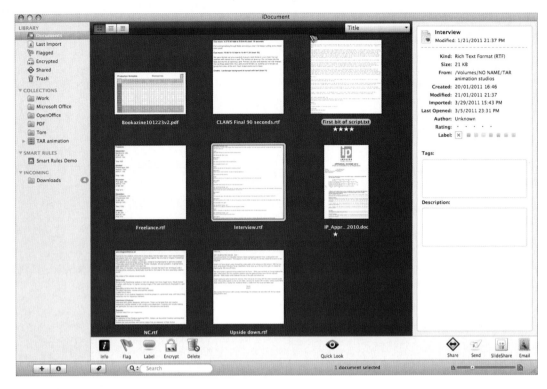

■ Send documents to other users on the same network.

■ Flag, label and encrypt documents on your Mac.

"A great way to browse every text document on your Mac"

Price: Free   **Developer:** Oscar Wu

iDocument Lite

Organise and manage every document on your Mac using this intuitive and free app

Keeping track of every document on your Mac can be a messy, time-consuming affair. Sure, you could always store every document in the Documents folder, but that's not always convenient or sensible if you are working with files that have separate uses and subjects. iDocument makes things much easier. It's a documents browser that can display TXT, DOC, PDF files and multiple interfaces, organise them into categories and share them, among other things.

When first opened, iDocument asks if you'd like to import files from specific folders, or whether you'd prefer to simply drag them from the Desktop onto the program's interface. It doesn't really matter which you choose, as there's no automated process for importing every document on your Mac. Nevertheless, it won't be long until you've gathered all your documents together in the program. Organising them is a breeze thanks to the Collections tab in the program's library panel. You can add a new collection at any point by clicking a plus icon in the bottom-left corner of the screen. Once a collection has been created, simply drag a document onto it and a new folder will be created within the collection that stores the file. It's a simple, intuitive affair, and the tricks for navigating its interface are easily picked up with a bit of practice.

Files can be labelled and flagged for easy reference using buttons located at the bottom of the screen, and it is possible to enable an Info panel that displays information about files such as size, date created and modified, author and rating. If security of your files is important then iDocument can encrypt every file stored within its library. The password can be as long or short as you wish, with a reminder in case you forget what words or numbers were used.

iDocument can't edit files, but to do so easily you can simply double-click on a file to open it in its default application. Files can also be previewed using Quick Look (the same function as when the Space key is pressed when a file is selected on the desktop). Sharing files is a little easier however, for example, it's possible to send a file to other iDocument users on the same network, email a file and upload it to SlideShare for quickly getting information across.

We do have some reservations about iDocument. It's not possible to remove a document from the library without moving it to the trash, individual documents can't be encrypted – only the entire library – and documents can't be edited within the program. These limitations aside, this is a great way to browse every text document on your Mac without having to navigate through myriad folders.

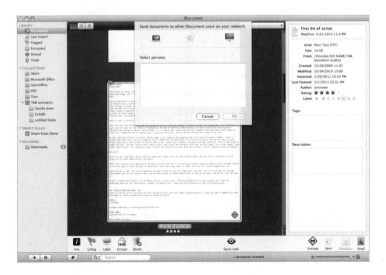

■ Files can be viewed as icons or lists.

Rating ★★★★☆

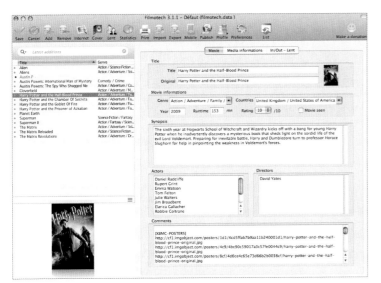

■ Filmotech can automatically enter every film detail.

■ You can even print covers to replace any originals that are damaged.

Price: Free **Developer:** Pascal PLUCHON

Filmotech

Manage your film collection and more with ease

The first step here is to create a database for your film collection. This is mostly an automated affair, although it's possible to select the default region setting, currency and media. Once set up and ready, you can add your first film. It's a surprisingly easy process – you simply need to enter a film title (or even a partial title) and let Filmotech search the web for the full information. It will fill in up to 17 available information fields, add a poster and complete the title, then add the film to your library. With such a fast, automated process, we were able to add dozens of films in next to no time. Once your collection has been added, it's then possible to export it in XML, CSV or XBMC formats, making it easy to share collections or transfer details to friends or other machines.

Managing a collection of movies isn't the only ability Filmotech has, as it includes some incredibly handy features that you wouldn't typically expect to find, such as a DVD cover creator, the ability to watch trailers, see statistics on your stored collection and even print out lists and catalogues.

With so many great features packed into one free app, Filmotech is by far the quickest and easiest way to manage your film collection; a must-have app for anyone with just dozens, not to mention hundreds of films.

Rating ★★★★★

Price: £5.99/$9.99 **Developer:** The Iconfactory

Twitterrific 4

Can some clever touches make this Twitter client stand out from the crowd?

The previous version of Twitterrific felt stagnant and out-dated, seemingly held back while the development team focused on the iPhone and iPad versions. With Apple's new push to bring some of the best iOS features to Mac in Lion, it appears the Twitterrific team are following its lead with this brand new version, packed with some clever touches and a new interface.

A new, inline and colour-coded aesthetic can be found in version 4, one that's easy to use and almost identical in appearance to the iOS iteration. That means when a user's icon is selected, an iPad-like ribbon appears over the interface. Conversations work in a similar manner too. Like the official Twitter app, Twitterrific runs entirely in a compact floating window on your screen, so tweets and images slide into view instead of opening in a browser. Replying to tweets is done via a context sensitive arrow that also enables you to translate tweets into other languages, email the tweet, copy it and save it to your favourites list. Version 4 also brings a multitude of customisation options including font size (important for those with large displays) and theme control for that personal touch.

Is this a better Twitter app than the official client? Not quite. Its customisation features go a long way to enhance the Twitter experience, especially on larger screens such as the 27-inch iMac, but it's not free, so justifying the asking price is determined by how much tweeting you do.

Rating ★★★★☆

■ It's a basic interface, but easy to use.

■ Quickly post a tweet without leaving the timeline.

Mac Apps

Price: Free **Developer:** Twitter, Inc.

Twitter

Join the social networking revolution with the intuitive official app

The success of Twitter is ultimately down to its sheer simplicity. Anyone can post and read tweets, there's no such thing as a private tweet and, like SMS messages, tweets have a limited character count (in this case 140). These may sound like unnecessary restrictions and limitations, but with such simple rules, everyone understands how they work and, ultimately, most people join in. Twitter has very literally become a revolution in social networking.

The official Twitter app for the Mac follows these same rules of keeping things simple. It's incredibly easy to use, with a permanent sidebar that enables you to switch between multiple accounts, and a timeline on the right. Similar in appearance to the iOS Twitter app, the timeline displays tweets in order of date (with the latest tweets from people you are following appearing at the top), and to scroll through the tweets you only have to scroll the mouse wheel or use two fingers on the trackpad. While on the subject of multi-gestures, the Twitter Mac app takes full advantage of these. It's possible to expand a tweet to view its full conversation by simply swiping with three fingers in a gesture to the right. You can then close the conversation easily by (you guessed it) swiping with three fingers to the left. Using a trackpad, it soon becomes second-nature to swipe through tweets and conversations with your fingers, quickly catching up on the hot topics.

Interacting with tweets is also incredibly easy. You don't have to click on a tweet or press any keys, simply move the cursor over the message. Several contextual buttons will fade-in, enabling you to reply, retweet, mark as a favourite or expand the conversation. With each interaction, a new panel slides into view to form a stack, and with the exception of pictures and web-links, you'll never see a pop-up window to interrupt the flow. Navigating these stacks with your fingers feels intuitive and natural, but when several are open it can become easy to get lost in a conversation or timeline.

You may have noticed from the screenshots that Twitter doesn't have a titlebar at the top of the window. This is a direct result of the developers keeping things simple, and it does work – but if you want to move the Twitter window around the screen, you'll need to click and hold the cursor anywhere within the sidebar. For most Twitter users, this is a great way to post and read tweets. Its multi-gesture interaction is smooth and intuitive, and the sliding panel interface is a joy to use. A bug currently exists for those that use Spaces, whereby the Twitter window appears in every Space, but this aside, the app will suffice for all but the most hardcore Twitter users.

Rating ★★★★★

■ View your own timeline in one window.

■ Everything is contained within one clean, stacked window.

■ Swipe with three fingers over a user to see all of their recent tweets.

"The official app will suffice for all but the most hardcore Twitter users"

Price: £5.99/$9.99   **Developer:** Apparent Software

Socialite

Visit your favourite social networking websites using only one app

Juggling every social networking website and service can be quite a task and for some it could very well be the only online activity they regularly do. Socialite makes the entire process much easier and more efficient than checking each site within a browser. It enables you to access Facebook, Twitter, Flickr, Google Reader, Digg and any RSS feeds without having to leave the program's interface.

Logging into each service is done entirely through the program and takes mere seconds. Once logged into Facebook, the sidebar updates with shortcuts for viewing status updates, friends' photos, your own photos and links. It's possible to update your status at any time via a bar at the bottom of the screen,

and shortcuts at the top of the interface enable you to upload photos. It works brilliantly, with content loading quicker than via a browser. There are a handful of severe limitations, however. It's not possible, for example, to message users, see your friends list, watch videos or chat in real-time. For some this could be a blessing in a disguise, preventing the multitude of distractions such as Farmville notifications from appearing on your feed, but for most these limitations will mean Socialite isn't a suitable replacement for the full website.

The Flickr functionality works in a similar manner. It's possible to upload and view your own photos, access your contacts and see interesting content from the website that's pulled in at random, but it's not possible to manually browse galleries on the website, nor can you message other users.

The Twitter features fare better, with a timeline that pulls in new tweets, a panel for quickly posting thoughts and shortcuts for replying, setting tweets as favourites, peeking at profiles and retweeting. Socialite also displays image attachments in a pop-up window, although web-links will still open your default browser. Twitter aside, accessing the Digg website is a handy feature, with links to each category of news. RSS feeds also work as expected, with support for Google Reader. Once feeds have been added, it's possible to browse the most recent unread articles, share them and add them to a favourites list.

Socialite makes managing your social network life considerably more efficient than simply using a browser, but it won't become your go-to application for every service, simply because it doesn't include enough functionality. This is a shame, because the ability to access every major social networking website through one window is genuinely useful. A free 14-day trial is available from **www.apparentsoft.com/socialite**. Give it a spin and see how you fare. After all, not everyone needs the constant distraction that is Facebook chat.

■ Catch up on the latest tweets through Socialite.

Rating ★★★★☆

■ Socialite also supports Digg and RSS feeds.

■ Upload and view Facebook photos through the app.

Price: £23.99/$39.99 **Developer:** Outer Level

Knapsack

Plan every aspect of your next trip
with this intuitive travel organiser

Travel often? If so, Knapsack could potentially save you time and stress. It's a get-things-done (GTD) app, one that focuses specifically on holidays and travel events. To begin, you add a trip and choose the dates that it covers. Knapsack will automatically add the required amount of days to the trip planner, leaving you to input activities and things that you plan on doing. Being a travel-themed GTD app, you can pinpoint the trip on a world map to help you quickly identify it. Those who go abroad often will quickly see pins dotting the globe and each can be clicked on to show a trip overview with description, thumbnail image and the last activity entry.

The interface makes adding and editing trips a joy, with large, labelled buttons at the top of the screen for quick access. It's possible to plan every day down to the minutest detail, with scheduled activities, addresses, photos, phone numbers and more. A permanent To Do list on the right-hand side of the interface enables you to add pre-trip check lists as well as notes for your packing (handy for remembering specific items), and each one can be checked off as you go.

If you've ever forgotten your toothbrush or like to plan activities for each day of your holiday in detail, in advance, then Knapsack is certainly worth a look.

■ Click on a pin to see an
overview of the trip.

Rating ★★★★★

Price: Free **Developer:** GOTOES.ORG

Sports Equipment Log

Monitor and catalogue your fitness equipment with this handy free app

For regular sports enthusiasts, keeping a log of your equipment is an important way to prevent injury or sudden expense when they develop a fault. Take running shoes for example; it's important to replace them after 500 miles of use. Cyclists will also need to monitor the mileage of the chain and tyres on their bike. Sports Equipment Log enables you to track every piece of sports equipment either manually or by syncing with Garmin Connect compatible devices such as the Forerunner 50 and FR60. The program can also import data from ANT+ GPS devices.

Adding a piece of equipment is a simple process, with the ability to import photos of each piece to help when identifying kit from a large list. Once an item has been added it can be updated with the distance used, date and time. To ease new users into the program, three built-in items are also included that can be updated and edited to get you started with the app.

Importing data from a Garmin device is also an easy affair, and once an import has been completed, Sports Equipment Log can automatically reference the import folder to update the equipment database, a really helpful time saver.

For those who love to regularly cycle and jog and want to keep up-to-date with their tools, this is a great solution for monitoring your equipment's life span. The ability to automatically import Garmin GPS data is just the icing on the cake.

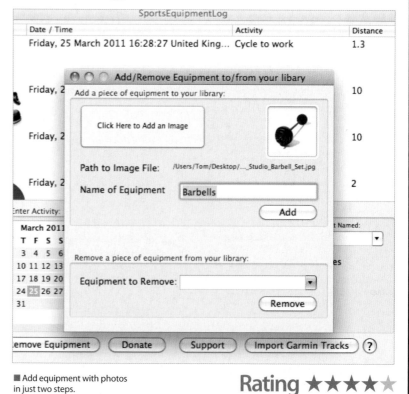

■ Add equipment with photos
in just two steps.

Rating ★★★★★

Price: £11.99/$19.99   **Developer:** Koingo Software, Inc.

MacCleanse 2

Give your Mac a spring clean with this powerful application

Over time your Mac will slowly fill with unnecessary junk such as log files, cache files, file histories and unused language files. As a result, giving it a spring clean using a cleaning app will enable it to run at full speed, preventing any slowdowns and long boot-up times.

MacCleanse is one such application, which can scan for file archives, cookies, application logs, Mail downloads, unused files and more.

When opened for the first time, you'll be presented with a blank window. By clicking the various search options in the left-hand pane, you can select files to scan for. Each has a description to inform you of the file types and use, so you needn't worry about erasing things that you may wish to reference at a future date. MacCleanse scans for a surprising number of files, so many in fact that it's tempting to simply click the Check All button. Once you're happy with the selection, hit the Scan & Delete button at the top of the screen and MacCleanse will automatically scan and delete any files it finds that meet your criteria, which in our case was more than 40GB of superfluous junk.

The program works incredibly quickly, much more so than other cleaning apps such as close competitor CleanMyMac. For anyone with an ageing Mac that's starting to slow down during everyday tasks or struggles with large files, MacCleanse could very well put a spring back into its step.

Rating ★★★★☆

■ Cleanup is lightning fast.

■ MacCleanse can scan and delete a wide range of files.

■ Hold down the right mouse button to enable gesture-actions.

Price: Free   **Developer:** Opera Software ASA

Opera

An alternative browser with some clever tab features and mouse gestures

Apple's Safari browser is arguably the best in the world, with blinding Java performance and full HTML5 support. So the question you need to ask yourself before installing Opera is: why bother? Well, it has some clever features that you won't find in any other browser. Take tab functionality for example. We're quite sure you're familiar with having too many tabs open at once, which results in them running off-screen, or in the case of Firefox, simply squishing in length. Opera aims to resolve this by enabling you to stack tabs on top of each other. If, for example, you have five tabs open for one website, you can stack them together to form one group which can be extended with a simple click. It works well and saves a considerable space at the top of the screen. Another great Opera functionality are the mouse-gestures. For quick navigation, simply hold down the right mouse button and a context sensitive window pops up that enables you to go back a page, forward, open a link in a new tab or stop a page from loading. It does save time with practice, but doesn't work so well on a trackpad.

When it comes to rendering speeds, Opera can open tabs quicker when compared to other browsers thanks to its Vega graphics library.

Pages also scroll incredibly smoothly, although we did experience hiccups when large images and videos came into view. Not the holy grail of browsers, but some great functional touches.

■ Stack tabs save space on a busy browser.

Rating ★★★★☆

■ This app is a far quicker way to access Mashable.

■ Never miss any important Apple news by checking out the Apple section.

Price: Free **Developer:** Mashable

Mashable! for Mac

Browse the entire Mashable website from an app on your Mac

 When the iPhone App Store was initially launched in 2008, it saw a slew of apps released that simply pulled in content from websites. Now we're seeing something similar in the Mac App Store with this news app, Mashable! for Mac. If you're a website developer or keen on following the latest web developments, then chances are you visit http://mashable.com on a daily basis. The website focuses on web development news, technology and gadgets. With more than 30 million page views each month, it's one of the world's most popular websites.

This Mac app simply pulls in content from **http://mashable.com** and presents it in an easy to use interface. It's entirely intuitive, with a panel on the left-hand side that displays news categories such as Social Media, Video, Mobile, Dev & Design and Business. Each has a number counter next to it that displays the amount of unread stories in that particular section. Once you've clicked on a category, stories appear in a secondary panel to the right, and once you've chosen an article, the content appears in the main window.

This app is a far more pleasurable way to browse Mashable than using the website through a browser. It's cleaner, loads content quicker and has a number of built-in features that make finding items easier. Whether you want a dedicated icon in the Dock just for browsing the Mashable website is determined solely by how often you visit the website.

Rating ★★★★★

Price: Free **Developer:** Smith Micro Software, Inc.

StuffIt Expander

Expand a wealth of file types using this free utility from Smith Micro

 Your Mac can already open ZIP files without the need for any third-party software, so you may wonder why you should download StuffIt Expander. Put simply, for the added ability to open a whole raft of further compression types. It's an important ability too, as files downloaded from the web can take the form of various compression types, each with their own pros and cons. Take RAR files for example. Compared to ZIP files they can be up to around 75 per cent smaller in file size, but ultimately will take longer to open.

StuffIt Expander will open nearly any file type, with support for ZIP, 7Z, AS, CAB, GZ, RAR, SIT, SITX, TAR, Z and more. It's an incredibly simple piece of software. After downloading from the App Store, it launches a small blue box in the centre of the screen. To open any compressed files, simply drag them onto this and they will unzip. You can also choose Expand from the Finder menu and locate a compressed file by hand.

That's the basics of this program, though it's possible to change a number of settings via Preferences. For example, you can instruct StuffIt to move files to the Trash after they have been opened, scan for viruses within a compressed file if any antivirus software is installed and assign or de-assign file formats. If you want to compress files to SITX format, however, you'll need to purchase StuffIt Mac, from **www.stuffit.com**.

Rating ★★★★★

■ This tiny window is the entire interface of the program.

■ You can determine which files automatically open in StuffIt from the Preferences pane.

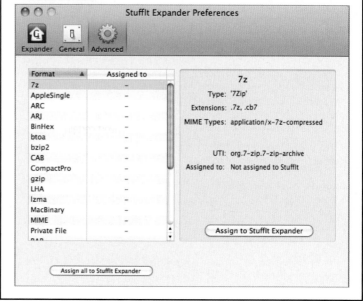

Price: £2.99/$4.99   Developer: Andrew Cook

Daylight

Watch nightfall approach in real-time using this fascinating app

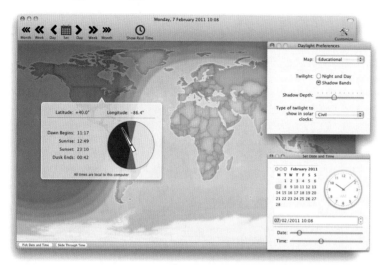

Already an existing app for both the iPhone and iPad, Daylight for Mac is a simple application that shows the progress of daylight across the globe in real-time. While that may sound a little odd, it's actually fascinating to see, with several bands of shadow that display twilight and nighttime. Leave the application running in the background and you can watch as nightfall slowly creeps across the map, which can be both enlightening and depressing if used during winter months. You're never restricted to seeing these effects solely in real-time however, as it's possible to change the date using a calendar and see how the Earth's tilt changes the rotation and therefore the time of daylight throughout the year.

Several map styles are built into the app, including a multi-coloured educational map, a natural green and blue version and one in a historic, *Indiana Jones*-style. By clicking on the map you can see any location's sunrise and sunset times, plus its latitude and longitude, and by using the Preferences panel you can subtly change the shadow depth and twilight style for a bit more customisation.

In all, this is a fascinating app to use. It's unlikely to stay installed on your Mac for long, but for those curious about day and nighttime cycles, it's certainly worth a download. Never again will you be wondering when the Sun will set in the immediate or near future, or a few years from now for that matter.

"You can watch as nightfall slowly creeps across the map"

Rating ★★★★☆

Price: Free   Developer: Participatory Culture Foundation

MiroVideoConverter

Convert videos to almost any format – for free

With the release of Snow Leopard came QuickTime X. Reprogrammed from scratch, it brought some much needed improvements, such as a border-less interface and real-time video screen capture. But it also introduced some limitations, the most notable being a lack of thorough export options. For typical users this isn't a problem, but for video editors and anyone who regularly converts video, QuickTime X isn't suitable for the majority of tasks.

Thankfully, MiroVideoConverter is here to help. It's a simple, free app that can convert nearly any video to H.264, MP4, WebM (vp8), Ogg Theora, or a number of presets that include the iPhone, iPad and Android devices. It's incredibly easy to use; simply drag a video onto its window, choose a device or video format, then click the Convert button. Whereas other applications such as MPEG Streamclip and QuickTime can struggle to convert certain MP4 and AVI files, MiroVideoConverter has never let us down. In fact, it has been in daily use on this reviewer's Mac for several months now. It lacks specific encoding options such as bit rate, custom video sizes and filters, and can't encode to Flash – but for basic video conversion, it does the job. If you ever need to convert a tricky video for playback in iTunes, on your Apple TV or iDevice, MiroVideoConverter will have you covered.

■ It's one of the simplest video converters around.

■ Convert any video to a wide selection of devices.

"A simple, free app that can convert nearly any video"

Rating ★★★★☆

Go creative with Mac, iPad & iPhone

Upskill today with the very best creative bookazines and DVDs

Mac for Beginners vol 3
Starting with the basics, this essential guide will teach you how to get to grips with every aspect of your Mac, from iLife and iWork to iTunes, Safari and Mail.

SRP: £12.99

iPhone Tips, Tricks, Apps & Hacks vol 4
Step-by-step tutorials and features covering the secrets of the iPhone and a jailbreaking guide make this a must-own.

SRP: £9.99

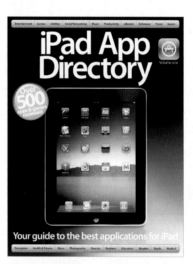

iPad App Directory vol 1
Save yourself time and money by using our definitive guide to the best apps on the App Store. Every category is covered and there are over 500 apps reviewed inside.

SRP: £9.99

iPhone App Directory vol 7
The world's best iPhone applications are reviewed right here, including the very best for iPhone 4, with every App Store category featured inside.

SRP: £9.99

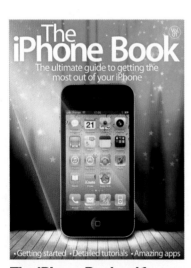

The iPhone Book vol 1
Whether you're brand new to the iPhone or have had one for a while, this book is the ultimate resource for getting the best from your favourite device.

SRP: £9.99

The Mac Book vol 6
256 pages of practical and creative tutorials and in-depth features that will take you through OS X, iLife, iWork and even third-party applications.

SRP: £12.99

iPhone Games Directory vol 2
The world's most comprehensive guide to iPhone, iPod touch and iPad gaming apps, with all gaming genres reviewed and rated.

SRP: £9.99

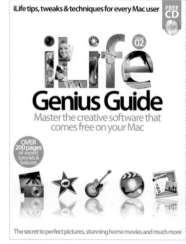

iLife Genius Guide vol 2
Easy-to-follow 256 page tutorial guide to the complete suite of Apple iLife apps including iPhoto, iMovie, iDVD, iWeb and GarageBand.

SRP: £12.99

your
ne

On your free disc

All the resources you need to master everything your Mac has to offer

Attached on the opposite page is your free Mac for Beginners disc. Here you'll find all the tutorial files you need to complete the tutorials in this book, as well as a wealth of other top resources. On offer are 11 top fonts, Pages templates, audio files, Mail templates, podcasts, video tutorials and much more! Everything is easy to access and downloads straight from the disc, meaning you can be experimenting with these fantastic tools in no time at all. So if you're raring to let your creative side run wild, pop the disc into your Mac and away you go!

11 free fonts

K-Type Fonts has kindly provided 11 excellent fonts for you to use, including the sci-fi-esque CyberScript. Be aware that these fonts are for non-commercial use

Navigate the disc

Upon start-up, this is the screen you'll be taken to. From here you can navigate your way around the disc, accessing all the free resources and assets for the book

Pages templates

Pages is a great tool for Mac users, and the tutorials in the book will show you how to perform some basic tasks in the application. But we've also included three full Pages templates from Inkd on the disc, including a newsletter, letterhead and postcard. There are also three branding kits for good measure…

Mail templates

If you wish to spice up your emails, these great resources will do the job. Jumsoft has provided ten free Mail templates for you to apply to your emails, all of which are part of its latest Mail Stationary 3.1 set.